CONCEPTUAL AND DISCOURSE FACTORS
IN LINGUISTIC STRUCTURE

CONCEPTUAL AND DISCOURSE FACTORS IN LINGUISTIC STRUCTURE

edited by
Alan Cienki
Barbara J. Luka
Michael B. Smith

CSLI
PUBLICATIONS
Center for the Study of
Language and Information
Stanford, California

Copyright ©2001
CSLI Publications
Center for the Study of Language and Information
Leland Stanford Junior University
Printed in the United States
05 04 03 02 01   1 2 3 4 5

Conceptual and discourse factors in linguistic structure / [edited by] Alan Cienki,
Barbara J. Luka, Michael B. Smith.
     p. cm.
     "This volume stems from the fourth such conference, CSDL-4, which was held
     at Emory University in Atlanta in October, 1998"--Pref.
     Includes bibliographical references and index.
     ISBN 1-57586-258-1 (paper : alk. paper) -- ISBN 1-57586-259-X (cloth :
     alk. paper)
     1. Grammar, Comparative and general--Congresses. 2. Semantics--
     Congresses. 3. Cognitive grammar--Congresses. 4. Functionalism
     (Linguistics)--Congresses. 5. Language acquisition--Congresses. I. Cienki,
     Alan J. II. Luka, Barbara J. (Barbara Josephine), 1966- III. Smith, Michael
     B., 1955- IV. Conceptual Structure, Discourse, and Language Conference
     (4th : 1998: Atlanta, Ga.) V. Title.

     P151 .C63 2001
     415--dc21

                                                                    2001025405

∞ The acid-free paper used in this book meets the minimum requirements of the
American National Standard for Information Sciences – Permanence of Paper for
Printed Library Materials, ansi z39.48-1984.

Please visit our web site at
http://cslipublications.stanford.edu/
for comments on this and other titles, as well as for changes
and corrections by the authors, editors and publisher.

Contents

Contributors

MICHEL ACHARD: Department of French Studies, Rice University, Houston, TX 77005
achard@rice.edu

TAMER AMIN: Department of Psychology, Clark University, 950 Main St., Worcester, MA 01610
tgamin@msn.com

BENJAMIN K. BERGEN: Department of Linguistics, University of California, Berkeley, Berkeley,CA 94720-2650
bbergen@icsi.berkeley.edu

NANCY BUDWIG: Department of Psychology, Clark University, 950 Main St., Worcester, MA 01610
nbudwig@clarku.edu

ROBERTA CORRIGAN: Department of Educational Psychology, University of Wisconsin-Milwaukee, Milwaukee, WI 53211
corrigan@csd.uwm.edu

FERDINAND DE HAAN: Department of Linguistics, University of New Mexico, Albuquerque, NM 87131
fdehaan@unm.edu

DIETER HILLERT: Department of Psychology, Biolinguistics Project, University of California, San Diego, La Jolla, CA 92093-0109
dhillert@ucsd.edu

CHRISTOPHER JOHNSON: Department of Linguistics, UC Berkeley, Frame-Net Project, International Computer Science Institute, Berkeley, CA 94720
crj@icsi.berkeley.edu

RONALD W. LANGACKER: Department of Linguistics, 0108, University of California, San Diego, La Jolla, CA 92093
rlangacker@ucsd.edu

KEVIN EZRA MOORE: Department of Linguistics and Language Development, San Jose State University, San Jose, CA 95192-0093
moore@socrates.berkeley.edu

ANNA PAPAFRAGOU: Institute for Research in Cognitive Science, University of Pennsylvania, 3401 Walnut Str., Suite 400A, Philadelphia, PA 19104
anna4@linc.cis.upenn.edu

MADELAINE C. PLAUCHÉ: Department of Linguistics, University of California, Berkeley, Berkeley, CA 94720-2650
mcp@socrates.berkeley.edu

REGINA PUSTET: Research Centre for Linguistic Typology, La Trobe University, Victoria 3086, Australia
pustet@lrz.uni-muenchen.de

IVO SÁNCHEZ: Department of Linguistics, University of California, Santa Barbara, Santa Barbara, CA 93106
isanchez@conversay.com

MICHAEL B. SMITH: Department of Linguistics, Oakland University, Rochester, MI 48309-4401
smith@oakland.edu

DAVID SWINNEY: Department of Psychology & Program in Neuroscience, University of California, San Diego, La Jolla, Ca. 92093-0109
dswinney@ucsd.edu

KIYOKO TAKAHASHI: Department of Linguistics, Chulalongkorn University, Phayathai Rd., Bangkok 10500, Thailand
kiyoko@keisen.ac.jp

LIANG TAO: Department of Linguistics, 383 Gordy Hall, Ohio University, Athens, OH 45701
tao@ohiou.edu

Preface

This publication reflects the commitment on the part of a growing number of linguists to give serious consideration to both conceptual and discourse factors in order to achieve a more complete account of linguistic structure. This commitment has led to an ongoing series of conferences on the theme of Conceptual Structure, Discourse, and Language (CSDL). This volume stems from the fourth such conference, CSDL-4, which was held at Emory University in Atlanta in October, 1998. Like all of the papers presented at the conference, the chapters of this volume represent a shared belief that there is an integral relationship between meaning and the form in which it is expressed in language. The works here reflect multiple perspectives, and represent further progress in the dialog between cognitive and functional approaches in linguistics. The range of topics represented in this volume can be broadly subsumed by four general topics: the relationship of lexical and grammatical meaning; metaphor and conceptual integration; functional considerations; and experimental and developmental approaches.

The first set of papers demonstrates how lexical form and grammatical form can be viewed as two points on one continuum, with each representing different ways of packaging meaning in language. Langacker tackles the difficult case of analyzing the meaning of the English *wh-* formative, the basis of both question words and relative pronouns (*what*, *when*, etc.). At the core of the analysis is the cognitive notion of establishing mental contact with one entity from a range of alternatives in the current shared (mental) discourse space. His account ultimately sheds light on the parallelism between *wh-* forms and demonstrative *th-* forms (*that*, *then*, etc.), and has broader implications for the analysis of interrogative and relative clauses cross-linguistically. Achard, using data from French, challenges the belief that the syntactic behavior of raising verbs can be directly ascribed to the specific underlying structures in which they occur. Rather, he argues that

the syntactic differences inherent in the raised versus unraised verb constructions are not merely structural, but are also a matter of construal (more objective versus more subjective construal), and thus he provides a motivated
explanation for the syntactic differences without appealing to underlying
levels of representation. Pustet's typological study investigates the factors
which determine whether lexical items may or may not combine with copu
las and finds that the relevant criteria do not necessarily coincide with the
dividing lines imposed by the traditional classification of nouns, verbs, and
adjectives. Rather they correspond to a number of semantic classes which
cut across the traditional parts of speech, but nevertheless reflect the hierarchy of time-stability of the concepts represented. Smith's paper examines
the separability of verb prefixes in German, and asks the question: Is there a
semantic motivation for prefix separation, or is the separability versus nonseparability of the prefixes simply an arbitrary feature of a particular construction? He argues for the former view, proposing a semantically-based
account for the word-order facts in German from the perspective of cognitive
grammar. Takahashi's paper examines Talmy's notion of access paths
(elsewhere known as 'fictive motion' or 'virtual motion') and contrasts an
analysis of them in English with how they are encoded in Thai. Takahashi
considers both the cognitive and functional motivations for access path expressions, describing how they are construed differently by speakers of Thai
and of English, providing a cross-linguistic comparison of the semantic
constraints on the form and the use of these expressions.

A second subset of the papers focuses on semantics in relation to processes of metaphorical mapping and conceptual integration. These phenomena can provide diachronic explanations of semantic change, as well as ex-
plications of synchronic polysemy. Amin's paper provides an account of
the English-speaking layperson's idealized cognitive model of thermal phenomena with a careful analysis of English data. Theoretically, the work represents a blend of approaches, beginning with Dowty's system of verb classification to explore the semantics of *heat* and *temperature*, then moving to
an exploration of metaphors for heat, and concluding with an analysis of
how we make sense of seemingly contradictory understandings of 'heat'
through processes of conceptual integration. Moore's paper addresses a re-
finement in our understanding of the linguistic expression of temporal
metaphor. Using data from English, he proposes that what has previously
been analyzed as a single Moving Time metaphor is actually two metaphors, with the difference critically depending upon recognizing the existence of both deictic and non-deictic expressions of time. He also considers
additional data from Wolof and Japanese which provide evidence that deixis
is not always relevant to the sequential relations implicit in the metaphor.

De Haan's paper surveys languages with visual evidentials and shows how evidentials typically do not derive from vision words, as might at first be thought, but tend to develop diachronically from demonstratives and tense/aspect markers. The author then provides plausible cognitive semantic motivations for this kind of grammaticalization process, whereby the markers likely evolved from deictic expressions which in some way linked the speaker to the event being witnessed visually. Bergen and Plauché's paper presents an analysis of French constructions containing the deictic locative expression *voilà* 'there is' and shows how such constructions are related to each other semantically as members of a radial complex conceptual category. The various senses of the construction are motivated by metaphor, metonymy, constructional grounding, and other cognitive mechanisms.

Research by a third subset of authors focuses on functional considerations in explicating grammatical phenomena, and highlights how factors integral to a discourse event play a role in determining linguistic structure. Sanchez presents empirical data which support the role of intonation units as a means of coding semantic integration between the two clausal constituents of complementation constructions in spoken Spanish. Prosody, in terms of intonation units, serves the dual function of signaling both the integration of complex constructions and the expression of canonical combinations of given and new information. The papers by Corrigan and Tao pay particular attention to the social context of language use. Corrigan reveals that in attributing causality in a verbal argument, we do not necessarily assume that the person instigating an event (usually coded as the grammatical subject) actually caused the event to occur. Rather, there are features independent of grammatical or thematic roles, such as contextual factors concerning the social identities of event participants, which play an important role when assigning causality. Tao, in a cross-linguistic study of the switch-reference pattern, proposes that grammatical coding of the pattern, versus the lack of it, may reflect how much inference speakers and listeners use in tracking referential meaning. Therefore, the more grammatical coding a language uses in its presentation of referential meaning, the less its speakers may rely on inference in processing discourse information, and vice versa. Elliptical reference, or zero anaphora, entails greater reliance on inference by the listener.

Experimental and developmental evidence for certain kinds of linguistic phenomena provides the basis for a fourth group of papers. Hillert and Swinney address the question of how idiomatic and literal meanings of compound nouns in German are accessed during real-time sentence processing. They present the results of two lexical priming experiments which support the conclusion that, for German nominal compounds, all meanings, both idiomatic and literal, are simultaneously and exhaustively accessed when the nominal compound is understood. Phrases with fixed meanings seem to be processed in much the same way as lexical ambiguities, blurring the distinction between syntactic, morphological, and lexical representation. Johnson's research addresses the processes children use to represent relations between constructions, using one form-meaning pair to motivate the acquisition of another related form in an overlapping discourse context. He illustrates the process of 'constructional grounding' with deictic and existential THERE-constructions. He proposes that children acquire the more concrete deictic constructions first and then extend these constructions to the more abstract existential uses. He finds support for this proposal in corpora of children's language usage. Papafragou provides conceptual motivation and empirical support for the hypothesis that central semantic and pragmatic aspects of language acquisition, in particular, the acquisition of epistemic modals and evidentials, presupposes certain advancements in children's ability to attribute mental representations to themselves and to others. Budwig's paper presents a developmental functional approach in its investigation of the grammatical acquisition of perspective in German and in English. Her research shows that errors children make in marking agency encode semantic and pragmatic aspects of scenes in systematic ways that vary across languages: children begin by using case markers to demarcate agency, and later use voice to signify more subtle distinctions. This research emphasizes that from the earliest stages of word combination, children represent and express viewpoints and perspectives, but that these expressions are sensitive to linguistic forms, cultural cues, and social contexts.

We believe the papers in this volume demonstrate the need to incorporate both conceptual and discourse factors in descriptions of linguistic form, and that, as such, they represent a valuable step forward in understanding human language. We would like to acknowledge in closing our sincere thanks the faculty, students, and staff who helped organize the conference at Emory University which gave rise to this volume. We also owe a debt of gratitude to the many anonymous referees who reviewed the papers submitted for publication. Their time, effort, and expertise helped make this volume possible.

Alan Cienki
Barbara J. Luka
Michael B. Smith

The Syntax of French Raising Verbs

Michel Achard

Rice University

1. Introduction

The study of raising figures prominently among the arguments advocating the need for an underlying level of representation in different models of generative grammar because of its seemingly structural character. Let us briefly review the facts with examples (1)-(3).

(1)   John seems to understand

(2)   John wants to understand

(3)   It seems that John understands

Despite their similar surface form, the sentences in (1) and (2) exhibit several semantic and syntactic differences. First, 'seem' apparently imposes no restrictions on its subject, but 'want' is usually restricted to animate subjects. Consequently, the only constraints imposed on the subject in (1) come from the complement verb, but in (2), the constraints imposed by the main and complement verbs need to be satisfied. Furthermore, a battery of syntactic tests well known in the literature (Perlmutter 1970; Ruwet 1972; *inter alia*) were argued to prove that while 'John' is the real subject of 'want', it is not the real subject of 'seem', but rather that of 'understand'. In order to explain these differences, generative linguists posited that the 'seem' verbs and the 'want' verbs are different in their underlying structure. The 'seem' or raising verbs were given the underlying structure in (4), and the 'want' (or first equi then control) verbs were assigned the underlying structure in (5). The representations in (4) and (5) are adapted from Ruwet

Conceptual and Discourse Factors in Linguistic Structure.
Alan Cienki, Barbara J. Luka and Michael B. Smith (eds.).
Copyright © 2001, CSLI Publications.

(1972: 60), where *ec* stands for an empty category. However, they are only presented as an example of the spirit of generative solutions.

(4)   [$_S$ *ec* seems [$_S$ John to understand]]

(5)   [John$_i$ want [$_S$PRO$_i$ to understand]]

The underlying form in (5) yields the surface form in (1) by the application of an optional subject raising rule by which John is promoted to the subject of seem. It the rule fails to apply, the empty subject position is filled by the dummy 'it', to satisfy the structural need for a surface subject. The resulting sentence is found in (3).

This kind of explanation was judged so convincing that in the early days of transformational grammar, it was widely used to promote the explanatory power of the newly developed theory. For example, in the introduction of the chapter on the syntax of subject raising verbs in his 1972 book, Ruwet (1972: 48) writes (translation mine):

> Les faits apparement très bizzares dont on va parler découlent naturellement de l'hypothèse que la compétence linguistique des sujets parlant une langue ne peut être décrite que par une grammaire qui comprend au moins un niveau de structure superficielle et un niveau de structure profonde, ces deux niveaux étant reliés par des transformations ordonnées.

> 'The seemingly bizarre facts we will be talking about naturally follow from the hypothesis that the linguistic competence of the subjects who speak a language can only be described by a grammar that contains at least a level of surface structure and a level of deep structure, these two levels being connected by ordered transformations.'

Although the mechanism of raising has considerably changed and reflects the sophistication of current syntactic theory, the belief that the behavior of the raising verbs is directly imputable to their specific underlying structure is still strong.[1] This paper uses data from French to challenge that belief on two fronts. First, I argue that the relation between the raised and unraised variants of a given verb (between (1) and (3) for example) is not a structural one, but one of construal (Langacker 1991). The speaker chooses one variant over the other, because the way in which it profiles the scene it describes is the most suitable to express her conceptualization and satisfy

---

[1] For example, in Chomsky's (1981) government binding model, the underlying structures of raising and control verbs are as follows:

(1)   [$_{NP}$ e] seem [$_{S'}$ COMP [$_S$ John INFL to understand]]

(2)   John pretend [$_{S'}$ COMP [$_S$ PRO INFL to understand]]

Furthermore, the subject raising rule has been replaced by the more general move Alpha and co-indexing mechanisms. However, the spirit of the solution is largely unchanged from the transformational days.

her communicative purposes. Secondly, I show that the syntactic behavior of the raising verbs can be explained by examining the interaction of the meaning of those verbs with that of the constructions that provide the environment for the tests. Consequently, following Langacker (1995), I claim that the syntax of the French raising verbs can successfully be described without positing underlying levels of representation.

The analysis makes use of the concepts developed within cognitive grammar (henceforth CG, Langacker 1987; 1991), and I assume basic familiarity with both the theoretical positions and the working constructs of the model. For the sake of brevity, I will focus exclusively on subject-to-subject raising (henceforth SSR), where the main clause subject is viewed as the logical subject of the complement verb, but the analysis can easily be extended to other kinds of raising constructions. The paper is structured in the following fashion. Section two briefly presents the French SSR verbs. Section three provides a CG analysis of the conceptual/semantic import of the SSR construction. Section four considers the syntactic behavior of the SSR verbs. Section five summarizes the results and concludes the paper.

2. French Raising Verbs

There are three verb classes that are uncontroversially considered SSR verbs in French. These are the aspectuals, modals (in their epistemic senses), and epistemic verbs, respectively illustrated in (6)-(8).

(6)   *Jean commence à comprendre*

        'John begins to understand'

(7)   *La voiture doit être réparée maintenant*

        'The car must be fixed now'

(8)   *Marie semble comprendre la linguistique facilement*

        'Mary seems to understand linguistics easily'

Note that among those verbs, only the epistemics admit both raised and unraised variants. Aspectuals and modals undergo the so-called obligatory raising, as illustrated in (9)-(11).

(9)   **Il commence que Jean comprend*

        'It begins that John understands'

(10)   **Il doit que la voiture soit réparée maintenant*

        'It must that the car be fixed now'

(11)   *Il semble que Marie comprend la linguistique facilement*

        'It seems that Mary understands linguistics easily'

Because this paper is mostly concerned with the relation between the raised and unraised variants of a given raising verb, I will restrict the analysis to the epistemic verbs, and particularly to *sembler* 'seem'. The issue of obligatory raising will be left for further research.

2.1 Syntactic Behavior of Raising Verbs

Among the battery of structural tests designed to identify a class of raising verbs, I will mostly focus on the one based on the behavior of the clitic *en* 'of it', because it is probably the most complex. It also represents in the words of Ruwet (1991: 56): "the most spectacular and most strictly syntactic", and thus the most recalcitrant to a conceptual account. Consider the examples in (12) and (13) (adapted from Ruwet 1983):

(12) a. *L'auteur (de ce livre) semble être génial*

'The author (of this book) seems to be brilliant'

b. *L'auteur (de ce livre) prétend être génial*

'The author (of this book) pretends to be brilliant'

(13) a. *Je ne sais pas qui a écrit ce livre, mais l'auteur semble en être génial*

'I don't know who wrote this book, but the author of it seems to be brilliant'

b. * *Je ne sais pas qui a écrit ce livre, mais l'auteur prétend en être génial*

'I don't know who wrote this book, but the author of it pretends to be brilliant'

The examples in (12) and (13) show that the clitic *en* can replace the prepositional phrase *de*-NP (*de ce livre* 'of this book') part of the subject NP of the subordinate verb, and be cliticized on that verb. However, this is only possible when the main verb is a raising verb. In the case of a control verb such as (13b), the cliticization of *en* on the subordinate verb is impossible.

Although it will not be considered in detail here, the raising verbs also cannot successfully be embedded in a causation/perception construction. Control verbs on the other hand are perfectly felicitous in that position, as illustrated in (14) and (15).

(14) **Marie fait sembler à Jean de ne pas douter de lui*

'Mary makes John seem not to doubt himself'

(15) *Marie fait promettre à Jean de ne pas douter de lui*

'Mary makes John promise not to doubt himself'

The raising verb *sembler* in (14) cannot occur in the causative construction. The same causative construction is perfectly acceptable when it includes a control verb such as *promettre* in (15).

These two tests, however, along with the others not mentioned here due to space considerations, fail to clearly distinguish between a raising and a control class of verbs on the basis of their syntactic behavior, because a fair number of verbs exhibit both control and raising properties (Ruwet 1983; Rooryck 1990). The most frequently mentioned of those verbs are *promettre* 'promise' and *menacer* 'threaten', but the list also includes among others *mériter* 'deserve', *avoir des chances* 'have chances', *s'avérer* 'turn out'. Let us use *promettre* as a representative example. As was shown in (13), the verb appears to be a control verb because it can successfully be embedded in a causative construction. However, as noticed in Ruwet (1983), it does not seem to impose restrictions on its subject, as illustrated in (16):

(16)   *La séance promet d'être houleuse*

         'The meeting promises to be stormy'

Furthermore, the cliticization of *en* seems to be at least partly symptomatic of raising. The example in (17) is from Ruwet (1983: 22).

(17)   *Les conditions (du traité) promettent d'en être satisfaisantes*

         'The conditions (of the treaty) seem of it to be satisfactory'

The inconsistent behavior of these verbs constitutes a problem for any account based on a structural difference between the control and raising verbs. None of the proposed solutions succeeds in reconciling the categorial nature of the control/raising distinction with the flexible behavior of the verbs mentioned above. The earliest (and still frequently invoked) follows Perlmutter (1970) in assigning two underlying structures to the verbs that are ambiguous between a raising and control interpretation. Consider the sentences in (18) and (19):

(18)   *Marie promet de devenir un grand musicien*

         'Mary promises to become a great musician'

(19)   *Jean menace de tout casser*

         'John threatens to break everything'

In these examples, both *promettre* 'promise and *menacer* 'threaten' have a control interpretation where the main subject performs the act of promising or threatening, as well as a raising reading where the speaker evaluates the future behavior of *Marie* and *Jean* as promising or threatening. Each interpretation is assigned a different underlying representation. In this solution, the structural nature of the raising/control distinction is preserved, but the arbitrariness of the assignment of a specific underlying representation is problematic.

The flexibility of the *promettre* type verbs has led other researchers to rethink the control/raising distinction more radically. For example, in his two analyses of the issue that follow his 1972 syntactic account, Ruwet gets further and further away from the idea of a structural difference between raising and control verbs, without however giving it up completely. He first (Ruwet 1983) recognizes the importance of the role of the main subject as a conceptualizing presence or an object of conceptualization. He notes that the difference between raising and control verbs is the greatest when the main subject of a control verb is presented as a conceptualizing presence, that is to say with verbs such as *penser* 'think' or *croire* 'believe', that present the scene in their complement from the viewpoint of their subject. These core control verbs stand in maximal contrast to the most common raising verbs such as *sembler* 'seem' or *paraître* 'appear' where the viewpoint from which the complement scene is conceptualized is unquestionably the speaker's. He proposes that those radically opposed verbs alone are generated in the grammar. In the remaining cases, namely when the subject of the main verb (human or not) is not presented as a conceptualizing presence, the line between raising and control verbs is blurry, and reducible to viewpoint phenomena. The consequences of his position, however, strike him as strange when he writes (Ruwet 1991: 78):[2]

> We would then arrive at the paradoxical situation of having only a fairly limited subset of the acceptable sentences of French being generated directly by grammar (essentially, the control sentences with a human subject, and the raising sentences involving *sembler* 'seem,' *paraître* 'appear', etc.).

Further reflection on this solution lead Ruwet to express even more doubts about the validity of a the raising/control structural distinction. In a previously unpublished postscript to the 1991 translation of his 1983 article, he writes (Ruwet 1991: 81):

> If we could develop a systematic and refined analysis in terms of point of view, and if it were not for the distribution of *en*, there would be very little reason left to keep to a double syntactic analysis (Raising, Control) of infinitival complementation: most of the facts that have been adduced in the past as arguments for raising (expletive subjects, specificational subjects, idiom chunks, etc.) would be explained in terms of an external point of view.

The analysis presented in this paper elaborates on Ruwet's insights to propose a solution where his "double syntactic analysis" is totally elimi-

---

[2] For convenience sake, the quote I am using here is taken from Goldsmith's translation of the 1983 article published in Ruwet (1991).

nated. I follow his initial suggestion that the difference between raising and control verbs is essentially one of viewpoint. In order to articulate that difference and make it systematic, I draw heavily on the growing CG literature on perspective (Langacker 1985; 1990; 1991), and its application to French sentential complementation (Achard 1996a; 1996b; 1998). I also show that Ruwet's last remaining syntactic stronghold, namely the distribution of *en* can also be successfully explained by a close analysis of the function of the *en* construction, and the evaluation of the compatibility of different verbs with that function. Consequently, the solution proposed in this paper differs radically from structural accounts because the syntactic behavior of the raising verbs is imputable to their semantic/conceptual specificity, and not their underlying structure. In the remainder of this paper, I first provide a semantic analysis of the raised and unraised variants of *sembler* 'seem', before turning to its syntactic behavior.

3. A CG Analysis of French Subject-to-Subject Raising

Following Langacker's (1995) analysis of English raising, I will claim that *sembler* is a polysemous verb, with different senses in different constructions. Its raised variant, that is to say, the one that occurs in the raising construction, is illustrated in (8). Its unraised variant, namely the one that occurs with a finite clause is illustrated in (11). Consistent with the CG methodology, I will now show that the meaning of each variant is best characterized by describing the specific construal it imposes on its conceptual base.

3.1 Conceptual Base

It has long been noticed (Ruwet 1972; 1983; Rooryck 1990) that the SSR verbs exhibit a great deal of semantic unity. To put it in the broadest possible terms, they pertain to the conditions of occurrence of some aspect of reality (event or proposition). The aspectuals profile the internal state of a process. The modal and epistemic verbs evaluate the conditions of occurrence of a given event or proposition. The meaning of these epistemics, the focus of this section, therefore needs to be characterized relative to our conception of reality.

An important aspect of our conception of reality is the fact that we are constantly guessing about its content. We are positive about the presence of certain elements because we perceive them, or have had irrefutable experiences with them. For others, we have to rely on our interpretation of various clues in our environment, and these clues provide us with different levels of certainty as to their presence in reality. The epistemic verbs provide the whole range of a conceptualizer's interpretative effort to determine the exact location of a given event or proposition. In the broadest sense of epistemic, these verbs also include control verbs such as *penser* 'think', *être certain de* 'be certain that', etc. Different epistemic verbs structure their base differently along different dimensions. Some of these dimensions are the following: i) presentation of the main subject as a conceptualizer or an object of conceptualization, ii) explicit mention of reality or a sub-part thereof, iii) expression of the participant in the observed process. We will see shortly that the meaning of the raising verbs needs to be characterized along these three dimensions.

Another aspect of our conception of reality concerns its dynamic nature, or in other words the fact that the way things are conditions and constrains the future course of events Langacker (1991: 277). The different epistemic verbs specify the tentative location of particular events or propositions in reality. For example, in *Jean semble comprendre* 'John seems to understand', the speaker's interpretation of John's behavior in current reality along with the comparison of that behavior with earlier relevant episodes allows her to consider the process of John's understanding as a valid candidate for insertion in current reality. Similarly, in *Marie s'avère être très sympathique* 'Mary turns out to be very nice', Mary's unexpected attitude is unveiled as a facet of current reality. Although this brief exposition doesn't do justice to the level of complexity of our model of reality, I hope it suffices to show how that model represents the conceptual base with respect to which the meaning of the raised and unraised variants of *sembler* needs to be characterized.

3.2 Profile of the Unraised and Raised Variants of *sembler*
The two variants of *sembler* structure the aforementioned base differently with respect to i) the specific mention of reality, and ii) the salience and discursive status of the main participant in the observed event.

Let us begin with the unraised variant illustrated in (11). As we mentioned earlier, the sentence profiles the speaker's evaluation of the proposition *Marie comprend la linguistique facilement* 'Mary understands linguistics easily' as a potential candidate for insertion into current reality. As it has also been pointed out, the speaker's opinion is deeply grounded in her observation and interpretation of the events of current reality. In Achard (1998: Chapter 7), I argue that impersonal constructions are existential in nature, in that they pertain to the presence of certain elements in reality (for us here, events or propositions). I also argue that the impersonal *il* 'it' represents an abstract setting subject (Langacker 1991), identifiable as the immediate scope of predication for the event/proposition profiled in the complement. This scope of predication consists of the sub-section of reality immediately required for the existence of the event/proposition in the complement to be identified. For example, in (11), the part of reality that includes the facts and behaviors that motivate the speaker's conclusion constitute the immediate scope of predication of the proposition *Marie comprend la linguistique facilement*. With unraised *sembler*, it is the abstract setting that is given focal prominence and thus marked as the subject. The event or proposition as a whole (and that includes its main participant) is viewed as the secondary figure and thus marked as the landmark. The verb therefore profiles a relation between a specific sub-part of reality and an event or proposition that can be identified within it. The important point here is that reality itself is put on stage and specifically invoked as a reference point with respect to which the event/proposition in the complement can be located.

In *sembler*'s raised variant illustrated in (8), the main character in the located event is taken as the trajector of the main relation. The process it participates in is viewed as the landmark of that relation. Unlike the case with the unraised variant, reality remains an unprofiled part of the base, or in other words, construed subjectively (Langacker 1985; 1990). The raised variant of *sembler* thus profiles the possible (apparent) participation of a thing in a given process. In order for *Jean* to be considered a true subject of *sembler*, Langacker's notion of active zones must be recognized. Recall that the active zone of an entity is "those facets of an entity capable of interacting directly with a given domain or relation (Langacker 1987: 485). In the raising construction, the complement process (*comprendre* in our example) represents the subject's (*Marie*) active zone with respect to its participation in the main relation. In other words, it is with respect to the process of *comprendre* that *Marie* can be considered the subject of *sembler*. This active zone relationship between the main verb and its subject enhances the latter's reference point function. The event in the complement can only be accessed via the initial location of its main participant.

If we generalize the analysis of *sembler* to all SSR verbs, we note that these verbs exhibit maximum transparency with respect to the choice of their subject. Langacker (1995: 40) characterizes transparency as follows: "any element that can occur in the appropriate position in the subordinate clause can likewise occur in 'raised' position in the main clause". That characteristic of raising verbs directly follows from their semantic characterization.

Let us consider the epistemic verbs. It was already mentioned in our earlier discussion of their conceptual base that we come to know things in the world in different ways. For example, we can actively seek knowledge, and specifically focus on the kind of epistemic effort that enables us to obtain it. This is often done with control verbs such as *se demander* 'wonder', *penser* 'think', etc. However, things have a way of unfolding themselves and reality often is perceived as revealing itself to us without any particular effort on our part. In that case, reality is viewed with some degree of independence from the specific conceptualizer who apprehends it. Raising Epistemics structure reality in that way. This semantic trait is particularly clear with verbs such as *s'avérer* 'turns out', *se trouver* 'happen' which do not even allow the specific mention of the conceptualizer responsible for the conceptualization, as illustrated in (20):

(20) a. *Il s'est avéré *(à Paul) que Marie avait menti*

'It turned out to Paul that Mary had lied'

b. *Il s'est trouvé *(à tout le monde) que personne n'avait rien compris*

'It happened to everybody that nobody had understood anything'

The verbs in (20) profile a property of reality, a facet of evolutionary momentum independent from any specific conceptualizer that unveils itself, and becomes available for everyone to notice. A more precise analysis of the middle marker *se* would emphasize the quasi agentive status of reality that allows it to be figuratively presenting itself, but this is well outside the scope of this presentation.

The other raising epistemics such as *sembler* and *paraître* profile less independent events or proposition, because they are less firmly established in objective reality. Their perception can be restricted to specific conceptualizers, and those can be specifically mentioned as illustrated in (21):

(21) a. *Il a semblé (à Paul) que Marie avait menti*

'It seemed to Paul that Mary had lied'

b. *Il a paru (à tout le monde) que personne n'avait rien compris*

'It appeared to everyone that nobody had understood anything'

However, like the more general *se trouver* and *s'avérer*, *sembler* and *paraître* are also primarily concerned with the properties of reality, or in other words with the way in which reality reveals itself, if only imperfectly and selectively. Importantly, those verbs do not profile any conceptualizer's effort to actively seek it out.

Given their semantic characterization, the transparency of the epistemic raising verbs is obvious. First, since they are concerned with the way in which reality reveals itself, the conceptualizer is not available as a main subject. The only elements that are available are part of the observed scene, and subject selection is a matter of focal prominence within that scene. If no element is particularly salient, the sub-part of reality that constitutes the immediate scope of predication for the event or proposition in the complement (profiled by *il*) represents a natural choice, and the unraised variant is chosen. On the other hand, we learn a lot about events involving things just by looking at those things. If some entity is salient enough to warrant our attention, it can also evoke a set of processes it has, will, or is likely to participate in. The use of the raised variant is thus also natural.

It is therefore clear that the relation between the raised and the unraised variant is not a structural one, but one of construal. This means that the distribution of these variants is determined by discourse and pragmatic factors, among which the topicality and salience of the main participant in the subordinate process figures prominently.[3]

3.3 Raising, Control, and Perspective

I have argued elsewhere (Achard 1996a; 1996b; 1998) that the dimension of perspective is crucial to the characterization of French sentential complements. Perspective (Langacker 1985; 1990) involves at the same time the vantage point from which the complement clause is conceptualized, as well as the kind of viewing arrangement that exists between the conceptualizer and her conceptualization (the complement clause). The overall picture of French complementation is presented in Figure 1 (from Achard 1996b: 1168)

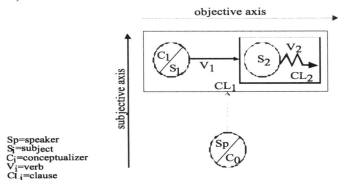

Sp=speaker
S_i=subject
C_i=conceptualizer
V_i=verb
Cl_i=clause

Figure 1. Complementation

In Figure 1, the outer rectangle CL_1 represents the sentence; V_1 represents the main verb. The inner rectangle CL_2 represents the complement structure, and V_2 represents the subordinate verb. The dual role of the speaker, as a speaker and a conceptualizer, is illustrated by Sp and C_0 respectively. The dotted arrow going from C_0 to CL_1 indicates the direction of conceptualization (the construal relation). It illustrates the fact that the whole sentence represents the conceptualization of C_0. The two arrows outside the diagram represent two axes of viewing arrangement.

---

[3] The current analysis makes the prediction that the raised variant of *sembler* should be found primarily when its subject has a high level of topicality (Langacker 1995). This prediction is indeed born out (Achard to appear), but this issue is beyond the scope of this paper.

The ground constitutes the default vantage point for the conceptualization of linguistic expressions. However, the internal complexity of certain multi-clause constructions presents an added level of difficulty. With the verbs whose subject functions as a conceptualizer with respect to the complement scene, the complement constructions include an additional conceptualizing relation. The profiled relation existing between the main subject S_1 and the complement clause CL_2 can be viewed as equivalent to that existing between the speaker and her conceptualization CL_1. For example, verbs such as *croire* 'believe' or *espérer* 'hope' present the mental stance of their subject vis-à-vis the CL_2 clause. The subject's role in conceptualizing the complement process can be likened to the construal relationship which ordinarily exists between the speech act participants and the conceptualized entity. In Figure 2, the potential dual role of the main clause subject, as a subject and a conceptualizer, is represented by S_1 and C_1 respectively. The arrow from C_1/S_1 to CL_2 illustrates the fact that the complement structure represents the conceptualization of C_1. With the verbs whose subject has an explicit conceptualizing role, the two construal relations define each of the two axes of viewing arrangement illustrated in Figure 2. The first occurs between the speaker and the objective scene, her conceptualization CL_1. Since it contains the primary subject of conceptualization, this axis is referred to as the "subjective axis". Secondly, as part of the viewed scene itself, there exists another kind of viewing relationship between the main clause conceptualizer C_1 and the complement clause CL_2. This second axis of viewing relationship is called the "objective axis" in Figure 2. The objective axis is of course only relevant if the main clause subject has a relevant conceptualizing role.

Perhaps the single most important difference between raising and control verbs concerns their different configurations of viewing arrangement. In Achard (1996a; 1996b), I draw a distinction between speaker-based and subject-based verbs. I argue that control verbs are subject-based, because they present the conceptualization of their subjects (along the objective axis). In keeping with the distinction, raising verbs are speaker-based, because conceptualization exclusively occurs along the subjective axis. The model briefly described here allows us to make more systematic Ruwet's initial intuition that viewpoint is more important than animacy to describe the constraints existing on the subjects of raising and control verbs. Regardless of whether or not the main subject of a raising verb is human, it is never a conceptualizing subject because of the viewpoint configuration of those verbs as speaker-based verbs.[4]

4. Syntactic Behavior of SSR Verbs

This section considers the distribution of *en* with the raising and control verbs. That distribution has strictly been used in the literature as a syntactic test, that is to say a systematic way of determining membership in either of the two verb classes. The use of *en*'s distribution as a test, however is rather strange given the highly sensitive ecology of the construction used for the test (that I will call the test construction). First, it is rare and very limited in scope. It is only when the cliticized PP is part of the subject NP of the subordinate verb that the control and raising verbs exhibit different behaviors. Compare for example (13b) to (22):

(22)   *L'auteur prétend en avoir expliqué tous les détails (de ce livre)*

'The author pretends of it to have explained all the details (of that book)'

Even though *prétendre* is a control verb, the sentence in (22) is felicitous because *en* stands for a PP part of the object NP of *expliquer* 'explain'. Secondly, it is heavily constrained by discourse pragmatic considerations, and its felicity often requires a very specific context. As a matter of fact, several of my consultants often questioned the validity of such paradigmatic examples as (12b). This indicates that the test construction is too context dependent to be used as a structural test where the sentences are evaluated in isolation. Finally, neither *en*'s meaning nor that of the test construction is ever taken into account to determine the felicity of the sentences.

This section shows that once all these factors are considered, *en*'s distribution naturally follows from the constraints imposed by the meaning of the test construction, and the way in which different verbs are compatible with these constraints. Obviously, this means that the analysis proposed in this section can only be suggestive of a way of reaching a definitive solution. The factors that influence *en*'s distribution are too broad, numerous, and intertwined to be given a truly exhaustive account within the scope of this paper.

---

[4] The two axes of viewing arrangement are motivated independently of the raising construction, and used elsewhere to describe different syntactic phenomena. In Achard (1996a), I show that the distribution of grammatical markers on the infinitival complement of modals can be explained by different configurations of viewing arrangement along the subjective axis. In Achard (1996b), I show that the difference between infinitival and finite complements in sentential complement constructions can be accounted for by different configurations of viewing arrangement along the objective axis.

4.1 The Meaning of *en*

From a purely descriptive standpoint, in the examples under discussion in this paper, *en* replaces a NP when the latter reoccurs as part of a PP headed by *de* embedded in another NP. This is illustrated in (23).[5]

(23) *Vous avez aimé la tarte, attendez, je vais vous en donner la recette (de la tarte)*!

'You enjoyed the pie, wait, I will give you the recipe of it'

In (23), the NP *la tarte* occurs as the object of *aimer*. It could also possibly occur in the PP *de la tarte* embedded under *la recette*. However, in order to avoid repetition, *de la tarte* is replaced by *en*.

In order to start the investigation of the meaning of the clitic, I suggest that *en*'s function is to make specific the intrinsic relation that exists between its referent and the head noun of the NP in which it is located. This hypothesis seems reasonable, because *en* replaces a PP introduced by the preposition *de*, and *de* has independently been argued to perform a similar function (Kemmer and Shyldkrot 1995; see also Langacker 1991 for English 'of'). The particularities of *en*'s meaning will emerge out of our investigation of the very nature of this intrinsic relation, as well as the specific strategy the speaker adopts to link the two NPs. To make things more concrete, I will use possession as an example of intrinsic relation. Compare the English and French examples in (24) and (25).

(24) John's book

(25) *Le livre de Jean*

'The book of John'

The different word orders in the two languages represent different strategies in identifying the possessed object with respect to the possessor. Langacker (1991; 1993) shows that these strategies are best described relative to the reference point model (RPM). The RPM is a cognitive model that articulates our basic strategies in accessing and locating objects. We know that some objects in the world are very salient, and they can be considered on their own. We also know that other less salient objects can only be identified with respect to more salient ones. Based primarily on English data, the RPM illustrates a specific strategy to access objects of low level of salience. Salient objects can be used as reference points for the location of less-salient ones, that is to say, the location of a non-salient object is calculated with

---

[5] *En* can also replace any expression of quantity. For example, *Je veux de l'eau* 'I want water' can be cliticized as *J'en veux*. 'I want of it'. It can also replace the argument of a verb if the preposition *de* is part of the structure dictated by the verb. For example, *J'ai peur des serpents* 'I am afraid of snakes' can cliticize in *J'en ai peur* 'I of it am afraid'. These constructions will not be considered here.

respect to a more salient one. The RPM is illustrated in Figure 2 (from Langacker 1991: 170).

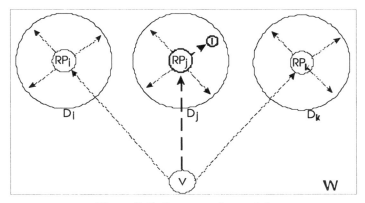

Figure 2. Reference-point model

In Figure 2, W stands for the world, V for the viewer, and T for the target, or in other words the entity the viewer is trying to locate. Each object that can potentially be used as a reference point anchors an abstract region defined as the set of objects it can be used to locate. This abstract region is called the reference point's dominion D. The viewer's mental path takes her to the target via the reference point with which she makes initial contact. The reference-point model is particularly well-suited to describe the English possessive construction in (24). The conception of John is expectedly more salient than that of the book. If the book is being located, it is more easily located through its being possessed by John (or any other salient conceptual relation it may hold to the reference point). In CG terms, John is used as a reference point, and the book is in his dominion. When a viewer wants to locate the book (the target), its conceptual path takes her initially to the reference point, and then to the target.

The *de* NP possessive construction in French reveals a different kind of strategy, although it can still be described within the RPM. In (25), *Jean* can still be viewed as a reference point, because the things he owns are still ultimately identified in their relation with him. However, he doesn't have the accessing function inherent to the reference point in English. The book is first accessed, and identified as a part of its owner's dominion by the preposition *de*. In a manner equivalent to the ''s' marker in English, the preposition *de* profiles the intrinsic relation (here possession) existing between John and the book (Langacker 1991).

Even though both *en* and *de* code intrinsic relations between nominals, they differ from each other in the accessing strategy used to establish that relation. *En* is closer to the English strategy in that it makes use of the accessing function of the reference point. *En*'s referent is used as a reference point with respect to which another entity is located. Let us consider again the example in (23). The initial mention of *la tarte* establishes it as a reference point. *La recette* is located in relation to that reference point, and can, in that sense, be said to be in its dominion.[6] We can therefore refine the preliminary definition of *en* given at the beginning of this section. *En* profiles the intrinsic relation existing between a reference point (its referent) and another entity identified as being part of its dominion.

Two important points emerge out of this definition. First, the uses of *en* considered in this paper are marked in French, because they involve an accessing strategy different from the one routinely used to express an intrinsic relation between nominals. Consequently, they will only be possible in specific situations. Secondly, because of its reference point function, the clitic's referent has enough prominence to be considered a local topic, a term quite simply used here to indicate what the sentence is perceived to be primarily about. However, because of the presence of another nominal in the construction (the head of the NP where *en* is located), there is the potential for competition for the position of local topic. *En*'s meaning needs to be considered in the context of that competition. By profiling the intrinsic relation existing between its referent and the other nominal, *en* enhances the topicality of its referent to ensure the latter wins out. It makes specific the fact that the head of the NP where it is located is only mentioned with respect to its referent.

4.2 *En* Part of a Subject NP

This section illustrates the clitic's role as a topic enhancer in the specific context of the construction where *en* replaces a PP part of a subject NP (the test construction).

First, whereas *de* can describe virtually any relation existing between two nominals, *en* is much more constrained. The relation it profiles must be highly central to its referent, and provide information crucial in identifying it. For example, Kupferman (1991) notes that in the case of concrete nouns, *en*'s referent and the head of the NP that contains the clitic most often stand in a part/whole relation. This is presented in (26) and (27).

(26)   a.   *La porte de ce frigo est cassée*

---

[6] This is confirmed by the presence of the definite article on the recipe. Note that the possessive *son* 'his/her' would be impossible in that case. The exclusive presence of the definite article can be explained because the possession relation is already implicitly present as part of the notion of dominion. These facts are similar in that sense to examples such as *Il a levé la main* 'He raised the hand' where the presence of the definite article corroborates the presence of the hand in the subject's dominion (Langacker 1991: 179).

'The door of that fridge is broken'

b. *Ce frigo est neuf, mais la porte en est cassée*

'This fridge is new, but the door of it is broken'

(27) a. *La viande de ce frigo est abîmée*

'The meat of this fridge is damaged'

b. **Ce frigo est froid, mais la viande en est abîmée*

'This fridge is cold, but the meat of it is spoiled'

The examples in (26) and (27) show that *de* can adequately describe the relations in (26a) and (27a). However, *en* is only felicitous with the part/whole relation in (26b). Kupferman (1991) argues that *en* must describe a stable relation, independent of a specific discourse. It is therefore infelicitous in (27b) where the relation between the meat and the refrigerator is strictly determined by the local discourse. Kupferman's explanation is perfectly compatible with the analysis proposed here where *en* enhances the topicality of its referent (it clearly shows the sentence is exclusively about the referent). The explicit mention of the relation between the door and the fridge enhances the latter's topicality because the door can only be viewed in relation with it.[7]

In addition to the constraints existing on its distribution, there is additional evidence that *en* enhances the topicality of its referent. Consider the examples in (28) and (29).

(28) *La maison est belle, mais le toit en est abîmé*

'The house is beautiful, but the roof of it is damaged'

---

[7] Similar constraints also exist with abstract entities. With nominalizations, the presence of *en* is most felicitous when a specific event is predicated of the head noun of the *en* phrase, as opposed to a stative or a mental process. This is illustrated in (1) and (2), adapted from Kupferman (1991).

(1) *Cet alphabet est maintenant bien connu, mais le décryptage en a été malaisé*

'This alphabet is now well known, but the deciphering of it was difficult'

(2) **Cet alphabet était autrefois bien connu, mais l'ignorance en est aujourd'hui générale*

'This alphabet was formerly well known, but the ignorance of it is quite general nowadays'

In (1) the deciphering describes a punctual event, an event with a beginning and an end, whereas the ignorance in (2) is presented as a more stable mental property, with no beginning or end. These fact go in the direction of the analysis proposed here. The mention of a well-known episode centrally associated with the reference point in (1) is very helpful in identifying that referent. This is not the case in (2), where the ignorance is merely accidentally associated with the reference point, and provides little help in identifying it.

(29)   *La maison est belle, mais le toit est abîmé*

'The house is beautiful, but the roof is damaged'

The examples in (28) and (29) show that the presence of *en* is not manda-
tory, and the PP *de la maison* can be omitted altogether. The relation existing between the two nouns is easily recoverable because of our world
knowledge.

    The difference in meaning between (28) and (29) clearly illustrates *en*'s
role in making explicit the relation that exists between the two nominals *la
maison* 'the house' and *le toit* 'the roof'. Obviously, the two sentences are
identical in their propositional content. Both convey a specific property of
one of the components (the roof) of the initial nominal (the house). However, they differ in the specific kind of relation existing between those two
entities. In (29), the sentence is understandable because we know that houses
have roofs, and if a roof is mentioned in connection with a house, in the
absence of a specific context, it will be interpreted as part of the house in
question. In (28), the presence of *en* makes the relation between the house
and the roof much more specific. It is explicitly mentioned that the damaged
roof belongs to the house being described. As a result, sentence (28) is perceived to be much more explicitly about the house itself, and how it is affected by the status of one of its parts. The state of the roof is only mentioned because of its effect on the global evaluation of the house. This sentence would be most appropriate discussing the condition of a vintage house
where each piece saliently contributes to the value of the whole.

    In (29), the house and the roof have a greater degree of independence.
The house is obviously central to the sentence, but the latter cannot be said
to be exclusively about the house. The statement in (29) could be, for instance, uttered by a potential buyer trying to decide if she should close the
deal. In that situation, even though the roof is obviously part of the house,
the state of the house and the state of the roof are independent elements that
influence the potential buyer in opposite ways. To phrase it differently, the
relation between the house and the roof in (28) is closely tied to a particular
object (the house), whereas in (29), it is more closely tied to a more general
situation. These examples illustrate the fact that *en* enhances the topicality
of its referent, because the clitic's presence specifically states that the property predicated of its part is solely being introduced for the purpose of showing the way in which the referent is being affected.

    Expectedly, the clitic's presence is increasingly necessary the most
highly topical its referent is. This is illustrated in (30).

(30)   a.   *Quand même, cette maison, le toît en est vraiment bien abîmé!*

        'Really, that house, the roof of it is totally damaged'

b.   ??*Quand même, cette maison, le toît est vraiment bien abîmé!*

'Really, that house, the roof of it is totally damaged'

In (30), the nominal *cette maison* is topicalized, and everything about the utterance (pauses, intonation) indicates that it is exclusively about the house. Given that high level of topicality, a looser association with the roof similar to the one in (29) is not sufficient. The connection between the two nominals needs to be explicitly stated.

4.3 *En* and Viewpoint

Finally, we need to consider the viewpoint constraints that exist on the distribution of *en* with sentential complement constructions. Ruwet (1983; 1990) notes when *en* is in the embedded clause, it can only refer to the main subject with certain specific verbs, as illustrated in (31) and (32), adapted from Ruwet (1990: 53, 55).

(31)   a.   **Emile$_i$ pense que Sophie en$_i$ est amoureuse*

'Emile thinks that Sophie of him is in love'

b.   **Emile$_i$ espère que Sophie en$_i$ tombera amoureuse*

'Emile hopes that Sophie of him will fall in love'

(32)   a.   *Un vieillard amoureux mérite qu'on en rie*

'An old man in love deserves to be made fun of him'

b.   *Ce livre mérite qu'on en parle à la télévision*

'This book deserves that one talks about it on television'

Coreference between the main subject and *en* is possible in (32) with the verb *mériter* 'deserve', but it is impossible in (31) with *penser* 'think'. Ruwet argues that the difference between the sentences in (31) and (32) is directly imputable to a difference between internal and external viewpoint. *En* (as well as *y*, another clitic not considered here) can only refer to the main subject if the latter doesn't constitute the vantage point from which the complement clause is conceptualized. He expresses this constraints as follows (1990: 56):

> Si en ou y se trouvent dans une proposition exprimant un contenu de con-science Cci, en et y ne peuvent être coréférentiels du N'' qui represente le su-jet de conscience Sci de ce Cci.

> 'If *en* or *y* are located in a proposition that expresses a content of con-sciousness Cci, *en* and *y* cannot be coreferential with the N'' that represents the subject of consciousness Sci of that Cci'.

Ruwet's analysis clearly shows that independently of its distribution with control and raising verbs, *en* is sensitive to the viewpoint from which the clause where it is located is conceptualized. In the next section, I argue that its behavior with control and raising verbs can also be viewed as a viewpoint phenomenon, and that Ruwet's proposal can be reformulated to cover those cases as well.

4.4 *En* with Raising and Control Constructions

The observations presented in the earlier sections do not do justice to *en*'s complex distribution, but they should make clear that the clitic's behavior with raising and control verbs cannot be considered a structural oddity. It simply emerges from the introduction of different types of verbs, each with their own conceptual structure, into a construction with a very complex ecology. Because they are conceptually different, the raising and control verbs react to the constraints imposed by the test construction with different degrees of felicity.

Recall from section 3 that the difference between control and raising verbs is primarily one of viewpoint. The subject of a control verb acts as a conceptualizer with respect to the complement scene, whereas the subject of a raising verb is not a conceptualizing subject. Consequently, the complement clause is conceptualized from the speaker's vantage point. It is therefore not surprising, given the sensitivity of the *en* construction to viewpoint phenomena, that it should react differently to the presence of verbs from these two classes. In fact, *en*'s distribution with raising and control verbs is closely related to the reference constraints on its distribution in sentential complements. I suggest that the rule in (33) covers the clitic's distribution in both instances.

(33)   *En* and its referent must both be located in a mental space set up by the speaker, or at least shared by the speaker.[8]

This formulation accounts for the reference facts presented in (31) and (32) in a direct way. With control verbs, the speaker does not set up any space of her own, but merely describes the main subject's mental space. For example in (31), the proposition *Sophie en est amoureuse* is presented as part of *Emile*'s mental space and not the speaker's. This is in obvious violation of the rule in (33), because neither the clitic nor its referent is located in a mental space set up by the speaker. In (32) on the other hand, the speaker does not describe the main subject's thoughts or ideas, but she sets up her own mental space composed of her thoughts and ideas associated with the main subject. That space is her sole creation, and it has no ties to what the main subject thinks or believes. This configuration satisfies the rule in (33), because both the clitic and its referent are located in that speaker generated space.

---

[8] The term 'mental space' is used here in the sense of Fauconnier (1985).

The rule in (33) also accounts for *en*'s distribution with the raising and control verbs presented in (12) and (13) in a straightforward manner. With the raising verbs, the speaker is the only conceptualizer in the sentence. *En* and its referent are thus necessarily in a mental space set up by her. On the other hand, because the subject of a control verb is a conceptualizing presence, and the complement content is situated in her own mental space, the clitic *en* cannot be in a mental space set up by the speaker. For example, in (13b), the complement content (*en être génial*) is located in the author's mental space and not the speaker's. The incompatibility of this configuration with the rule in (33) explains the infelicity of the sentence.

A final problem remains. The preceding section has shown that the constraint in (33) accounts for the viewpoint phenomena that govern *en*'s distribution in different constructions. However, it is still unclear what purpose that constraint serves, or more precisely how it relates to the clitic's basic function. In the remaining part of this section, I argue that the reason why the viewpoint constraint expressed in (33) exists is to allow *en* to perform its function presented in sections 4.1 and 4.2, namely to enhance the topicality of its referent.

The methodology adopted to confirm this hypothesis is similar to that proposed in section 4.2. Recall that *en* is not necessary in the test construction, and its omission from (13a) yields the sentence in (34).

(34)   *Je ne sais pas qui a écrit ce livre, mais l'auteur semble être génial*

'I don't know who wrote this book but the author seems to be brilliant'

Both (13a) and (34) are grammatical sentences, but I would claim that the one in (13a) is more obviously about the book than the one in (34), which could also be about the author. In order to substantiate that claim, consider the utterances in (35) and (36).

(35)   a.   *Je ne sais pas qui a écrit ce livre, mais l'auteur semble être génial. La structure est solide et le suspense ne se relâche jamais.*

'I don't know who wrote this book, but the author seems to be brilliant. The structure is sound, and the suspense never lets off'

b.   *Je ne sais pas qui a écrit ce livre, mais l'auteur semble être génial. Il manipule l'intrigue de main de maître, et le lecteur ne s'ennuie jamais.*

'I don't know who wrote this book, but the author seems to be brilliant. He manipulates the plot masterfully, and the reader never gets bored'

In both situations in (35), the clitic is omitted. The local topic in (35a) is the book, as indicated by the characteristics described in the second sentence. In (35b), the author can be viewed as the local topic for similar reasons. The book is only considered as the manifestation of her craft. Both utterances are perfectly grammatical and pragmatically felicitous. However, compare the utterances in (35) to their counterparts in (36) that include *en*.

(36) a. *Je ne sais pas qui a écrit ce livre, mais l'auteur semble en être génial. La structure en est solide et le suspense ne se relâche jamais*

'I don't know who wrote this book, but the author seems of it to be brilliant. The structure of it is sound, and the suspense never lets off'

b. *?? Je ne sais pas qui a écrit ce livre, mais l'auteur semble en être génial. Il manipule l'intrigue de main de maître, et le lecteur ne s'ennuie jamais*

'I don't know who wrote this book, but the author seems of it to be brilliant. He manipulates the plot masterfully, and the reader never gets bored'

Whereas the examples in (35) are equally felicitous whether they are primarily about the book or about the author, the presence of *en* in (36) makes the utterance where the author is the local topic more difficult to accept. My consultants did not think (36b) was ungrammatical, but pragmatically strange. One of them indicated it was too "loose", as if the different pieces did not fit together well. Their intuitions fit nicely with the analysis proposed here. *En*'s function, namely to enhance the topicality of its referent, conflicts with the presence of another nominal as the local topic and thus produces pragmatic discomfort.

The situation is quite different with the control verbs. In the test construction that holds the potential for competition for local topic between *en*'s referent and the head of the NP that contains the clitic, their subject will invariably be the local topic due to its status as a conceptualizing subject. This is illustrated in (37) and (38).

(37) *Je ne sais pas qui a écrit ce livre, mais l'auteur prétend être génial*

'I don't know who wrote this book but the author pretends to be brilliant'

In the absence of *en*, the sentence is perfectly grammatical. However, it is not about the book, not about the speaker's view of the author either, but about what the author said, as shown in the examples in (38).

(38)   a.   *Je ne sais pas qui a écrit ce livre, mais l'auteur prétend être gé-
            nial. La structure est solide et le suspense ne se relâche jamais

            'I don't know who wrote this book, but the author pretends to be
            brilliant. The structure is sound, and the suspense never lets off'

       b.   *Je ne sais pas qui a écrit ce livre, mais l'auteur prétend être gé-
            nial. Il manipule l'intrigue de main de maître, et le lecteur ne
            s'ennuie jamais

            'I don't know who wrote this book, but the author seems to be
            brilliant. He manipulates the plot masterfully, and the reader
            never gets bored'

       c.   Je ne sais pas qui a écrit ce livre, mais l'auteur prétend être gé-
            nial. Il dit que jamais personne n'a décrit l'âme humaine comme
            lui

            'I don't know who wrote this book, but the author pretends to be
            brilliant. He says that no one ever described the human soul as he
            did'

The infelicity of en with the control verbs in the test construction is therefore clear. Those verbs are incompatible with the clitic's basic function (to
enhance the topicality of its referent), because in the specific context of the
test construction, their subject is the local topic by virtue of its conceptualizing role. This result is not surprising. It merely reflects the interest humans have in other humans, particularly in their thoughts, opinions, and
desires. The raising verbs do not present the same difficulty. Because of
their transparency, their subject doesn't pose any threat to the topicality of
en's referent.

5. Recapitulation and Conclusion

Let us recapitulate the results obtained throughout this paper. Two claims
were made in the introduction. The first one was that the relation between
the raised and unraised variants of the raising verbs is not a structural one,
but one of construal. It was shown that each variant of sembler has its own
meaning, and that meaning is characterized by the specific construal it imposes on its conceptual base (our folk model of reality). The connection
between the two variants is obvious, they both structure the same scene, but
the choice between them is essentially a matter of focal prominence. If the
main participant in the conceptualized scene stands out, its choice as subject
with the raised variant is most natural. If no element of the scene has focal
prominence, the immediate scope of the event or proposition expressed in
the complement, that is to say the sub-part of reality necessarily invoked for
its identification is marked as the subject with the unraised variant.

The second claim was that the syntactic behavior of the raising verbs is explainable without resorting to underlying levels of representation. I have shown that the distribution of *en* can be explained by the careful examination of the different elements that compose the test construction, namely *en*'s meaning, the specific ecology of the construction, and the meaning of the raising and control verbs. It was shown that *en*'s distribution results from the different ways in which the respective conceptual structures of raising and control verbs are accommodated in the test construction. Much work needs to be done to exhaustively describe the syntax of the raising verbs, but I share Ruwet's optimism that the other syntactic behaviors characteristic of those verbs can be accounted for in similar fashion.

This solution eliminates the arbitrariness associated with the *promettre* 'promise' and *menacer* 'threaten' verbs. In their control sense, the main subject of these verbs respectively issue a specific promise or threat. In their raising sense, the speaker pronounces an epistemic judgment on the nature of things to come. The control senses are unproblematic. The subject consciously performs a promise or a menace to perform the event expressed in the complement. The raising sense of *promettre* and *menacer* are similar to the other epistemic verbs (although they are clearly future directed). The speaker observes some current facts about the subject, and that observation allows her to evaluate the probability of occurrence of future events involving it. The subject represents the most salient figure in the scene in which it participates, and its coding as subject is unproblematic. Note that this analysis does not merely list the two senses of *promettre* and *menacer*, but characterizes the relation between them as one of subjectification. In the control cases, the act of promising or threatening is objectively construed, strongly anchored by the main subject along the objective axis. The latter is the clearly outlined locus of the speech act. From this position along the objective axis, the speech act force gets realigned toward the speaker (along the subjective axis) in the raising cases. The speech act relation is no longer an objectively construed separate relation, but it is virtually indistinguishable from the speaker's interpretation of the evolutionary momentum of reality. From external and anchored by the main subject, it becomes subjective and speaker internal. The mechanism described here is virtually identical to other well-known instances of subjectification such as the main verb constructions becoming modals (Langacker 1991; Achard 1998).

As a final note, the analysis presented in this paper does not seek to eliminate the differences between the raising and control verb classes, simply what Ruwet called their "double syntactic analysis". The syntactic behavior of the raising verbs does differ from that of the control verbs, and those differences need to be explained. However, rather than being the output of structural mechanisms, they naturally emerge out of the verbs' different conceptual configurations in specific contexts.

References

Achard, Michel. To appear. The Distribution of French Raising Constructions. *Proceedings of the 26th Meeting of the Berkeley Linguistics Society*. University of California: Berkeley.

Achard, Michel. 1998. *Representation of Cognitive Structures: Syntax and Semantics of French Complements*. Berlin, Mouton de Gruyter.

Achard, Michel. 1996a. French Modals and Speaker Control, in A. Goldberg, ed., *Conceptual Structure, Discourse, and Language*. Stanford: CSLI.

Achard, Michel. 1996b. Perspective and Syntactic Realization. *Linguistics* 34. 1159-1198.

Chomsky, Noam. 1981. *Lectures on Government and Binding*. Dordrecht: Foris.

Fauconnier, Gilles. 1985. *Mental Spaces. Aspects of Meaning Construction in Natural Language*. Cambridge, Mass.: MIT Press/Bradford.

Kemmer, Suzanne, and Hava Bat-Zeev Shyldkrot. 1995. The Semantics of 'Empty Prepositions' in French, in E. Casad, ed., *Cognitive Linguistics in the Redwoods*. Berlin: Mouton de Gruyter.

Kupferman, Lucien. 1991. L'aspect du Groupe Nominal et l'Extraction de *en*. *Le Français Moderne* 59:113-147.

Langacker, Ronald W. 1985. Observations and Speculations on Subjectivity, in J. Haiman, ed., *Iconicity in Syntax*. Amsterdam: John Benjamins.

Langacker, Ronald W. 1987. *Foundations of Cognitive Grammar*, vol. 1: *Theoretical Prerequisites*. Stanford: Stanford University Press.

Langacker, Ronald W. 1990. Subjectification. *Cognitive Linguistics* 1:5-38.

Langacker, Ronald W. 1991. *Foundations of Cognitive Grammar*, vol. 2: *Descriptive Application*. Stanford: Stanford University Press.

Langacker, Ronald W. 1993. Reference-point Constructions. *Cognitive Linguistics* 4. 1-38.

Langacker, Ronald W. 1995. Raising and Transparency. *Language* 71:1-62.

Perlmutter, David. 1970. The Two Verbs *Begin*, in R. A. Jacobs and P. S Rosenbaum, eds., *Readings in English Transformational Grammar*. Waltham, MA: Ginn and Co.

Rooryck, Johan. 1990. Montée et Contrôle: Une Nouvelle Analyse. *Le Français Moderne* 58:1-27.

Ruwet, Nicolas. 1972. *Théorie Syntaxique et Syntaxe du Français*. Paris: Editions du Seuil.

Ruwet, Nicolas. 1983. Montée et Contrôle: Une Question à Revoir? in *Analyses Grammaticales du Français: Etudes publiées à l'occasion du 50e anniversaire de Carl Vikner. Revue Romane*, no. spécial 24:17-34.

Ruwet, Nicolas. 1990. *En* et *Y*, Deux Clitiques Pronominaux Antilogophoriques. *Languages* 97:51-81.

Ruwet, Nicolas. 1991. *Syntax and Human Experience*. Chicago: University of Chicago Press.

A Cognitive Linguistics Approach to the Layperson's Understanding of Thermal Phenomena

TAMER G. AMIN
Clark University

1. Introduction

The central objective of this paper is to provide a language-based characterization of the English speaking layperson's idealized cognitive model (Lakoff 1987) of thermal phenomena. The focus is on characterizing the core causal schema that can be expected to apply across all such phenomena. This work constitutes part of a larger study aimed at understanding the mechanism of conceptual change implicated in the transition from novice to expert in the domain of thermal physics (Wiser 1995; Wiser & Amin 1998). From the perspective of this larger study the analysis presented here contributes to the characterization of the layperson's understanding of thermal phenomena prior to formal instruction. I make use of the framework of cognitive linguistics (see e.g., Fauconnier 1997; Lakoff 1987; 1990; 1993; Langacker 1987) to achieve this characterization. First, on the basis of an analysis of the syntactic contexts of the lexical items *heat* (as verb), *heat* (as noun) and the noun *temperature*, as well as metaphors implicit in everyday language, a conceptual schema can be characterized, what I will call the "minimal cognitive model" of thermal phenomena. Second, the process of "conceptual integration" (Fauconnier 1997; Turner & Fauconnier 1995), claimed to take place as discourse unfolds, provides a useful analytical tool

Conceptual and Discourse Factors in Linguistic Structure.
Alan Cienki, Barbara J. Luka and Michael B. Smith (eds.).
Copyright © 2001, CSLI Publications.

for research on conceptual change in science. In particular, the framework of conceptual integration is applied to a student's conceptualization of the ontology of 'heat'. The suggestion will be that this conceptualization is not part of the layperson's minimal cognitive model of thermal phenomena but rather emerges in specific contexts of explanation.

2. A Language-based Characterization of the Minimal Cognitive Model of Thermal Phenomena.

In this section I examine aspects of the syntactic contexts of *heat* (as verb), *heat* (as noun) and *temperature*, and identify the corresponding semantic components that make up a minimal cognitive model of thermal phenomena. First, an argument is developed for classifying the verb *heat* as an accomplishment verb. This will suggest a basic semantic structure as a starting point for characterizing the minimal cognitive model sought. This is then followed by an analysis of the syntactic contexts of the nouns *heat* and *temperature* suggesting further semantic elaboration of the model.

2.1 The Syntax and Semantics of the Verb *Heat*

The starting point for this analysis is the classification of the verb *heat* with respect to the four verb classes: states, achievements, activities, and accomplishments (see Dowty 1979). Dowty suggested that verbs can be classified in terms of the basic aspectual structure implicit in their meaning. That is, verbs in each of the four aspectual class share a small set of basic units of meaning such as DO, BECOME, and CAUSE. State verbs are specified simply in terms of what Dowty called "stative predicates" where some entity is specified as being in some state (e.g., knowing). Achievement verbs involve elaborating the basic predicate with some sense of coming into being or becoming (e.g., notice). Activity verbs involve elaboration of a predicated entity with some sense of agency or doing (e.g., walk). Finally, accomplishment verbs share an aspectual structure which can be thought of as an agentive act causing the becoming of some state. The following table[1] from Foley and Van Valin (1984) summarizes these four aspectual structures.

Verb class	Logical structure
State	predicate (x)
Achievement	BECOME predicate (x)
Activity	DO (x, [predicate (x)])
Accomplishment	(causal event) CAUSE (BECOME [predicate (x)])

---

[1] The accomplishment verb entry is modified slightly for clarity.

Dowty (1979) lists a set of syntactic and logical entailment tests that establish the membership of a verb in one of these aspectual classes. In what follows, I summarize the application of these tests, establishing *heat* as an accomplishment verb. First, I quickly exclude the classification of *heat* as an achievement or state verb. Excluding the classification of *heat* as an activity verb is less straightforward and will require a slightly more extended discussion of the relevant tests.

Three tests met by state, activity, and accomplishment verbs are met by *heat*, but exclude its classification as an achievement verb. All three tests reflect the fact that state, activity and accomplishment verbs refer to events that are extended in time: (i) *heat* takes adverbial prepositional phrases with *for*, as in (1) below, (ii) *heat* can occur with *spend an hour*, as in (2), (iii) *heat* can appear as a complement of *stop*, as in (3).

(1)   John heated the soup for an hour.

(2)   John spent an hour heating the soup.

(3)   John stopped heating the soup.

A series of tests exclude the classification of heat as a state verb. First, in contrast to state verbs *heat* has a habitual reading in the simple present tense.

(4)   John heats the soup (for every meal).

In addition, *heat* meets an additional five "non-stative" tests listed by Dowty (1979: 55): (i) *heat* appears in the progressive, as in (5), (ii) *heat* appears as a complement of *force* and *persuade,* as in (6), (iii) *heat* appears as an imperative, as in (7), (iv) *heat* appears with the adverbs *deliberately* and *carefully,* as in (8), (v) *heat* appears in pseudo-cleft constructions, as in (9).

(5)   John is heating the soup.

(6)   John forced/persuaded Harry to heat the soup.

(7)   Heat the soup!

(8)   John deliberately/carefully heated the soup.

(9)   What John did was heat the soup.

The tests surveyed thus far narrow down the classification of *heat* to one of two classes, activity and accomplishment verbs. A series of tests were listed by Dowty (1979) that distinguish these two classes. Applying these tests indicates that *heat* should be classified as an accomplishment verb (with a slight qualification to be noted below). Semantically these tests reflect the fact that accomplishment verbs designate goal directed events. This is reflected in the following contrasts between *heat* and the activity verb *walk*:

(10) a.   *John walked in an hour.

       b.   John heated the soup in an hour.

(11) a.   *It took John an hour to walk.

       b.   It took John an hour to heat the soup.

(12) a.   *John finished walking.

       b.   John finished heating the soup.

In addition, two logical entailment tests were listed by Dowty (1979) as distinguishing activity and accomplishment verbs. On applying these tests, *heat* is found to behave as an activity verb, in apparent contradiction to the classification suggested by (10) – (12), as shown in (13) and (14) below. For each, I list three cases incorporating in turn an activity verb, *heat,* and an accomplishment verb.

(13) a.   John walked for an hour.
           Entails: John walked at all times during that hour.

       b.   John heated the soup for an hour.
           Entails: John heated the soup at all times during that hour.

       c.   John painted a picture for an hour.

           Does not entail: John painted a picture at all times during that hour.

(14) a.   John is walking.

           Entails: John has walked.

       b.   John is heating the soup.

           Entails: John has heated the soup.

       c.   John is painting a picture.

           Does not entail: John has painted a picture.

    The tests in (13) and (14) result in the classification of *heat* as an activity verb in contrast to the classification indicated by tests (10) – (12). In (10) – (12) the behavior of *heat* as an accomplishment verb reflects the goal directedness of the event it designates. It is precisely this goal directedness that is supposed to preclude the logical entailments in (13b) and (14b), as it does for *paint a picture* in (13c) and (14c). I suggest that the behavior of *heat* as an activity verb in (13) and (14), reflects a semantic property of the event designated by *heat,* where the goal is defined on an ordinal scale that is internally homogeneous. The abstract semantic structures of *heat the soup* and *paint a picture,* differ in the degree of internal homogeneity of the designated event. Indeed it is this homogeneity that distinguishes prototypical activity verbs (e.g. walk) from prototypical accomplishment verbs (e.g. build). What distinguishes *heat* from activity verbs is a goal directedness that results not from a fundamentally distinct final state, but from the existence of a series of distinct states along an ordinal scale. Thus, the goal is defined in relative terms, allowing the entailments expressed in (13b) and (14b).

This aspect of the semantics of *heat* is implicated in another test mentioned by Dowty (1979): the different effects of the adverb *almost* on activity and accomplishment verbs. (15a) and (15c) incorporate prototypical accomplishment and activity verbs, respectively.

(15)   a.   John almost painted a picture.

       b.   John almost heated the soup.

       c.   John almost walked.

Dowty (1979:58) points out that (15a) has two possible readings: either that the idea of painting a picture was entertained but no painting took place, or the painting of the picture was begun but was not completed. In (15c) only the first reading is possible. Now in (15b) I suggest that there are two readings, classifying *heat* as an accomplishment verb. The second reading in the case of *heat*, while less likely than in (15a), can be reinforced by the context (e.g. dinner is being prepared). That is, *heated the soup* refers not to *any* increase in the hotness of the soup but an increase that makes it ready for dinner. This can be seen in the common co-occurrence of the verb *heat* with certain prepositional phrases as a complement suggesting that a unique state (or at least a limited range of states) along the ordinal scale is often entertained. Consider (16a-c):

(16)   a.   Heat gently *until the sugar has melted.*

       b.   I could heat up the rest of the chicken *for supper.*

       c.   She heated up a kettle of pool water *to do the washing up.*

To conclude, the results of applying a series of syntactic and logical entailment tests indicate that *heat* should be classified as an accomplishment verb. This classification justifies characterizing a semantic structure designated by the verb *heat* in terms of a state predicate, HOT, and the appropriate string of operators corresponding to the class of accomplishment verbs. Following Dowty, this may be expressed as [causal event] CAUSE [BECOME HOT(X)]. The discussion above, however, suggests that we interpret the predicate HOT as specifying some state along an ordinal scale. Moreover, (16a-c) suggest an additional semantic component: a unique point (or limited range) along the ordinal scale made unique by virtue of its functional consequences. Therefore, the semantic structure may be elaborated as follows:

[causal event] CAUSE [BECOME HOT$_i$(X)]

where: HOT$_{i-1}$ < HOT$_i$,

HOT$_c$ = a critical degree of hotness

The following two sub-sections examine syntactic properties of the nouns *heat* and *temperature* and the implied semantic elaboration of the core structure just described. The sentences used to illustrate these syntactic properties were obtained from the British National Corpus, a 100 million word data-base of current English usage. This is a corpus of English sentences compiled so as to be representative of current English usage from a broad spectrum of domains: novels, newspapers, TV programs etc.

2.2 The Syntax and Semantics of the Noun *Heat*

The semantic structure expressed above includes an unspecified causal event as the causal source of a change in the state of hotness. I will suggest in this section that the noun *heat* is used to designate a spatially localized entity that is the causal source of hotness, elaborating this unspecified causal event. In addition, the noun *heat* occasionally designates the state of hotness itself.

That heat designates a causal entity is reflected in the prepositions that take *heat* as a complement as in (17).

(17) a. It was Rosie, red-faced from running, and *from* the heat of the kitchens.

   b. The contents and décor of the kitchen were severely damaged *by* heat and smoke and the rest of the ground floor suffered smoke damage.

This causal entity is spatially localized as seen in the prepositional phrases that the noun *heat* takes as a complement, as in (18), and the prepositional phrases in which *heat* participates, as in (19)

(18) a. The heat *in the room* was already intensely humid.

   b. The excitement was there, the burning heat *inside her*, but also there was peace, belonging.

   c. Once, she caught Chrissie with her head down, drying herself in the heat *from the fire* with her hair hanging over her eyes.

(19) a. As soon as the thigh meat is ready, remove it *from the heat*.

   b. For a few moments the clouds open and we lie *in the heat of the hazy sun*, our efforts justly rewarded.

   c. Connelly, barely conscious now, felt as if his blood was boiling, as if his bones were calcifying *under the incredible heat*.

d.   Some washed under the pump before cooking rice and vegeta-
bles, while others seated *by the heat of the cooking fire* then
washed before eating.

In addition to the causal and spatial properties of the entity designated
by *heat* reflected in the linguistic evidence just cited, the syntactic behavior
of *heat* as a mass noun, as in (20), indicates that the entity designated is unindividuated.

(20)   a.   With the tent flap closed, the *heat* had been building up under the
canvas.

b.   *With the tent flap closed, the *heats* had been building up under
the canvas.

In (17) - (19) the noun *heat* is being used to designate a spatially localized causal entity that is independent of the object whose hotness is in
question. In contrast, participation of *heat* in the prepositional phrases in
(21) below, suggests that it is designating the state of hotness itself, and
making reference to the consequences of that state of hotness.

(21)   a.   I was giddy *with the heat* and a little flown with the wine.

b.   Go home dear girl, you will die *of heat* on your bicycle.

The contrast I refer to can be seen by comparing the sentences in (17) to
those in (21). There seems to be a difference between the entity designated
by *heat* in (17a) and (17b), on the one hand, and (21a) and (21b) on the
other. In (17a) there is a distinction implied between the external entity
'heat' and the 'state of hotness'. This is reflected in the possessive preposition *of* marking the association of 'heat' with 'the kitchen' marking it as
distinct from the 'state of hotness' of 'red-faced Rosie'. Moreover, in (17b)
the preposition *by* marks the entity 'heat' as an agent, suggesting an independent entity, not a passive 'state of hotness' that simply results in damage. In contrast, the prepositions *with* and *of* in (21a) and (21b) respectively,
suggest that the 'state of hotness' itself is designated by the noun *heat*.
These considerations support the inclusion of two distinct semantic components in the cognitive model to be proposed (see section 2.4): an entity
'heat' that is the causal source of hotness, and the 'state of hotness' itself.

Finally, in the sentences in (17) and (21), *damaged, red-faced, giddy,*
and *die* all refer to consequences (especially undesirable) of the state of hotness. This reinforces the inclusion of 'a critical degree of hotness' as a
component in the semantic structure described in subsection 2.1 above.

2.3 The Syntax and Semantics of *Temperature*

The linguistic properties of the noun *temperature* differ markedly from that
of the noun *heat.*

Temperature participates in locative prepositional phrases suggesting
that temperature is conceived as a location in space.

(22) a. Stir thoroughly, then allow to cool *to room temperature.*

   b. Maintain the water *at a temperature of 19-24°C* and feed the fish on flake, tubifex, insects and earthworms.

Moreover, the possible locations are limited to a single, vertical dimension and *temperature* can designate an entity moving along it, as in (23).

(23) a. With almost clear skies and very little wind, the *temperature will fall* sharply this evening.

   b. Although the days were still warm and sunny, the evenings closed in early and the *temperature soon began to dip* as darkness approached.

In contrast to *heat, temperature* is a count noun, indicating that it designates an individuated entity.

(24) There is a large range of temperatures suitable for human life.

2.4 A Minimal Cognitive Model of Thermal Phenomena

The results of subsections 2.1-2.3 suggest the components of a conceptual structure that underlies the use of *heat* (as verb), *heat* (as noun) and *temperature*. This minimal cognitive model underlying the usage of *heat* and *temperature* as discussed above is represented in figure 1. This is a *minimal* model in the sense that it incorporates only those semantic elements that apply to a variety of specific thermal phenomena. The model can be described in terms of its basic components as follows: There is an unindividuated entity occupying an extended region in space (shaded circle). Its spatial contiguity with an object is the causal source of the increased hotness of that object (the square in the diagram). This hotness, conceptualized as a location along a vertical dimension, can range in intensity (represented by HOT_i). One point (or a limited range of points) are singled out as critical (HOT_c). The suggestion here is that the lexical items *heat* (as verb and noun) and *temperature* designate different aspects of this model. The verb *heat* designates the whole model. The noun *heat* may designate the spatially localized entity that is the causal source of hotness, or occasionally the state of hotness itself. *Temperature* designates the degree of hotness, conceptualized as a location along a vertical scale.[2]

---

[2] The distinction between the whole cognitive model and the designations of the individual lexical items correspond to Langacker's (1987) domain/profile distinction.

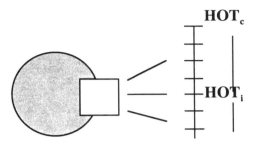

Figure 1: The minimal cognitive model of thermal phenomena

The cognitive model just described models the phenomenon of an object becoming hotter at a fairly schematic level. That is, emphasis has been placed on characterizing it in terms of conceptual notions like space, cause, states and linear scale. This is not surprising since the model was characterized by performing a grammatical analysis and it is precisely such notions that are encoded grammatically (Slobin 1997). Thus this characterization turns out to have emphasized what Lakoff and Turner (1989) have called the event (or "generic-level") structure of the conceptual domain. This model can be described purely in generic terms as follows: spatial contiguity between two entities is the cause of a change of state where that change occurs along a vertical scale with a certain point singled out as functionally significant

Lakoff and Turner (Lakoff 1993; Lakoff & Turner 1989) have suggested that generic-level structure is what is preserved across metaphorical mappings from one conceptual domain to another. Therefore, the accuracy of the above characterization can be checked by examining whether the generic-level structure of the model proposed is indeed preserved across mappings from the source domain of heat to other domains. I address this point next.

2.5 Two Sets of Conceptual Mappings as Corroborating Evidence
In this subsection I discuss two sets of conceptual mappings found in English implicating the domain of heat as a source domain. The first involves an extension of the use of the noun *heat* in American slang, in particular, language in use in the criminal world. The second is a coherent set of metaphorical expressions, unified by the conceptual metaphor ANGER IS HEAT, identified by Lakoff and Kövecses (Kövecses 1990[3]). In both cases the mapping preserves the generic-level structure described above.

---

[3] Chapter 4, "Anger", was co-authored with George Lakoff.

I begin with the first set of mappings underlying the use of the noun *heat* in the slang of the world of crime. The sentences that are used to develop the argument are compiled from dictionaries of American slang.

Consider the sentences in (25) - (27).

(25) a. If you pack heat, you've got to know what you're doing. (pack heat = carry a gun).

b. Drop the heater and leave the jewel case where it is, I don't want any unpleasantness. (heater = gun)

c. I was packing about as much heat as you find in an icicle. (heat = gun)

d. Try operating an American city without the heat. (heat = police)

(26) a. We better stop purse-snatching while the heat is on. (heat = pressure of police)

b. The heat is on dope. (heat = pressure of police)

(27) a. He will soon feel the heat of their threats.

b. I had to take the heat for his mistake.

c. He gave him the heat. (= He shot him.)

I suggest that these three groups of sentences reflect the role of generic-level schema in motivating the mapping between the domain heat itself and the criminal world.

In (25) *heat* either designates a gun or the police in analogy to the use of heat to designate the entity heat which is the causal source of hotness as discussed earlier. A gun (or the police) and the entity heat constitute counterparts, both being instantiations of an entity that is spatially localized and is causally relevant to a change of state.

In (26a) and (26b) *heat* designates the pressure applied by the police on a particular target. While this applied pressure is the effect of police presence, it plays a distinct semantic role. So the suggestion here is that 'degree of hotness' and 'applied police pressure' are counterparts, both instantiations of another aspect of the generic level schema: the effect of one entity on another is conceptualized with respect to an intensity scale.

Finally, the uses of *heat* in (27) implicate the final component of the generic level schema contrasting slightly with (26). In (27a), *heat* designates 'that point at which gradually intensifying threats become particularly troubling'. In (27b) it designates 'repercussions of a mistake by one person intense enough to negatively affect another'. In (27c) the 'threat by a gun culminated in the threatened being shot'. Thus, the claim is that the usage of the noun *heat* in (27) involves designations in the criminal domain that are counterparts of 'a critical degree of hotness' in the domain of heat, both instantiating a critical degree of intensity with significant functional consequences. I say that the usage "involves" this designation implying a slight qualification. Notice that in (27b) and (27c) the constructions *to take the heat for* and *gave him the heat* suggest that *heat* designates a localized entity. In both cases there is the conception of transfer of an entity to a recipient who comes to possess that entity. These usages need to be distinguished from those in (25), however. This is because the constructions in (27b) and (27c) are examples of the EXPERIENCES ARE POSSESSIONS metaphor (see Lakoff 1990). It seems reasonable, therefore, to emphasize that the usage of *heat* (certainly in conjunction with the grammatical constructions in which it is embedded) involves a designation that involves a critical degree of intensity with functional (experiential) significance.

The second mapping that I will consider here is one that underlies much of the language about anger in English. Lakoff and Kövecses (Kövecses 1990) identified a conceptual metaphor that renders coherent many English sentences about anger. They point out that the combination of the metaphor ANGER IS HEAT when applied to fluids, with the metaphor THE BODY IS A CONTAINER FOR THE EMOTIONS, produces the central metaphor ANGER IS THE HEAT OF A FLUID IN A CONTAINER. What is of particular interest here is the specific aspects of the source domain (i.e. HEAT OF A FLUID IN A CONTAINER) that participate in the mapping. We find Lakoff and Kövecses (see Kövecses, 1990: 54-56) organizing their examples into the following groups (I give one example from each. For more examples see Kövecses 1990: 54-56).

i. WHEN THE INTENSITY OF ANGER INCREASES, THE FLUID RISES:

(28)   His pent-up anger *welled up* inside him.

ii. INTENSE ANGER PRODUCES STEAM:

(29)   Billy's just blowing off steam.

iii. INTENSE ANGER PRODUCES PRESSURE ON THE CONTAINER:

(30)   I could barely contain my rage.

iv. WHEN ANGER BECOMES TOO INTENSE, THE PERSON EXPLODES.

(31)   When I told him, he just exploded.

v. WHEN A PERSON EXPLODES, PARTS OF HIM GO UP IN THE AIR

(32)   She flipped her lid.

vi. WHEN A PERSON EXPLODES, WHAT WAS INSIDE HIM COMES OUT

(33)   His anger finally came out.

The groupings identified by Lakoff and Kövecses can be further collected into two more schematic groups: those referring to points on the intensity scale and those referring to a limit having been reached. Hence we find the following comment in Kövecses (1990), summarizing the central metaphor:

> In the central metaphor, the scale indicating the amount of anger is the heat-scale. But, as the central metaphor indicates, the anger scale is not open-ended; it has a limit. Just as a hot fluid in a closed container can only take so much heat before it explodes, so we conceptualize the anger scale as having a limit point. We can only bear so much anger, before we explode, that is, lose control. (p. 56)

This mapping between the source domain, HEAT OF A FLUID IN A CONTAINER and ANGER is structured according to the components of the abstract schema mentioned at the beginning of this subsection. I have pointed out the fundamental role played by the intensity scale and the critical point of this intensity scale as reflected in the two groups of metaphorical expressions. In addition, *anger*, in analogy to *heat*, plays the dual role of designating an entity that is a spatially located causal source of intense agitation as implied in (34), and the state of intense agitation itself as in (35).

(34)   Try to get you anger out of your system.

(35)   She was shaking with anger.

Thus in the two mappings discussed the generic level schema extracted from the minimal cognitive model proposed in section 2 are preserved. This constitutes corroborating evidence for the existence of that model.

3. The Ontology of Heat as an Emergent Product of Conceptual Integration

I consider the model proposed to be a good starting point for a characterization of the core of the layperson's understanding of thermal phenomena. Certainly people have a lot of other related specific knowledge (e.g., that water boils when heated for some time and that we sweat under intense sun). The model proposed incorporates the basic causal structure of the layperson's understanding that can be applied across contexts. Another aspect of what might constitute such generalizable knowledge is the ontology of the entity 'heat', what type of thing heat is. In this section I will argue that a stable assignment for the ontology of 'heat' is absent from the layperson's core understanding, but rather emerges in specific explanatory contexts.

I develop this argument by examining two segments of an interview where an experimenter (I) was interviewing a high-school student (S) with the purpose of revealing the student's pre-instruction understanding of thermal phenomena. These segments come from interviews that form part of a series of studies conducted by Marianne Wiser (see Wiser 1995) in which she has been examining the relationship between high-school students' pre-instruction knowledge and textbook knowledge about thermal phenomena and its implications for characterizing the process of conceptual change involved in this domain.

Segments (i) and (ii), quoted below, reflect the same student's understanding of insulation and conduction, respectively (these segments occur within minutes of each other). The first suggests that the student believes the entity heat is a material substance. The second segment contradicts that conclusion. I present these segments below, then address the question of how these apparently contradictory conceptualizations can be interpreted given the minimal cognitive model described in section 2 above and the process of "conceptual integration" described by Fauconnier and Turner (see Fauconnier 1997; Turner & Fauconnier 1995).

Segment i - Insulation:

I: ... Do you know how insulation works?

S: Not really.

I: What does that word mean to you when you hear "insulation"?

S: Keeping stuff at the same temperature. Warming something up.

I: All right. So keeping stuff at the same temperature or warming something up. OK, say I have two cups of water, one of them is made of out of Styrofoam and one of them is made out of cardboard. Well, what I want to ask is: we use Styrofoam cups to keep things warm, what do you think it is about Styrofoam that keeps what's inside warm?

S: I don't know. Maybe it's like thicker material that has a better insulation, or something. 'Cause, if you keep it at the same temperature, it's insulated.

I: OK, but what is it about the Styrofoam itself? I mean, water inside the Styrofoam cup stays hotter than water which was, in the beginning, at the same temperature inside the cardboard cup.

S: The Styrofoam can keep it heated better.

A few exchanges later ...

I: ... Do you think that insulation has anything to do with molecules?

S: Yeah.

I: In what way?

S: The molecules are more smushed, so the heat can't escape.

Segment ii - Conduction:

I: Now this is a copper bar and we've got a candle here at one end, and there's a blob of wax, or a pellet of wax, at the other end. The wax is eventually going to melt, right, do you think that's true?

S: Yeah.

I: OK. How does the heat get from one end of the bar to the other. We've got this little candle heating up this end. How does it get to the end of the bar?

S: Well, this end would probably be hotter, 'cause that's where it started, but the molecules would just, the heat would just keep pushing down onto the molecules after a while, but this end would probably be hotter, but eventually this end would get pretty hot and it would melt the wax.

A few exchanges later ...

I: ...Do you think water would be able to pass through the bar in the same way?

S: No, I don't think so. Water could pass through the bar? No.

I: No? What about a gas for example? Would that be able to pass through the bar?

S: I don't think so.

I: What about air?

S: I don't know. I don't think it could go through. I don't think so.

I: OK, so water and a gas and air would not travel through the bar, but heat would. What's different about heat, that would make it travel?

S: I don't know, it kinda just spreads through, I don't know why it would travel, I just think it would.

I: So, what kind of a thing is heat, then, it's different from those other things, like water and air?

S: I don't know, you can't really see it, it just heats up the particles and then, it's not like the fire is inside the bar, but it gives it the hotter temperature.

In the first segment in which the student's understanding of insulation is explored, the student displays an understanding of the entity heat as a material substance, which "can't escape" because molecules of Styrofoam, the good insulator, are "more smushed". The student's responses seem to be based on a cognitive model in which the water stays hot because the material entity heat is unable to pass through a substance made of tightly packed molecules. In contrast, in the second segment of the interview the student resists granting material substances like water or gas the ability to pass through a copper bar, an ability granted to heat. Moreover, she does not describe a process in which heat travels *between* molecules of the conductor, it "just spreads through". The understanding of the process of conduction and the melting of the wax is expressed in terms of spatial location of the entity heat, the gradually increasing temperature at points along the bar and the eventual melting of the wax when that end gets hot enough. That is, the explanation of conduction is formulated in terms of the minimal cognitive model with a rejection of a material substance interpretation of the entity heat.

Fauconnier and Turner's account of "conceptual integration" and "emergent" meaning in blended conceptual spaces can help make sense of the apparently conflicting observations mentioned above (see Fauconnier 1997; Turner & Fauconnier 1995). Figure 2 illustrates how the framework of conceptual integration can be used to understand how the material substance ontology of heat can emerge in the context of a student's explanation of insulation. Input space 1 includes the minimal cognitive model proposed earlier. Input space 2 corresponds to specific knowledge about insulation: that some insulating substance (I) maintains the hotness of a contained liquid (L). The integration of the conceptual content of each of these two spaces is motivated by correspondences established by the generic space. The projected structure from input spaces 1 and 2 to the blend can be characterized as: the insulator maintains the desired temperature of the liquid by preventing the spatial dislocation of the entity heat that is responsible for the desired state of hotness. I suggest that this projected structure is further elaborated by a force-dynamic frame that is part of our early developing knowledge in which a solid object blocks the passage of another solid object. This elaboration is a result of the process of "completion" described by Fauconnier (1997) where elements in a blend can prompt the conceptualizer to elaborate the conceptual structure in the blend with background knowledge frames. The resultant emergent structure in the blend will contain the conceptualization of heat as a solid material substance unable to pass through the solid insulator and it is this that explains why the hotness of the liquid is maintained.

Thus, within the context of discussing insulation, the schemas that are evoked and integrated result in an emergent conceptual structure in which the entity heat is interpreted as a material substance. However, the material substance ontology is a temporary component of the cognitive model dynamically constructed by the student while reasoning about insulation. Its lack of entrenchment allows the ontologically unelaborated minimal cognitive model to drive reasoning in response to questioning about conduction a few minutes later.

Generic Space

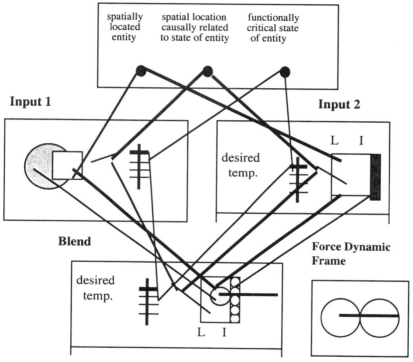

Figure 2: Emergent material substance ontology of heat as a result
of conceptual integration. (L = liquid, I = insulator)

Interpreted thus, the apparently contradictory findings regarding the student's understanding of thermal phenomena turn out to be quite consistent, as far as cognitive theorizing is concerned. Much of the research on conceptual change in science has, however, assumed that the task is to identify static knowledge structures. For example, Chi and colleagues (e.g. Slotta, Chi & Joram 1995) have suggested that an important source of difficulty in learning science concepts (including heat) is the pre-instruction classification of these concepts within the material substance ontological category. A static view of this pre-instruction classification does not accord with the kind of variability observed in the interview segments presented above. It is the assumption that it is static knowledge structures that are driving student responses which makes the above segments appear to constitute contradictory findings regarding the student's knowledge. Granting the possibility of the dynamic construction of cognitive models through online conceptual integration provides a framework within which to interpret the absence of stability in pre-instruction understanding of physical phenomena.

4. Conclusion

I hope to have illustrated how the framework of cognitive linguistics can contribute to the characterization of a layperson's core understanding in a physical domain. This contribution can be seen as twofold. On the one hand, cognitive linguistic tools for the analysis of semantic structure implicit in language use can help characterize particularly stable aspects of conceptualization. On the other hand, fluctuating conceptualizations can be understood as dynamic constructions at the moment of use interpreted within the framework of conceptual integration and the emergence of conceptualization in blended spaces. Together these can prove to be a useful set of tools for characterizing pre-instruction knowledge in science.

5. References

Dowty, David. 1979. *Word Meaning and Montague Grammar*. Dordrecht: Reidel.

Fauconnier, Gilles. 1997. *Mappings in Thought and Language*. Cambridge: Cambridge University Press.

Foley, William A., and Robert Van Valin. 1984. *Functional Syntax and Universal Grammar*. Cambridge Studies in Linguistics 38. Cambridge: Cambridge University Press.

Kövecses, Zoltan. 1990. *Emotion Concepts*. New York: Springer-Verlag.

Lakoff, George. 1987. *Women, Fire and Dangerous Things: What Categories Reveal About the Mind*. Chicago, IL: University of Chicago Press.

Lakoff, George. 1990. The Invariance Hypothesis: Is Abstract Reason Based on Image-schemas? *Cognitive Linguistics* 1:1.39-74.

Lakoff, George. 1993. The Contemporary Theory of Metaphor, in A. Ortony, ed., *Metaphor and Thought*. Cambridge: Cambridge University Press.

Lakoff, George and Mark Turner. 1989. *More Than Cool Reason: A Field Guide to Poetic Metaphor*. Chicago, IL: University of Chicago Press.

Langacker, Ronald. 1987. *Foundations of Cognitive Grammar. Vol. 1, Theoretical Prerequisites*. Stanford, CA: Stanford University Press.

Slobin, Dan. 1997. The Origins of Grammaticizable Notions: Beyond the Individual Mind, in D. I. Slobin, ed., *The Crosslinguistic Study of Language Acquisition, Vol. 5: Expanding the Contexts*. Mahwah, NJ: Erlbaum.

Slotta, James, Michelene Chi, and Elana Joram. 1995. Assessing Students' Misclassifications of Physics Concepts: An Ontological Basis for Conceptual Change. *Cognition and Instruction* 13:3.373–400.

Turner, Mark and Gilles Fauconnier. 1995. Conceptual Integration and Formal Expression. *Journal of Metaphor and Symbolic Activity* 10:3.183–204.

Wiser, Marianne. 1995. Use of History of Science to Understand and Remedy Students' Misconceptions about Heat and Temperature. In D. N. Perkins, J. L. Schwartz, M. M. West & M. S. Wiske, eds., *Software Goes to School: Teaching for Understanding with New Technologies*. Oxford: Oxford University Press.

Wiser, Marianne & Tamer G. Amin. 1998. *Routes to Ontological Change in Science*. Paper Presented at the Twenty-Eigth Annual Symposium of the Jean Piaget Society, Chicago, IL.

Voilà *voilà*: Extensions of Deictic Constructions in French

BENJAMIN K. BERGEN AND MADELAINE C. PLAUCHÉ
University of California, Berkeley

1. Introduction

French deictic locatives *voilà* 'there is' and *voici* 'here is' occur at first glance with greatly varying meanings and somewhat less varying syntax, as the examples in (1) attest. Their extensive variation defies classical categorization in terms of grammatical or discourse elements.

(1) (a) Nous y voilà, enfin arrivés.
          We've finally arrived.

     (b) Voici son sac.
          Here's his bag.

     (c) Voilà le moment que nous attendions.
          Here's the moment we've been waiting for.

     (d) Voilà deux heures que ça pue la vache.
          That's two hours it's smelled like cow.

     (e) Voilà que la fin approche.
          Now the end is coming.

     (f) Voilà mon oncle content.
          Now there's my uncle happy.

     (g) Voilà des étudiants de Berkeley.
          There are some Berkeley students.

Conceptual and Discourse Factors in Linguistic Structure.
Alan Cienki, Barbara J. Luka and Michael B. Smith (eds.).
Copyright © 2001, CSLI Publications.

(h) En voilà des étudiants!
Now there are some students (for you)!
(i) Voici le but de la discussion...
Here's the point of the discussion...

The present study is a cognitive semantic analysis of the different senses of *voilà* and *voici* found above, as well as their syntax.[1]

1.1 Some Historical Background on *voilà* and *voici*

Voilà and *voici* derive historically from imperative forms of the verb 'to see', which in Modern French has the form *voir*, plus a deictic locative adverb, either *ci* 'here' or *là* 'there', both of which still exist as clitics in Modern French. Very early attested forms maintained verbal inflection and permitted certain pronouns to come between the verbal form and the locative clitic (2).

(2)   veez me là
'Here I am' (from *Le Mort le Roi Artu*)

At least as early as the 14th century, however, these forms both lost their inflection and merged into a single lexical item, as their orthography and invariability of form in (1) show.

Additionally, *voilà* and *voici* were historically used to differentiate between proximal and distal relations, as *ci* and *là* still do (3). At present, *voilà* and *voici* are mostly interchangeable without semantic effect, with *voilà* generally used and *voici* becoming less common among younger speakers.

(3)   (a) Tu parles de ce type-là?
Are you talking about that guy there?
(b) Non, de ce type-ci!
No, about this guy here!

1.2 Previous Accounts

Previous accounts of *voilà* and *voici*, as Moignet (1969) points out, have labelled them according either to traditional parts of speech ("syntactic" properties) or discourse function ("pragmatic" properties) (4):

(4)   (a) Prepositions (Girault-Duvivier 1851)
(b) Adverbs (Brunot & Bruneau 1969)
(c) Verbs (Moignet 1969)
(d) Presentatives (Grenoble & Riley 1996; Lambrecht 1981)

---

[1] For those constructions where *voici* displays the same behavior as *voilà*, we will focus on *voilà*. For those cases where they differ, we will make explicit mention of that divergence.

(e) Interjections (Nyrop 1914)

(f) Factives (Damourette & Pichon 1927)

We argue that grammatical classifications based on classic categorization like those described above are insufficient since *voilà* displays both non-prototypical behavior in terms of traditional grammatical categories and a sufficiently wide range of semantic and pragmatic "senses" to defy a monotonic classification of its meaning.

1.3 Structure of the Present Analysis

The present analysis involves: (1) positing distinct word senses where semantic, pragmatic, and syntactic properties between uses differ (Brugman 1981; Lakoff 1987); (2) categorizing each sense of *voilà* based on its own behavior, rather than trying to determine a single grammatical class for it (van Oosten 1986); and (3) determining the systematic relations between the different senses of a given word, including metaphor, metonymy, and constructional grounding (Lakoff & Johnson 1980; Sweetser 1990; Johnson 1998).

Our goal is to: (1) give semantic, pragmatic, and syntactic descriptions of the multiple senses of *voilà*; (2) show how some syntactic properties follow from semantic and pragmatic properties; and (3) show how the independent senses are related or independently motivated.

The cases of *voilà* and *voici* are particularly suited to a radial category analysis because they constitute a family of constructions that are related through metaphor, metonymy, constructional grounding, and other cognitive mechanisms. More importantly, these forms display close ties to the speech contexts they occur in and the pragmatic information they convey for the simple reason that they communicate more than just a proposition. As deictics, they are grounded in space and time relative to the speaker and/or hearer. Additionally, they entail communicative acts relying upon the current state of the interlocutor and instructions to change that state. Thus, the pragmatics of the speech context in which each sense is used and the particular semantics of the domain to which it is extended motivate the properties of each extension.

2. The Central Deictic

2.1 So You Say You Found the Central Case...

Following Lakoff (1987), we will describe the central sense of locative deictics in terms of an Idealized Cognitive Model (ICM) (*ibid.*) or primary scene (Grady & Johnson 1997) of "Pointing Out" (☞). This is an experiential gestalt that is common and crucial in young children's linguistic and non-linguistic interaction.

It is assumed as a background that some entity exists and is present at some location in the speaker's visual field, that the speaker is directing his attention at it, and that the hearer is interested in its whereabouts but does not have his attention focused on it and may not even know that it is present. The speaker then directs the hearer's attention to the location of the entity (perhaps accompanied by a pointing gesture) and brings it to the hearer's attention that the entity is at the specified location [...] (Lakoff 1987:490).

Of the elements in this ICM, *voilà* and *voici* explicitly encode both a directive to focus attention (*voi-*) and the location of the entity (*-ci* or *-là*). Their direct object is the entity pointed out. Uses of *voilà* and *voici* corresponding to this sense can be found in (5) below:

(5)　(a)　Voilà les clés que tu cherchais.
　　　　　There are the keys you were looking for.

　　(b)　Voici son sac.
　　　　　Here's his bag.

There is no generally accepted means for determining the central sense of a radial category. Nevertheless, as demonstrated below, direction of historical change, relative experiential complexity, and synchronic cognitive organization all yield the same results for *voilà* and *voici*. First, diachronic developments can reflect the directionality of cognitive processes (Sweetser 1990). Etymologically, *voilà* and *voici* are composed of *voi* 'see-IMP' and *là* 'there' or *ci* 'here'. Historically, then, they belong to the domain of spatial perception, suggesting the sense in (5) is a primary or central one. Second, a central case can be defined as one which stems from a basic experiential domain. If spatial location is thought to be a more concrete experiential domain than, for example, discourse, then the spatial senses of *voilà* and *voici* qualify as central. Third, if two senses of a construction are related through a single metaphorical mapping, we can assume the central case is identified with the source, and not the target domain of that mapping. In general, in French, as in other languages, space acts as a source domain for metaphors that map onto discourse, time, and other conceptual domains. In the case of *voilà* and *voici*, all of the above indicators identify the spatial sense in (5) as the central one.

2.2 The Syntax

The basic structure of the Central Deictic is a construction with the following minimal specification: a deictic locative adverb (i.e. *voilà* or *voici*) and a noun phrase (which we show to be the direct object of the construction). In this section we will discuss some of the formal properties of the Central Deictic, including its relation to the declarative and imperative verbal modes, and the possibility of embedding it.

2.2.1 *Voilà*: Declarative or Imperative (or Both)?

The Central Deictic's NP can be either a pronominal or a full NP, which can optionally include modifiers of all sorts and can be definite or indefinite (6).

(6) (a) modifier + N   Voilà ton petit frère.
                                          There's your little brother.

     (b) indefinite determiner + N   Voilà un(des) oiseau(x).
                                          There's (are) a (some) bird(s).

     (c) definite determiner + N   Voilà le roi.
                                          There's the king.

     (d) N + relative clause   Voilà Paul qui pleure.
                                          There's Paul crying.

     (e) N + gerundial phrase   Voilà Marie travaillant.
                                          There's Marie working.

The pronominalization of the NP in the Central deictic shows that the NP is the direct object of *voilà* and that its syntax is like a declarative sentence, though the action of "pointing out" functions similarly to an imperative. The pronoun used in the *voilà* construction is a direct object pronoun placed before *voilà* (7a), like the declarative (7b), but unlike the affirmative imperative, which places the pronoun after the verb (7c). Note that the negative imperative (7d) places the direct object pronoun before the verb.

(7) (a) Voilà les clés que tu cherchais.   Les voilà.
          There are the keys you were looking for.   There they are.

     (b) Je vois les clés que tu cherchais.   Je les vois.
          I see the keys you were looking for.   I see them.

     (c) Apporte les clés que je cherchais.   Apporte-les.
          Bring the keys I was looking for.   Bring them.

     (d) N'apporte pas les clés.   Ne les apporte pas.
          Don't bring the keys.   Don't bring them.

This is also true for the cases where the NP is preceded by an indefinite article (partitive NPs), where the pronoun *en* 'some', patterns like the direct object pronouns above, coming before the verb for declarative and *voilà* constructions, but after the verb in imperative constructions.

(8) Voilà des étudiants de Berkeley.   En voilà.
     There're some Berkeley students.   There are some.

A possible explanation for *voilà*'s acquisition of declarative pronominalization patterns is that it expresses conventionalized propositional content, rather than simply encoding a directive. Specifically, its content is not just 'look at that thing there,' as the imperative might express, but additionally, 'that thing is there'. The conventional presence of this proposition can be shown by the *Oui, je sais* test (Jones 1996:181). If a sentence can be answered with *Oui, je sais* 'yes, I know', then a proposition has been expressed. Note that this works for both declarative (9a) and *voilà* constructions (9b), but fails for imperatives (9c).

(9)   (a)   -Je lui ai parlé hier.   -Oui, je sais.
                I talked to her yesterday.   Yes, I know.

        (b)   -Voilà tes clés.   -Oui, je sais.
                There are your keys.   Yes, I know.

        (c)   -Regardez les petites vaches!   -*Oui, je sais.
                Look at the cute little cows!   Yes, I know.[2]

The *voilà* construction differs from other declarative sentences in some respects, however. One of the more obvious ways is that there is no explicit subject, which is true for the imperative, as well. This suggests that the pragmatics of the "pointing out" scene surfaces in the syntax of the construction. In pro-drop languages, the subject pronoun can be omitted when the subject is known to the speaker and interlocutor. The same is true for imperatives and *voilà* constructions in French (which is not pro-drop) because of their semantics; both have understood subjects, namely, the interlocutor. The central *voilà* construction was historically an imperative, which may also account for the origin of the lack of an explicit subject.

The central *voilà* case also does not allow indirect objects, thus behaving like a strict transitive verb (10).

(10)   (a)   Regarde-moi ce livre.
             See (look at) this book for me.

       (b)   *Voilà-moi ce livre.   or   *Me voilà ce livre.
            There's that book for me.

       (c)   *Il m'y a ce livre.
            There is this book for me.

We claim that this constraint, which is neither like a declarative nor like an imperative, derives from the semantics of the Pointing-Out ICM. In French, most any construction can acquire an indirect object via the well-documented benefactive/adversative construction, exemplified in (10) (Smith 1997). The semantics of these indirect object adding constructions, however conflicts with the propositional content of *voilà*, which describes a state of affairs. The same is true for *il y a*, the French existential construction, which in essence describes a state of affairs, and whose semantics is not compatible with the idea of performing an action for the benefit of, or to the detriment of, another participant.

---

[2] This sentence would only be felicitous if the speaker were confirming the illocutionary meaning indirectly expressed: "I want you to look at the entity" or "There is some reason to look at the entity". However, it is not possible to respond affirmatively to the directive itself.

Another way in which the pragmatics of the Pointing-Out ICM surfaces is that speakers tend not to use the first person as the direct object in the Central Deictic, unless it is in a different mental space (in a picture, movie, narrative, etc...), where the first person is not the speaker but a representation of the speaker (11).

(11) (a) Me voilà l'été dernier [pointing to a picture].
           There I am last summer.
      (b) ?Me voilà/voici.
           There/here I am.

Note that the questionable sense we mean in (11b) is not the case where it indicates the recent arrival of the speaker, which we discuss below as the Now Deictic, but the case where the speaker is present, has been present, and indicates his or her location to the interlocutor. English 'there' shows the same distribution. This constraint may derive from the pragmatics of the ICM: *voilà* presupposes that both speaker and hearer know the location of speaker and hearer. Therefore, if the location of the speaker is not known, which would be presupposed by *me voilà* 'here I am', *voilà* is incompatible with the speech context.

2.2.2 Embedding

Like other verbs expressing propositions, *voilà* can be embedded in a relative clause, modifying its subject, direct object, or indirect object (12). The meaning of this combination of constructions is predictable from their compositional semantics, namely, the relativized main clause NP is in the speech context and is pointed out parenthetically.

(12) (a) L'homme que voilà est mon amant.
           The man (who is) there is my lover.
      (b) Mon frère a vu l'homme que voilà dans un quartier riche.
           My brother saw that man (who is) there in a rich neighborhood.
      (c) J'ai parlé à la femme que voilà.
           I talked to that woman (who is) there.

This is another way in which the central *voilà* construction patterns with declaratives, as imperatives can not be placed in relative clauses:

(13) (a) *J'ai vu l'homme que regarde!
           I saw the man who look (imperative) at him!
      (b) *Je l'ai donné à l'homme que frappe!
           I gave it to the man who hit (imperative) (him)!

Other cases where the verb does not express a proposition, such as questions and exhortations also defy relativization:

(14) (a) *J'ai vu l'homme que connais-tu?
           I saw the man whom do you know?

All of this is evidence that (1) *voilà* is acting as a verb with a direct object in terms of relative clause structure, and (2) that it expresses a proposition.

In terms of synchronic behavior and in terms of historical development, the Central *voilà* construction has some aspects of imperatives, some aspects of declaratives, and some unique properties. We have shown above that the distribution of these aspects is non-random but rather is based on pragmatic and semantic factors, which suggest an account for the historical retention and acquisition of certain features of the syntax.

2.3 The Event Deictic

Voilà can also be used to point out an event, rather than an object. Syntactically, in this construction, *voilà* is followed by *que* (a complementizer) and a finite clause.[3] This is much like the central case, except that instead of a simple noun phrase indicating an object, *que* + finite clause (15) or NP + infinitival phrase indicates an event or action (16).[4]

(15) (a) Je savais que Marie embrassait Paul.
         I knew that Marie was kissing Paul.

      (b) Voilà que Marie part.
          There's Marie leaving.

In French, the event expressed as the direct object of *laisser* 'to leave' and verbs of perception can alternatively be realized as an infinitival phrase. *Voilà* patterns with verbs of perception either because it is preserving formal aspects of *voir* or because the "pointing out" part of its semantics has to do with perception. However the *que* + finite form seems to be preferred by speakers, perhaps for functional reasons: (1) they are identical to simple declaratives; and (2) they are less restricted than their infinitival counterparts and appear more frequently in the language in general (in part because they are not restricted to perceptual verbs).

(16) (a) Paul a laissé parler le président.
         Paul let the President speak.

      (b) Voilà Marie partir (partir Marie).
          There's Marie leaving.

The above patterning is related to a less central aspect of the Pointing Out ICM that also surfaces in English: that of pointing out not only an object but an event it is taking part in. This is a characteristic not simply

---

[3] Just as with expressions of objects in the Central Deictic, events are not anchored exclusively to the present perceptual space, but, rather, can exist in alternative mental spaces, such as in a narrative: *Voilà que nous sommes dans la forêt...* 'There we are in the forest...'

[4] A negative exclamation of the Event Deictic is also used by some speakers: *Ne voilà-t-il pas qu'il se fâche!* '(I'll be damned) If he isn't getting mad!'

of the Pointing-Out ICM, but rather of expressions of perception in general, as is the case for English. Additionally, the possibility of expressing events as objects with nominal properties derives from Events are Objects (Event Structure Metaphor).

An interesting difference between the object Central Deictic and the Event Central Deictic is that the object case will serve as a source domain for many of the extensions from the Central Deictic discussed below, as well as for one non-metaphorical extension (the Now Deictic, Section 3.3). In the metaphorical extensions, the metaphor that selects the source domain takes some aspect of the spatial domain with reference to objects, and not to events, while the Now Deictic is an extension which is derived through metonymy and pragmatics, and does have to do with events. In the next section, we discuss these extensions from the Central Deictic in detail.

3. Extensions

Radial categories (Lakoff 1987; Brugman 1981; Lindner 1981) are polysemy networks where connections between senses are created through metonymy, metaphor, and other cognitive processes. The rest of the meanings discussed in this paper will be shown to extend directly or indirectly from the Central Deictic and so will preserve most of the structure we have discussed above. Our observations will confirm Moore's (1998) claim that deixis is retained in metaphorical extensions.

3.1 The Discourse Deictic

An important extension from the Central Deictic is to the domain of discourse. The Discourse Deictic inherits the syntactic structure of the Central Deictic, with restrictions that derive from its particular pragmatics.[5] This extended sense of *voilà* is mapped through the metaphors: Discourse Space is Physical Space, Discourse Elements are Entities, Discourse is Motion Along a Path, Immediately Past Discourse is in Our Presence at a Distance From Us, and Discourse in the Immediate Future is Moving Towards Us. These are attested elsewhere both in English and in French (17).

(17) (a) Quand arrive-t-on à la partie interessante de l'histoire?
           When are we going to get to the interesting part of the story?

      (b) Je n'ai pas pu suivre la discussion.
           I couldn't follow the discussion.

As has been previously shown for other languages (Lakoff 1987; Fillmore 1997), the proximal form, *voici*, is used to indicate discourse

---

[5] Note that we are omitting discussion here of the isolated interjective use of *voilà*, which is extremely frequent in spontaneous discourse (Bergen & Plauché submitted).

elements that will occur in the near future (18a), whereas the distal form, *voilà*, points to discourse elements that occurred in the recent past (18b). Note that although the Central Deictic allows a somewhat free exchange of the proximal and distal forms, here the distinction is maintained. This is most likely related to the continued presence in French of the contrast between locational clitics *-ci* (and *ici*) 'here' and *-là* (and *là*) 'there' (Plauché & Bergen 1999).

(18)   (a) Voici deux exemples.
           Here are two examples (to come).
       (b) Voilà un bon point.
           There's a good point (that's just been made).

It should be noted that the use of these metaphors is not unique to the domain of discourse. *Voilà* and *voici* can be used in a similar way with other domains which involve sequences of events occurring over time, such as events in movies or games (19).

(19)   (a) Voici la partie du film dont je t'avais parlé.
           Here's the part of the film I told you about.
       (b) Voilà le point crucial du jeu.
           There was the crux of the game.

3.2 The Central Time Deictic

Another minor extension of the Central Deictic is what we refer to as the Central Time Deictic. This sense is mapped by the metaphors TIME IS SPACE, POINTS IN TIME ARE POINTS IN SPACE. It is used to refer to points in time with the same structure that we use to refer to objects in space. This metaphor is also common in other constructions throughout the French language.

Because the structure of the Central Time Deictic is so closely related to the ICM of pointing out, some interesting restrictions apply. Recall that the Central Deictic is used to point to elements within the field of vision of the speaker and hearer. The metaphors TIME IS SPACE, and POINTS IN TIME ARE POINTS IN SPACE map the location of the speaker and hearer onto a one dimensional "time line," thus the only elements, or instants, that are within their field of vision are those points on the line that the speaker and hearer occupy. We find that this metaphor only works for points in time (20a), not spans of time (20b), unless the span of time is used to refer metonymically to its onset. Moreover, this metaphor is limited to points in time that are anchored to the speech time (20c).

(20)   (a) Voilà l'instant que nous attendions tous.
           Here's the moment we've all been waiting for.

(b) ?Voilà la journée que j'attendais.[6]
Here's the day I've been waiting for.

(c) *Voilà l'instant où tu vas arriver.
There's the instant when you will arrive.

Due to the pragmatic restrictions on this construction, pronominalization of the NP and unmodified NPs are possible but pragmatically dispreferred. This results from the fact that in order to pronominalize or use an unmodified NP, both the speaker and hearer must be previously aware of this referent.

3.3 The Now Deictic

The next extension of the Central Deictic is not a metaphorical mapping, but one that is derived from both metonymy and pragmatics. The Now Deictic is the sense of *voilà* that we translated as "now" in (1e) and the meaning includes the idea of the present time, as opposed to the Central Deictic. It has a particular intonation pattern in many cases, with a rise in pitch across the word *voilà*. The clause is often preceded by *et* 'and' or *mais* 'but' to emphasize the consequentiality of the clause.

When we point out an element to a listener who was previously unaware of it, this is often because this element has recently arrived in our field of vision, and was not present there a moment before. The fact that two states of affairs (i.e., presence and arrival) are commonly co-associated with this construction and that the sentence is frequently ambiguous between the two senses can give rise to a secondary meaning. Other works (Sweetser 1990; C. Johnson 1998) discuss this process more thoroughly. Proof that this is indeed an independent sense from the Central Deictic and not merely implicit in it comes from its divergent syntax and pragmatics.

The Now Deictic, as opposed to the Central Deictic, requires the locational complement to be specified, whether pronominalized (21b) or not (21a).[7]

(21) (a) Nous voilà au labo.
Now here we are in the lab.

(b) Nous y voilà.
Now here we are.

That this sense is different from the Central Deictic is shown by the possibility of referring to an object or event that is not necessarily in the perceptual realm of the speaker, but when the state described by the NP is expected to obtain at a certain time (22).

(22) (a) Voilà mon prof au labo.

---

[6] Native speakers disagree on the felicity of this utterance, even in its metonymic reading.

[7] The sentences in (21) might be uttered by a tour guide.

Now my prof is in the lab [looking at watch].

(b) Voilà que mon frère part.
Now my brother's leaving.

Recall that in the Central Deictic, the use of first person was uncommon, due to conflicting presuppositions of the context and the potential construction. The first person is commonly used in the Now Deictic (21), however, another indication that the construction has a different set of presuppositions from the Central Deictic, as it is an independent sense of *voilà*.

3.4 Stative Deictic

A characteristic of radial categories in general is that extensions can give birth to second-degree extensions. In other words, not all extensions of a radial category must be directly extended from that central case; they can be extensions from other extensions. While this phenomenon has been discussed for lexical polysemy networks (Lakoff 1987; Brugman 1981) and for subjecthood (Van Oosten 1986), the idea that families of constructions might also display this behavior is a novel one (although inheritance of inherited constructions is discussed for the SAI construction in Fillmore 1998).

The Stative Deictic is mapped through the metaphor STATES ARE LOCATIONS from the Now Deictic. It inherits the structure, the stress pattern, and the tendency to occur with *et* 'and' or *mais* 'but' from the Now Deictic. Instead of a specified locational complement, it requires a stative complement, such as an adjective or the *qui*+verb construction (functionally similar to the gerund in English). The meaning that emerges is that a person is now in a state that (s)he previously was not in.

(23) (a) Voilà mon oncle content.
Now my uncle's happy.

(b) Voilà mon frère qui pleure.
Now my brother's crying.

(c) Me voilà partie.
Now I'm gone.

Note that the sentence in (23b) can also have a Central Deictic meaning if the *qui*+verb is modifying the noun phrase, where the speaker is pointing out this brother as opposed to some other brother (restrictive). It can also have the central meaning when the *qui*+verb is actually a descriptor of an action being pointed out (non-restrictive). These two uses are distinguished from the Now sense by the fact that in the Now sense the speaker doesn't have to be pointing at the object performing the action; moreover, the object doesn't even have to be in the visual field of the speaker or hearer.

The metaphor responsible for the Stative Deictic, STATES ARE LOCATIONS, is rampant elsewhere in both French and English (24). In the *voilà* sentences in (23) above, the fact that *voilà* takes a state descriptor in place of the locative descriptor from the Central Deictic shows that this metaphor is present. In the examples below, prepositions and verbal predicates encode this replacement, but this is a general fact about the expression of states in French.

(24)   (a)   Elle est en colère.
             She's angry.

       (b)   Il est tombé dans les pommes.
             He passed out. (literally, 'he fell in the apples')

3.5 Span of Time/Distance Deictic

As additional evidence of the phenomenon of second-degree constructional extensions, we present the Span of Time/Distance Deictic, which motivates sentences like those in (25).

(25)   (a)   Voilà deux heures que ça pue la vache.
             Now it's been stinking cow for two hours.

       (b)   Voilà deux kilomètres que ça pue la vache.
             Now it's been stinking cow for two kilometers.

We analyze this construction as a blend, based on the fact that there exists one other construction that shares the particular syntax of these forms: X NP[span of time] *que* finite phrase. (We know of no others.) We will call this the Span of Time Construction. Specifically, X can be either *ça fait* 'it's been' or *il y a* 'it's been', as in (26).

(26)   (a)   Ça fait deux ans que je vous attend.
             It's been two years that I've waited for you.

       (b)   Il y a deux ans que j'habite dans ce quartier.
             I've been living in this neighborhood for two years.

The explanation of the motivation for this sense of *voilà* is more complicated than for the previous examples. We claim that once *voilà* has aquired the meaning of 'now', as in the Now Deictic, it is available to undergo a kind of constructional blend with the time constructions in (26) above. On the semantic side, this blend essentially takes this sense of *voilà* ('now') and adds to it the sense associated with the Span of Time Construction ('it has been X time that Y'), yielding 'it has now been X time that Y'. In other words, while *ça fait* and *il y a* can be placed in the future or past (27a and c), *voilà* is anchored in the time of the utterance, and therefore cannot felicitously co-occur with a future or past tense verb (27b and d). On the syntactic side, the syntax is identical to that of the Span of Time Construction.

(27)   (a)   Il y aura/Ça fera deux ans qu'on se connaitra.
             It will be two years that we will have known each other.

       (b)   *Voilà deux ans qu'on se connaitra.
             Now it will be two years that we will have known each other.

       (c)   Il y avait/Ça faisait deux ans qu'on se connaissait.
             It was two years that we had known each other.

       (d)   ?Voilà deux ans qu'on se connaissait.
             Now it was two years that we had known each other.

The attentive reader will have noticed from (25) that not only time, but also space can be used as a measure in this construction. On our analysis, it is not necessary to posit another sense, extended off of the Span of Time sense to the domain of space (which would be theoretically interesting as metaphors are claimed to be unidirectional). Rather, this is a case of metonymy in which a distance stands for the time it takes to travel that distance, as in English 'We've been singing for thirty miles'.

3.6 Paragon

Another extension of the Central Deictic is used for the purpose of pointing something out because it is somehow distinct from other members of its category, often because this object is a paragon example of the group (Lakoff 1987). The Paragon Deictic exhibits the syntactic restriction of only accepting partitive NPs, either full or pronominalized using *en* 'some' (28).

(28)   (a)   Voilà de la bonne littérature.
             Now there's good literature.

       (b)   En voilà des étudiants!
             Now there's some students (for you)!

This construction uses the intonation pattern found in general with the expression of awe or paragon status (bolded in (29)), as exemplified in other constructions expressing awe. Instrumental analysis shows that this intonational pattern corresponds to a Low to High pitch contour over the word *voilà*, with a quick drop onto the rest of the low pitch sentence (Bergen & Plauché submitted).

(29)   (a)   **Ça** c'est une bonne idée.
             Now, **that's** a good idea.

       (b)   Si **Marco** n'y va pas, eh ben, moi non plus.
             If **Marco** isn't going, well then, me neither.

Partitive noun phrases are the only ones permitted in the Paragon *voilà* construction, which can be shown to derive once again from the pragmatics of this particular sense. The Paragon Deictic specifically picks out one member (or set of members) from a category. This is most aptly expressed syntactically with the partitive, which selects a part of a group. Coupled with the "pointing out" sense of the deictic, this construction yields a "pointing out" of the paragon members of a group, with appropriately limited syntax.

6. Conclusion

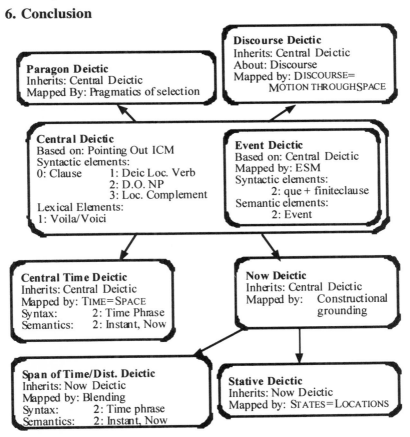

Figure 1: Radial category of *voilà* constructions

We have been able to motivate the relations between a family of constructions (Figure 1), through reference to general cognitive mechanisms, such as metaphor, metonymy, blending, and constructional grounding. Considering the pragmatic and semantic constraints on *voilà* constructions has additionally allowed us to explain aspects of their syntactic behavior that are problematic for traditional grammatical analyses.

As deictics, *voilà* and *voici* are singular in their inherent groundedness in the time and place of the utterance. Nevertheless, we believe the methodology we have adopted to investigate the cognitive motivation for the constructions' syntax and inter-relatedness will prove equally fruitful for families of constructions which are grounded in other aspects of human experience.

References

Bergen, Benjamin K. and Madelaine C. Plauché. Submitted. Extensions of Deictic and Existential Constructions in French: *voilà*, *voici*, and *il y a*.

Brugman, Claudia. 1981. *Story of Over*. M.A. Thesis. University of California, Berkeley. Indiana University Linguistics Club.

Brunot, Ferdinand, and C. Bruneau. 1969. *Précis de grammaire historique de la langue française*. Paris: Mosson.

Damourette, Jacques and Edouard Pichon. 1927. *Des mots à la pensée: Essai de grammaire de la langue française*. Paris: d'Artrey.

Fillmore, Charles J. 1997 [1971]. *Lectures on Deixis*. Stanford: CSLI Publications.

Fillmore, Charles J. 1998. Inversion and Constructional Inheritance, in Gert Webelhuth, Jean-Pierre Koenig, and Andreas Kathol, eds., *Constructional and Lexical Aspects of Linguistic Explanation*. CSLI Publications, 113-128.

Girault-Duvivier, Charles Pierre. 1851. *Grammaire des grammaires, ou Analyse raisonnée des meilleurs traites sur la langue française*. Paris: A. Cotelle.

Grady, Joe and Chris Johnson. 1997. Primary Scenes, in Jeri Moxley and Matt Juge eds., *Proceedings of the 23rd Annual Meeting of the Berkeley Linguistics Society*. Berkeley: BLS.

Grenoble, Lenore and Matthew Riley. 1996. The Role of Deictics in Discourse Coherence: French *voici/voilà* and Russian *vot/von*. *Journal of Pragmatics* 25:819-838.

Johnson, Chris. 1998. Constructional Grounding: On the Relation between Deictic and Existential *there*-Constructions in Acquisition. Paper Presented at CDSL-4.

Jones, Michael A. 1996. *Foundations of French Syntax*. Cambridge: Cambridge University Press.

Lakoff, George. 1987. *Women, Fire and Dangerous Things*. Chicago: University of Chicago Press.

Lakoff, George and Mark Johnson. 1980. *Metaphors We Live By*. Chicago: University of Chicago Press.

Lambrecht, Knud. 1981. *Topic, Focus, and the Grammar of Spoken French.* Unpublished Ph.D. Dissertation. UC Berkeley.

Lindner, Susan. 1981. *A Lexico-Semantic Analysis of Verb-Particle Constructions with Up and Out.* Ph.D. Dissertation. University of California, San Diego.

Moignet, Gerard. 1969. Le verbe *voici-voilà. Travaux de Linguistique et de Littérature* 7:189-201.

Moore, Kevin E. 1998. Deixis and the 'front/back' Component of Temporal Metaphors. Paper presented at CSDL-4.

Nyrop, Kristoffer. 1914. *Grammaire historique de la langue française.* New York: Stechert.

Plauché, Madelaine C. and Benjamin K. Bergen. 1999. The Evolution of Binary Spatial Deictics: French *voilà* and *voici*, in Steve Chang et al, eds. *Proceedings of the 25th Annual Meeting of the Berkeley Linguistics Society.* Berkeley: Berkeley Linguistics Society.

Smith, Tomoko. 1997. How 'give' and 'receive' Provide Structure for Abstract Notions: The Case of Benefactives, Adversative, Causatives, and Passives, in Benjamin Bergen, Madelaine Plauché and Ashlee Bailey, eds., *Proceedings of the 24th Annual Meeting of the Berkeley Linguistics Society.* Berkeley: BLS.

Sweetser, Eve. 1990. *From Etymology to Pragmatics.* Cambridge: Cambridge University Press.

Van Oosten, Jeanne. 1986. *The Nature of Subjects, Topics, and Agents: A Cognitive Explanation.* Bloomington: Indiana University Linguistics Club.

Perspective, Deixis and Voice: Developmental Reflections

NANCY BUDWIG

Clark University

1. Introduction

The notion of perspective and the role of language in construing reality has received much attention from cognitive linguists and cognitive anthropologists (see Taylor & MacLaury 1995 for review). In such work, it is frequently claimed that the ability to adopt perspectives is innate. But at the same time, it has only been recently that developmental psycholinguists have concerned themselves with this issue (see for instance Bowerman 1985; Budwig 1995; Slobin 1985; in press; Tomasello 2000 for reviews). One notable exception to this is Werner and Kaplan's (1963/1984) consideration of Bühler's (1934/1990) discussion of symbolic fields from a developmental perspective. Bühler's notion of symbolic fields, which shares much in common with Lakoff's (1987) "Idealized Cognitive Models" and Langacker's (1987) use of "schema," highlighted the extent to which the use of particular linguistic forms, embedded in specific linguistic fields plays a significant role in structuring reality. Werner and Kaplan (1963/1984), picking up on Bühler's work, suggested that language development could be viewed as one example of a more general developmental process. This trend suggested that children desire to conceive of the world first in terms of "formula-like schemata" and only later in terms of more freedom from the concrete perceptual-motor contexts. It was not, though, until developmental psycholinguists began turning to the work of cognitive linguists that the topic of perspective and event construal made its way back into the discus-

Conceptual and Discourse Factors in Linguistic Structure.
Alan Cienki, Barbara J. Luka and Michael B. Smith (eds.).
Copyright © 2001, CSLI Publications.

sion of grammatical development. It is this topic that will be the focus of the current chapter.

In order to address the issue of perspective and event construal, I will review findings from a series of cross-linguistic studies that I have conducted over the last few years. In this work I have developed a framework which I refer to as a developmental-functionalist approach. It draws simultaneously on work in functional linguistic theory, and a Wernerian perspective on development. In this chapter, I begin with a consideration of issues related to perspective and agency. Next I examine two domains of grammatical development which include deixis and voice. In doing so, I will draw upon cross-linguistic data of the early phases of children's acquisition of English and German. A central question will be whether children begin with a universal set of perspectives that they adopt, or whether children from the start begin with perspectives that already show sensitivity to typological factors of the languages they are acquiring. Answers to this question will place us in a better position to understand the developmental unfolding of perspective during the early phases of grammatical development. In addition to looking at whether perspective is marked in the earliest word combinations of young children, I also report on findings looking at the developmental unfolding of this ability by children acquiring English and German.

2. Perspective and Agency: Theoretical Starting Points

2.1 Functionalist Approaches to Child Language

Cognitive linguistic perspectives have had an influence on child language work only in the last decade. This can be traced to how the notion of function was treated by developmental psycholinguists over time. During the 1970's, child language researchers primarily provided catalogs or inventories of the various communicative functions of children's utterances. By the 1980's, the notion of function began to be related to children's grammatical development in two ways. First, some researchers began to consider the role of language function in influencing the *order* of acquisition. Here the central question was: In what order do various linguistic forms develop, and how can one account for them by appealing to functional notions? For instance, Form X might appear before Form Y in a particular language because it served a particularly salient or accessible function. A second view of function that developed during that time focused on the notion of developmental histories of given form-function patternings, looking both at changes in forms and changes in functions. The focus here was not so much on developmental order, but rather, emphasis was placed on overall functional shifts. For instance, such research has noted that children first use linguistic forms unifunctionally and only later plurifunctionally (see Karmiloff-Smith 1979), or children tend to use forms in more context-restricted ways before using them more abstractly (see Budwig 1995; Ervin-Tripp 1996). Those adopting this second view of function began borrowing from cognitive linguistic views, and it is this turn that influenced my own framework. I will turn now to consider one example of a way this theorizing has influenced theoretical developments in child language research. The area that this has had the most impact is the topic of perspective and agency.

2.2 Perspective and Agency

Over the last two decades there has been increased focus on the claim that children might mark distinct perspectives with diverse linguistic forms. Given prior work suggesting that agent-action relations were among children's first word combinations cognitive linguists' views concerning prototypical agency seemed worth examining. DeLancey (1984) summarizes work carried out by a variety of people in the following quote:

> The general claim is that there is a crosslinguistically valid prototype for true transitivity which involves (among other things) a direct causation schema with proximate and ultimate cause both residing in the same volitionally acting causer. The prototype definition of agent is part of this schema, i.e. the prototypical agent is just such a volitional causer. Deviations from the semantic prototype are coded by deviations from prototypical transitivity. (DeLancey 1984:185)

Work on prototypical agency was first picked up by Slobin in his crosslinguistic comparisons of early child grammar. Slobin (1985) suggested that certain scenes provide early wedges into grammar for the child. One scene, the manipulative activity scene, is clearly related to DeLancey's comments. Slobin describes the scene as:

> The experiential gestalt of a basic causal event in which an agent carries out a physical and perceptible change of state in a patient by means of direct body contact or with an instrument under the agent's control (Slobin 1985: 1175).

While such work reflected an exciting paradigm shift in child language researchers' views of function, it was not without criticisms (see Bowerman 1985). One issue included the fact that such work did not acknowledge cognitive developmental research that suggests that the very notion of agency undergoes rapid developments between the ages of 1 and 5. For instance, around the age of 2, children are said to be working primarily with a notion of personal agency rather than a more global notion of independent agency (see Budwig 1995 for review).

More recently, I have revised Slobin's original proposal by suggesting a developmental-functional approach to child language with special reference to the linguistic marking of agency (see Budwig 1989; 1995). Following Werner and Kaplan's (1963/1984) discussion of the orthogenetic principle, this work focuses on changes in form-function pairings. Development is studied by examining the ways forms for marking agency relate to one another over time, but also cluster with various semantic meanings and pragmatic functions. In addition to looking at the development of the marking of prototypical agency, emphasis also has been placed on various deviations marked by children over time. In the remainder of this chapter I will illustrate this by examining two areas of grammatical development, namely deixis and voice, making use of data I have collected from children acquiring English and German.

3. Deixis: An Examination of the Early Use of Personal Pronouns

3.1 The Berkeley Sample

It has long been reported that children make errors in their use of personal pronouns in acquiring the complexities of case marking when learning English (see Budwig 1995 for review). While error-like patterns had been noted, I began to be curious whether the patterns noted for children during the early phases of acquiring personal pronouns might best be understood in terms of an attempt by the children to mark prototypical agency and various deviations. In developing this hypothesis I was influenced by Slobin's (1985) reports concerning the cross-linguistic marking of agency in child language, and work I did in collaboration with Deutsch (see Deutsch & Budwig 1983) concerning English-speaking children's early use of possessive pronouns.

Slobin (1985) reported that children acquiring typologically distinct languages showed the same underextension of marking transitivity in the early phases of child language. Early on the children limited the use of ergative and accusative inflections to a scene in which an agent brought about a change. This he referred to as the "Manipulative Activity Scene." Around the same time, when examining the early linguistic marking of possession, Deutsch and Budwig (1983) noted that the American children they studied formally distinguished two kinds of pragmatic perspectives when talking about possessions. The children used *My* when taking a volitional perspective – for instance in acts of requesting and demanding objects. In contrast they used a nominal form "*Name*" when taking a constative perspective — for instance when referring to objects where possession was not in question. This resulted in minimal pairs such that a child named Adam uttered *Adam car* when asserting a car was his own, but said *My pencil* when attempting to gain control of the researcher's pencil. Noting related uses of pronouns in subject position (e.g., *My make a boat, Me jump*) led me to systematically examine whether these instances were similar to those reported by Slobin for other languages. In other words, I examined whether children were making use of various personal pronouns in subject position in their attempts to mark something like prototypical agency and various deviations.

To assess this possibility I gathered longitudinal language samples from six English-speaking children growing up in and around Berkeley, CA in the early 1980's. The children ranged between the ages of 18 and 30 months of age at the onset of the study. I examined the early use of personal pronouns by the children as they played once a month with a caregiver and a peer across a four-month period. By the end of the longitudinal study four months later, all children had given up their special use of first person pronouns. The central finding of the study can be summarized as follows. The children who were just beginning to combine words went through an extended phase of referring to themselves with multiple self reference forms often in ways that deviated from adult English (e.g., *I want that, My cracked the eggs, Megan ride bicycle, Me all done*). Before the time the children regularly referred to others, they "borrowed" first person pronominal forms to situate themselves differently with regard to their perspective on their role in ongoing action frames.

At first glance the children seemed to be marking something like a semantic agency prototype and various deviations. When referring to themselves as experiencer they used the nominative pronoun *I*, for instance uttering *I like peas* or *I think so*. In contrast, when they referred to themselves as prototypical agents, they switched to using the genitive *My,* for instance, saying *My built the tower* as they completed building a structure with wooden blocks. Affected agency, that is instances where the child was both the agent and recipient of the action described, was marked by use of *Me* as for instance when the child said, *Me jump* as she was jumping up and down. Finally, in instances where reference was made to depicted action which the children were not currently experiencing they used "*Name.*" For instance Megan said *Megan wear a t-shirt* as she looked at a photograph of herself in a T-shirt.

The special patterning of pronominal forms was not simply clustered around semantic notions of agency. There were instances, for example, of children using both *I* and *My* with the verb *want*. The semantic analysis would only have predicted the use of *I*. The children's use nevertheless was not random. Instead, the children (like those studied by Deutsch & Budwig 1983), developed a pattern of also using *My* in requests and commands, while *I* was found in less dynamically charged instances. For instance, *I want that one* was said as an assertion by a child as she was lifting up a container with a nut inside, while her mother sat passively watching her play. In contrast, *My want it* was frequently heard as the peers disputed over rights to control a shiny red toy helicopter. In sum, the children contrastively made use of self reference forms to take distinct perspectives on their role in human action. The semantic and pragmatic uses seemed to cluster together into a larger gestalt. For instance, both the semantic and pragmatic uses of *My* were found in a scene where the children tried to bring about change either physically or through using language as an instrument.

3.2 The Berlin Sample

After focusing on the American sample I decided to collect a comparable sample from German-speaking children. I was particularly interested in whether children growing up in East Germany, where notions of personal agency did not seem to be a primary socialization theme, would also specially mark prototypical agency. In addition, German provided an interesting contrast because it is quite close to English, and yet at the same time, allows more flexibility in use of case marking pronouns, especially in spoken language. For instance, while German-speaking children would be receiving input of the sort *Ich denke* (I think) or *Ich laufe* (I run), they would hear *Mir is kalt* and *Mir ist was passiert*. What is interesting in these examples is the use of *Mir* preverbally meaning something like "To me is cold" or "To me something happened." It seemed the German children might be receiving input that might actually encourage them to make use of case marking to adopt distinct perspectives on agency. I studied three German children growing up in former East Berlin around the time of reunification adopting methods similar to those used with the American children. The children were matched to be at the same level as the children studied in Berkeley who made special use of pronominal forms. All the German children were also at the earliest stages of word combinations at the onset of the study.

What was surprising was the infrequent use by the German-speaking children of self reference pronouns. In contrast to the American children, who used hundreds of such forms in each session, the German children used only a handful of pronominal forms combined. Nevertheless, there were some interesting patternings when pronominal forms were employed by the German children. These both compared and contrasted with the uses of the American children. Most notable was the absence of the form *Ich* (nominative first person pronoun) in the early sessions. Though the American children were noted to primarily refer to themselves, the German children regularly referred to others. In addition, no specific marking of what has been described as prototypical agency was found. The German children did make regular use of their own and other's names in reference to self and other as actors in acts of labeling where no intentional stance was taken. *Meine* (first person possessive) was used in conjunction with references to objects the child wanted to gain or maintain control of, but this form was not used as a subject pronoun in the way the American children extended the use of *My*.

What was most intriguing about the German children's talk about agentivity at this stage was their precocious use of the impersonal construction *man* ("one"). The use of *man* was employed by the children to refer to their own actions from a generic perspective. For instance, as one child began to lift up nuts in a plastic spoon while playing with toy dinnerware this child said *Löffel, Löffel kann man mal* implying something like "one can spoon them." In comparable instances in the Berkeley sample the children would have said "My spoon the nuts." The German children distinguished themselves from the American children in the perspectives they took on agency in two ways. First, the German children did not seem to mark the notion of prototypical agency, and second, they frequently referred to what I have called a generic perspective on their own ongoing actions which was absent in the Berkeley children's talk.

3.3 Summary

In sum, both the American and German children first restricted the use of self reference forms in subject position to a cluster of semantic and pragmatic perspectives dealing with agentivity. While there was good overlap between the children, there also were some important differences between the American and German children. Most notable was the extent to which the Berkeley children went beyond the patterning of English to mark prototypical agency. At a time before they regularly used case marked pronouns, they borrowed the first person forms to adopt distinct vantage points on self with respect to the ongoing context. While the Berlin children did not mark prototypical agency, they did link the use of the impersonal form *man* with a scene in which they adopted a generic point of view on their own actions. Accounting for these differences is beyond the purpose of this paper (see though Budwig 2000). Rather I will move on to discuss a second kind of instance of children's linking of grammatical forms with specific perspectives.

4. Voice

4.1 Voice Contrasts: Actives, Middles, and Passives

While there is quite a lot of developmental psycholinguistic work on children's early talk about prototypical agency (see Budwig 1995 for review), significantly less is known about children's growing ability to talk about nonagent subjects. As part of my continuing interest in children's linguistic marking of event perspectives I have more recently examined the children's talk about nonagent subjects in both the Berkeley and Berlin samples described above (see Budwig, Stein, & O'Brien, in press). As the children gave up their special use of pronominal forms in subject position, one finds the onset of regular talk about nonagent subjects. Although occasionally the use of nonagent subjects occurred in active transitive constructions (often cases of metonymy) the children most regularly contrasted between intransitive and middle diathesis constructions. In keeping with Klaiman (1988) and Acre-Arenales, Axelrod, and Fox (1994), I will consider middle diathesis sentences those with "syntactically active subjects which are semantically affected by the action of the verb" (Acre-Arenales et al. 1994:1). After looking at the use of nonagent subjects in these two kinds of constructions in both the English-speaking and German samples, I will briefly consider some related work on passives.

4.2 Active Intransitives versus Middles: A Developmental Examination of English and German

The question that I was concerned with involved whether there was any evidence that the children distinguished between intransitive constructions like *It (=dump truck) dumps* and middle diathesis constructions like *The doors won't open*. Following Kemmer (1994) I assumed that although formally intransitive, middle marking has its own semantic properties. The difference between these examples is subtle, namely in the first utterance it is the dump truck that carries out the action described by the verb. Yet in the second example, the child was actually attempting to open the doors referred to and to this extent the doors in the second example are semantically affected (or not affected!) by the action denoted by the verb (see Budwig, Stein, & O'Brien, in press, for further details). Similar to the children's early use of deictic forms, the children first limited the use of active intransitive and middle diathesis constructions to particular activity scenes. We will turn first to consider the findings from the Berkeley children.

The English-speaking children's first uses of nonagent subject in active intransitives co-occurred with their announcements of bids for novel play frames. Rather than focussing on their own active manipulation of objects as in their use of active transitive constructions, the children changed to focus on an event perspective which shifted focus to ways in which objects could be introduced into the play frame (e.g., *It flies, The bulldozer picks up*). In contrast, the nonagent subjects occurring in middle diathesis constructions co-occurred with utterances functioning to describe "goal blockings" or "resistance from the environment" (see Savasir 1984 for a related discussion in Turkish children). In these instances the children often had announced desires to act in particular ways, tried and were in some way unable to complete the sequence (e.g., *The doors won't open, That fell over*). In sum, the use of the middle diathesis constructions appeared in instances where the child's desires to manipulate objects in particular ways failed. To this extent, the middle diathesis constructions offered another deviation from prototypical agency.

The German children appeared to have a very similar pattern for nonagent subjects appearing in active intransitive constructions. For instance after describing their own manipulations of objects, they then switched perspective to talk about the toys, in particular to introduce new play frames. For instance one child said *"Fährt sie jetzt gleich wieder zurück"* (She [=the toy train] drives now once again back). While the middle diathesis constructions provided an alternative for the German children, such uses did not link up with goal blocking, as was noted for the American children. Given that the German children did not mark prototypical agentivity in the first place, the lack of marking of goal blocking should hardly be surprising. For the German children, the middle diathesis constructions occurred with a normative perspective. Here they appealed to normative reasons for why objects should be located in particular ways. For instance the children said things like *Da kommen die hin* (*There they fit there*) or *Das gehört dem Teller* (That belongs (with) the plate). Thus, the contrast for the Berlin children was one of using non-agent subjects to announce play frame bids versus normative perspectives on relationships between objects.

In sum, in addition to adopting various perspectives on agentivity, the children also were able before the age of three to consistently adopt a variety of perspectives with nonagent subjects. Here children switched between active intransitive and middle diathesis constructions to mark alternative vantage points. Interestingly, the children in neither sample made use of passive constructions. We will turn now to other work I have done that highlights that by the age of three children also can use passives to adopt other perspectives on events. As we will see, the sorts of events marked with such constructions are not the sort best captured when a researcher brings in appealing toys for the children to manipulate.

4.3 Passives: A Developmental Examination of English

Although the children I studied failed to make use of passive constructions, there are reports in the literature of young children using passives (see Bowerman 1990; Budwig 1990; Slobin 1994). I have examined the use of passive constructions found in Bowerman's diary records of her daughters' Eva and Christy and in addition, have designed some empirical studies to test hypotheses derived from this examination with a wider group of subjects (Budwig 1990). As was the case in our discussion above, shifts away from agentive transitive clause structure marked deviations from prototypical agency. Bowerman's daughters distinguished two kinds of nonprototypical agency when using passives, one perspective co-occurred with *get* passives and the other co-occurred with *be* passives. The *get* passives were used as a perspective taking device to focus on actions that have painful or negative consequences. Between the ages of 30 months and five years of age the children said things like *If Deedee don't be careful, she might get runned over from a car, I just got pinched from these pointed stuff, We will get striked by lightening,* and *And he got punished with the teacher- by the teacher spanking him hard.* In all these instances, the child places focus on the negative consequence of the action described by the verb. As I have described elsewhere (Budwig 1990), this pattern of using *get* passives to take an affective stance on happenings is not limited to these children and has been reported by others (see Givon & Yang 1994 for a historical review of the *get* passive construction).

In contrast to marking adversity, *be* passives appear in conjunction with reference to events in which the agent is generic, irrelevant, or unknown. In these instances the child is not particularly concerned with WHO is performing the action described and is intrigued with communicating the result. These examples also begin before the third birthday and continue across the diary studies. For instance Eva queries at age 2;8 *Does the cream of wheat need to be cooled?*, and also before the age of three asks *Do you think that flower's supposed to be picked by somebody?*. Christy comments at age 4;2 *Hair needs to be brushed.* A particularly novel example created by Eva at age 6;7 included *I'm gonna have a will and it's gonna say that I wanna be ashed.* In each of these cases the children have used the *be* passive to downplay agency, in particular because it is not relevant.

4.4 Summary

The work with the passives highlights even further perspectives the children take on events. In addition to marking prototypical agency, announcing play bids, and marking resistance from the environment or goal blocking, English speaking children use the passive to adopt two further perspectives: negative consequence and generic agency. In sum, I have argued in this section that before the age of three, children use voice contrasts to adopt distinct perspectives on scenes. In keeping with Werner and Kaplan (1963/1984) I have suggested that these perspectives are very much tied to their ongoing actions with objects and fairly concrete goals of ongoing play practices.

5. Conclusions

Three conclusions can be drawn from the work summarized in this paper. First, the material reviewed adds to the growing amount of evidence that at least from their earliest stages of word combinations children alternate linguistic forms to communicate distinct perspectives on events. As Clark (1990) has suggested, learning viewpoints is an essential part of the language learning task. The findings reviewed here from children acquiring both English and German suggest that all the children from the start concerned themselves with perspective taking. Although this might be viewed as evidence for some innate, broader cognitive urge, the data also suggest that the ability to adopt perspectives undergoes development itself and that the developments witnessed are not the same for children living in distinct cultural communities that speak different languages. An open question remains whether all children begin with what Clark (in press) has referred to as "emergent" categories that quickly are reshaped into the conventional vantage points of specific languages or whether children really do start verb-by-verb using a conservative strategy of not generalizing beyond input heard as Tomasello has suggested (see Tomasello 2000 for review). Only with careful naturalistic observations of a larger number of children will such a question get sorted out.

It is clear that much more research is needed to clarify the nature of the developmental paths traveled by children from their earliest word combinations to adult-like usage. Tomasello's work (see Tomasello 2000 for review) suggests that children begin with quite conservative procedures, listening carefully to the input and starting with very concrete input driven usage patterns. My own research, reviewed above suggests a related, but nevertheless, distinct developmental path. The findings from my own cross-lingustic work suggest that children rather start with formula-like perspectives marking scenes that are salient based on their experiences in communicative practices. For instance the Berkeley children integrated a notion of using language as an instrument of control into their marking of prototypical agency.

This study also suggests that children may first make use of lexical means (such as the contrastive use of pronominal forms) before they make use of construction variations (e.g., shifts from actives to passives) when marking perspective. Other evidence for young children's ability to lexically mark distinct perspectives has also been noted by Clark (1997). More cross-linguistic work would help better understand the relationship between the use of various kinds of linguistic markers and the scenes with which children link them when adopting various perspectives over developmental time.

Finally, the present study suggests the need to further examine cross-linguistic and cultural differences in the nature of the perspectives adopted. Although we did find all children marked perspectives, the specifics of such markings varied for the children acquiring English and German. What remains to be seen is whether the distinctions are best related to differences in socialization practices that exist between cultures or differences in typological factors of the input the children received. That is, further work needs to be done to sort out why the Berkeley children were concerned with the marking of prototypical agency, while normativity played a more salient role for the Berlin children. Much of the work on perspective from a developmental psycholinguistic perspective has involved the detailed analysis of children acquiring a particular language. It is clear that carefully planned comparisons of children receiving different kinds of input are very much needed to sort out this complex issue.

In concluding, I would like to emphasize the point that cognitive and functional linguistic theories have played a tremendous role in understanding the nature of children's early grammatical development. At the same time, one point that needs to be kept in mind is that children's language development is *protracted* and therefore there is not always a one-to-one fit between cognitive linguistic or functional theories and developmental onset. As Werner and Kaplan (1963/1984) pointed out long ago, children's use of linguistic forms is more likely to begin with concrete markings. My own work has highlighted the extent to which children make use of broader activity scenes that cut across what has traditionally been thought about as semantic and pragmatic levels of analysis. Thus it remains necessary to further consider the relationship between cognitive linguistic theorizing and developmental theorizing.

In closing, I also would like to suggest that the study of language development might serve an important role for developing cognitive linguistic theories. For instance, analyses of children's language development might offer fresh insights into the connection between particular grammatical constructions. In this chapter, I have argued that the children moved from using case markers to mark a fairly global distinction between various kinds of agency, to a more refined use of voice to mark further distinctions. In addition, the developmental work suggests ways children link pragmatic aspects of scenes (such as requesting) to their marking of agentivity in ways that might be fruitful for cognitive linguists to consider. In sum, such research highlights the importance of linking cognitive linguistic and developmental theorizing when considering the linguistic marking of perspective.

References

Acre-Arenales, Manuel, Melissa Axelrod and Barbara Fox. 1994. Active Voice and Middle Diathesis: A Cross-linguistic Perspective, in B. Fox and P. Hopper, eds., *Voice: Form and Function*. Amsterdam: John Benjamins Publishing.

Bowerman, Melissa. 1985. What Shapes Children's Grammars? in D. Slobin, ed., *The Crosslinguistic Study of Language Acquisition* (Vol. 2). Hillsdale, NJ: Lawrence Erlbaum Associates.

Bowerman, Melissa. 1990. *When a Patient is the Subject: Sorting Out Passives, Anticausatives, and Middles in the Acquisition of English*. Paper presented to Voice Symposium, University of California, Santa Barbara.

Budwig, Nancy. 1989. The Linguistic Marking of Agentivity and Control in Child Language. *Journal of Child Language* 16:263-284.

Budwig, Nancy. 1990. The Linguistic Marking of Non-prototypical Agency: An Exploration into Children's Use of Passives. *Linguistics* 28:1221-1252.

Budwig, Nancy. 1995. *A Developmental-Functionalist Approach to Child Language*. Mahwah, NJ: Lawrence Erlbaum Associates.

Budwig, Nancy. 2000. Language and the Construction of Self: Linking Forms and Functions Across Development, in N. Budwig, I. C. Uzgiris, and James V. Wertsch, eds., *Communication: An Arena of Development*. Greenwich, CT: Ablex.

Budwig, Nancy, Serena Stein and Catherine O'Brien. In press. Non-agent Subjects in Early Child Language: A Cross-linguistic Comparison, in K. Nelson,

A. Aksu-Koc & C. Johnson, eds., *Children's Language: Vol. 10. Language in Use, Narrative and Interaction.* Mahwah, NJ: Lawrence Erlbaum.

Bühler, Karl. 1934. *Sprachtheorie.* Jena-Stuttgart: Gustav Fischer.

Bühler, Karl. 1990. Theory of Language: The Representational Function of Language. [Translation of *Sprachtheorie*, by Donald Goodwin] Amsterdam: John Benjamins.

Clark, Eve. 1990. Speaker Perspective in Language Acquisition. *Journal of Linguistics* 28:1201-1220.

Clark, Eve. 1997. Conceptual Perspective and Lexical Choice in Acquisition. *Cognition* 64:1-37.

Clark, Eve. In press. Emergent Categories in First Language Acquisition, in M. Bowerman & S. C. Levinson, eds., *Language Acquisition and Conceptual Development.* Cambridge: Cambridge University Press.

DeLancey, Scott. 1984. Notes on Agentivity and Causation. *Studies in Language* 8:181-213.

Deutsch, Werner and Nancy Budwig. 1983. Form and Function in the Development of Possessives. *Papers and Reports on Child Language Development* 22.36-42.

Ervin-Tripp, Susan. 1996. Context in Language, in D. I. Slobin, J. Gerhardt, A. Kyratzis, & J. Guo, eds., *Social Interaction, Social Context, and Language.* Mahwah, NJ: Lawrence Erlbaum.

Givon, Talmy and Lynne Yang. 1994. The Rise of the English GET-Passive, in B. Fox and P. Hopper, eds., *Voice: Form and Function.* Amsterdam: John Benjamins Publishing.

Karmiloff-Smith, Annette. 1979. *A Functional Approach to Child Language.* Cambridge: Cambridge University Press.

Kemmer, Suzanne. 1994. Middle Voice, Transitivity, and the Elaboration of Events, in B. Fox and P. Hopper, eds., *Voice: Form and Function.* Amsterdam: John Benjamins.

Klaiman, M. H. 1988. Affectedness and Control: A Typology of Voice Systems, in M. Shibatani, ed., *Passive and Voice.* Amsterdam: John Benjamins.

Lakoff, George. 1987. *Women, Fire, and Dangerous Things: What Categories Reveal About the Mind.* Chicago: University of Chicago Press.

Langacker, Ronald. 1987. *Foundations of Cognitive Grammar* (Vol. 1). Stanford: Stanford University Press.

Savasir, Iskender. 1984. *How Many Futures?* Unpublished Masters Thesis, University of California Berkeley.

Slobin, Dan. 1985. Crosslinguistic Evidence for the Language-Making Capacity, in D. Slobin, ed., *The Crosslinguistic Study of Language Acquisition* (Vol. 2). Hillsdale, NJ: Lawrence Erlbaum Associates.

Slobin, Dan. 1994. Passives and Alternatives in Children's Narratives, in B. Fox and P. Hopper, eds., *Voice: Form and Function*. Amsterdam: John Benjamins.

Slobin, Dan. In press. Why are Grammaticizable Notions Special? — A Reanalysis and a Challenge to Learning Theory, in M. Bowerman & S. C. Levinson, eds., *Language Acquisition and Conceptual Development*. Cambridge: Cambridge University Press.

Taylor, John and Robert MacLaury, eds., 1995. *Language and the Cognitive Construal of the World.*. Berlin: Mouton de Gruyter.

Tomasello, Michael. 2000. *The Cultural Origins of Human Cognition*. Cambridge, MA: Harvard University Press.

Werner, Heinz and Bernard Kaplan. 1963/1984. *Symbol Formation*. Hillsdale, NJ: Lawrence Erlbaum Associates.

Semantic Influences on Attributions of Causality in Interpersonal Events

ROBERTA CORRIGAN

University of Wisconsin-Milwaukee

1. Introduction

In our everyday lives we are often curious as to why people behave as they do. Often, their behaviors are described orally or in print rather than being observed directly. Therefore, it is important to understand how causality is conveyed through language. If I hear that a customer in a department store yelled at a salesperson, I may wonder why. Had the clerk done something to elicit the customer's behavior or was the customer generally an irritable person? Social psychologists describe causal attributions made about others' behaviors in terms of whether the event was caused by something external to the person (the situation was provocative) or internal to the person (a trait or disposition). Psychologists have suggested that some verbs bias attributions of causality to the subject of simple SVO sentences describing events and others bias attributions to the object, a phenomenon known as 'implicit verb causality.' Sections 2 and 3 of this paper describe 'implicit verb causality' and the initial research on which it is based. Section 4 presents arguments from linguistics and social psychology suggesting that implicit causality is not solely in the verb, but is a function of the semantics of the entire sentence/event. This section also presents empirical data showing that judges do not always attribute responsibility for an action to the sentence subject. In section 5, I ask how these data can be reconciled with suggestions that 'responsibility' or 'causality' as the central characteristic of agency. I conclude that implicit causality is not just a function of the verb and its thematic roles, but is also a function of the underlying semantic dimensions of the lexical items filling those roles. The first participant in

Conceptual and Discourse Factors in Linguistic Structure.
Alan Cienki, Barbara J. Luka and Michael B. Smith (eds.).
Copyright © 2001, CSLI Publications.

an action event, usually the subject in a simple sentence, initiates the event, but does not necessarily cause it.

2. The Phenomenon of Implicit Verb Causality

When people are presented with sentences such as (1) and (2) and are asked to judge who caused the interactions, they are most likely to attribute the event in (1) to Ann and in (2) to Sally. That is, in simple, active-voice sentences, people consistently make causal attributions to the sentence subject for sentences containing some verbs and to the object for others.

(1)   Ann harassed Sally.

(2)   Ann admired Sally.

Sentence processing research has found that implicit verb causality influences things like anaphora and reading times (Garvey, Caramazza & Yates 1976; McKoon, Greene & Ratcliff 1993). Implicit causality effects have been examined in many languages including Chinese, Dutch, English, Italian, Japanese, and German (see Lee and Kasof 1993 for a bibliography).

3. The Background

Garvey and Caramazza (1974) were first to claim that some verbs bias causal judgments about sentence participants to the sentence subject and some to the sentence object. They argued that implicit causality is a semantic feature of the verb. Brown and Fish (1983) recognized that action verbs give greater weight to the sentence agent and state verbs give greater weight to the sentence stimulus, (to the sentence subject for stimulus-experiencer verbs and to the object for experiencer-stimulus verbs).[1] Their basic argument was that causality is attributed to the agent with action verbs because anyone can be acted upon, while the category of persons who can act is more restricted. For example, anyone can be cheated, but few people are predisposed to cheat. Likewise, with state verbs, anyone can experience a state, but fewer people can evoke the state. The more unusual, more restricted category is the one to whom causality is attributed.

At first blush, the Brown and Fish (1983) findings are reasonable. The division of verbs into state verbs and action verbs (including activity, achievement, and accomplishment verbs) has been widely acknowledged since Vendler (1957[1967]). Sentences such as (1), used by Brown and Fish to elicit causal judgments, described transitive events and the prototypical transitive event involves a volitional agent who carries out a physical activity which transmits energy to a patient, causing it to undergo a change of state (Langacker 1991:210). The prototypical agent is therefore the person

---

[1] What Brown and Fish (1983) label as 'state' verbs are often labeled as transitive Psychological verbs. Alternative labels for "stimulus" include 'theme,' 'cause,' 'object of emotion' or 'target of emotion' (Levin 1993).

responsible for the action. As stated by DeLancey (1984:182), "the fundamental sense of agentivity involves causation of an event."

Sentences used by Brown and Fish such as (2) described psychological states. Croft (1993; see also Van Valin & LaPolla 1997) notes that state verbs really belong to multiple classes. Stimulus-Experiencer verbs such as 'please' or 'frighten' are causative verbs because the stimulus causes the experiencer to enter a mental state, as shown in (3a-b). As causatives, they describe processes and are comparable in many respects to other action verbs.

(3)   a.   John frightened Ted.

        b.   John caused Ted to be afraid.

On the other hand, Experiencer-Stimulus verbs such as 'like' or 'fear' share properties with other verbs of cognition and perception. There are two processes involved in possessing and changing a mental state. The experiencer directs her attention to the stimulus, which then causes the experiencer to be in the state. Croft's (1991) representation of this relationship is shown in (4).

(4)   Experiencer   Stimulus

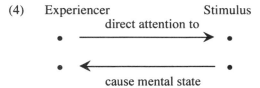

4. Do Action Verbs Always Elicit Causal Attributions to the Agent?

In sum, Brown and Fish's arguments (1983) are sensible in the context of the sentences they used in their experiments, where the only information on which to base a causal judgment was whether the verb was an action or an experiencer verb. But most real-world events contain semantic information about the participants in an event via the labels that are used to describe them. The remainder of this paper focuses on action verbs rather than state verbs and asks whether, as Brown and Fish suggested, action verbs always bias attributions to the agent (the sentence subject in the simple sentences presented in their studies).

A major problem with much of the current psychological literature is that the verb is viewed as a separate entity rather than as part of an entire sentence/event (see Fiedler & Semin 1988, for similar arguments). A sentence in a text or in natural discourse is embedded in a context. Only in psychology experiments do we hear or read about neutral, same gender individuals interacting. In everyday life, if we are told about a fight between John and Sam, we usually know *something* about John and Sam: for example, their ages, their genders, personality characteristics, their social roles (father-child), their professional roles (teacher-student,) and we know something about fighting (the conditions under which it is likely to occur, typical types of aggression that can occur, etc).

There are several exceptions in the implicit causality literature that look at the effects of event context. Although she does not study contextual factors directly, Au (1986) suggests that understanding verb causality involves activating a scene and focusing on certain parts of it, similar to suggestions by Fillmore (1977). Characteristics of event participants such as their gender, animacy or social status have been found to influence attributions of who caused an event (Corrigan 1988; 1992; 1993; Garvey, Caramazza & Yates 1976; LaFrance, Brownell & Hahn 1997).

4.1 Linguistic Arguments: Causal Chains and Thematic Roles

Of course, many cognitive linguists agree that comprehending a sentence requires understanding an entire event and that causal understanding is critical for that event understanding. Croft (1991; 1994) argues that events are defined by their causal structure. Event structures described by sentences are 'causal chains' (See also Langacker 1991), which are idealized cognitive models (ICMs) of single events (Lakoff 1987) in which event participants are linked by causal relations whereby one individual transmits force of some kind to another. A verb denotes a segment of the causal chain.

Van Valin and LaPolla (1997:84) note that participants in events have roles that do not exist independently of events. Dowty (1991:572) suggests that two, cluster concept proto-roles, proto-agent and proto-patient, subsume all other thematic roles. The grammatical argument with the greatest number of proto-agent properties will be lexicalized as the subject of the predicate and the argument having the greatest number of proto-patient properties will be lexicalized as the direct object.

Recently, McRae, Ferretti, and Amyote (1997) indicated that thematic roles encode specific information about who typically does what to whom. Expectations of experimental participants who were presented with sentences that were initially ambiguous (they could either be main clauses or reduced relative clauses) were affected by the presence of adjectives that biased the sentence-initial nominal concept toward being a good agent or a good patient. For example, readers expected 'The shrewd heartless...' to be part of the main clause in (7a) rather than part of the reduced relative clause in (7b) and they expected 'The young naïve...' to be part of the reduced relative clause in (7d) rather than the main clause in (7c).

(7)   a.   The shrewd heartless gambler manipulated the dealer.

b. The shrewd heartless gambler manipulated by the dealer...

c. The young naïve gambler manipulated the dealer.

d. The young naïve gambler manipulated by the dealer...

In other words, some identities were better agents for a given verb than others even though both filled the same thematic role.

4.2 Psychological Arguments: Universal Dimensions of Word Meaning

One social psychology theory that addresses the question of whether there are general semantic factors that can account for effects of both verbs, nouns and their interactions is Affect Control Theory (Heise 1992; MacKinnon 1994). Although *all* elements in a social interaction contribute to people's interpretation of it, in sentences such as (1) and (2), if the only information available concerns the verb, then people will necessarily use it to make judgments. However, if additional information is available, then information about the entire event will be used to make judgments.

Affect Control theorists argue that all social cognitions involving people, their behaviors and their properties evoke universal affective/connotative dimensions of word meaning: Evaluation, potency, and activity (Osgood, May & Miron 1975). Evaluation is the degree to which people and their associated activities are good or bad; potency is the degree to which people or events are strong, powerful, or large; activity is the degree to which a person or action is dynamic or energetic. Within Affect Control Theory, evaluation, potency, and activity (EPA) ratings are assessed via semantic differential rating scales which range from –4 to +4. EPA responses are shared within a community so that an average EPA response to a person or behavior is a measure of that community's affective response to an entity (Heise 1992). For example, Mackinnon (1994:18) reports that for a sample of male Canadian university students, the EPA rating for 'professor' was 1.47, 1.36, and -.55 while for 'student' it was 1.18, .20, 1.86. This means that this community views the typical professor as "between slightly and quite good, slightly powerful, and edging towards slightly slow, old, and quiet." On the other hand, a student is slightly good, neutral in potency, and quite lively.

The social identities of both participants in an interaction restrict the types of actions that are likely to be performed. When an actor behaves in a way that deviates from expectations, observers judge the event to be abnormal and use a variety of methods to reconcile the contradiction. One way of handling inconsistencies is to attribute causality to factors outside the actor (Vonk 1995), for example to the sentence patient. In (8a), violence toward an enemy is expected, but violence toward a child in (8b) is not. Bad, forceful behaviors toward bad, potent objects seem justified while such behaviors toward good, weak objects seem ruthless (Heise 1992). Most people would deem the enemy to be to be at least partially responsible for the event described in (8a) because negative, potent individuals elicit negative actions; they would judge the soldier to be responsible for the event described in (8b), because children do not deserve to be the object of such negative actions.

(8)   a.   The soldier shot the enemy.

        b.   The soldier shot the child.

4.3 Experimental Evidence

Thus far, I have suggested that interpretations of events are not made solely on the basis of the verb. I will now present evidence from two experiments described in detail in Corrigan (1998) to show that when sentences contain more than minimal information about the characteristics of the event participants, causal attributions are not always made to the subject.

Prior to the experiments described here, 59 college students rated the evaluation, potency, and activity of 46 *action* verbs on scales from − 4 (very negative/ bad, very weak/ powerless, or very inactive) to + 4 (very good/positive, very strong/ powerful, or very active/dynamic). They also rated the evaluation and potency of 92 nouns labeling social identities such as *criminal* or *juror*. The experiments investigated the effects of evaluation, potency, and activity on goodness of thematic role and on causal attributions to events described by sentences.

4.3.1 Experiment 1: Judged Likelihood of Generic Actions

Another 37 students judged (on a 7– point scale) the likelihood that these identities engaged in generic positive or negative actions, as shown in (9).

(9)   a.   How likely is it that a grandmother will to do something positive/ negative to another person?

        b.   How likely is it that another person will do something positive/ negative to a grandmother?

Results of a series of regression analyses indicated that the perceived evaluation and potency of noun identities had large effects on whether or not they were judged to be good agents or patients. Negative, potent individuals were judged more likely to do negative things (with evaluation accounting for 65% of the variance and potency an additional 11%); positive identities, regardless of potency were more likely to engage in positive actions (R^2=.75). Negative identities, regardless of potency were likely to have negative things done to them (R^2 =.47) and positive, non-potent identities were most likely to have positive things done to them (with evaluation accounting for 65% of the variance and potency accounting for an additional 3%). In sum, knowing nothing at all about the specific action involved in an event (except its evaluation), judges differentiate between participants' likelihood to fill different thematic roles based on their social identity labels.

4.3.2 Experiment 2: Who Caused the Event?

The stimuli for Experiment 2 consisted of sentences which paired specific action verbs with the social identities from Experiment 1. In these sentences, each verb was included with two different noun–pairs, each noun–pair was included with two different action verbs, and the same nouns were included in subject position with the same verb in one sentence and in object position in another sentence, as shown in (10a-b) and (11a-b).

(10) a. The teenager praised the elder.

     b. The elder praised the teenager.

(11) a   The teenager harassed the elder.

     b. The elder harassed the teenager

55 college students judged on a 7-point scale how likely it was that each of the identities caused the events, as shown in (12).

(12) The teenager praised/harassed the elder.

    Did the teenager cause the event because teenagers are the kind of people that praise/harass people?

Very Likely						Very Unlikely
1	2	3	4	5	6	7

    Did the elder cause the event because elders are the kind of people that others praise/harass?

Very Likely						Very Unlikely
1	2	3	4	5	6	7

To determine whether semantic characteristics of the nouns and verbs interacted to affect causality ratings, a stepwise regression analysis was computed. First, a goodness of agent/ patient measure was constructed for each noun pair by subtracting the likelihood judgment from Experiment 1 of the patient identity having had something done to it from the likelihood of the agent identity doing something. For example, in (10a), 'praise' is a positively evaluated verb. The mean likelihood that a teen will do something good was 3.91, while the likelihood that an elder would have something good done to him/her was 5.1. The goodness of thematic role for this sentence was therefore −1.19, indicating that for this pair, an elder is a better patient than a teen is an agent. In (10b), the likelihood that an elder will do something good is 5.2, while the likelihood that a teenager will have something good done to him or her is 4.36, indicating that for this pair, the elder is a better agent than the teen is a patient.

The stepwise regression on causality difference ratings used noun evaluation and potency, verb evaluation, potency, and activity and goodness of thematic role as quantitative variables. Together they accounted for 44% of the variance. Most variance in causal ratings (25%) was accounted for by how good an agent and patient a particular noun pair was for a generic positive or negative action. An additional 16% of variance was accounted for by the relative evaluation of the agent and patient as negative or positive.

If implicit verb causality was the major determinant of causal attributions, then causality should be attributed to the subject in sentences containing action verbs, regardless of the identity of the participant. Instead, goodness of agent–patient information was the best predictor of attributions. An elder is a better agent than a teen and is also a better patient (regardless of whether s/he is praising or doing something else positive) and attributions therefore go to the elder, regardless of sentence position. Recall from experiment 1, whether an identity was a good agent or patient was related to the evaluation of the identity compared to that of the verb and to the potency of the identity ($r = .34$, $p < .05$).

In sum, though previous research had found that judges typically attribute causality to agents in sentences where there is minimal information about the event participants, attributions of causality are often made to the sentence patient when information about social identities is available. Taken together, results of the two experiments indicate that causality can be attributed **either** to the identity judged to be the better agent (relative to the patient) **or** to the identity judged to be the better patient (relative to the agent). These judgments in turn are related to the evaluation and potency of the identities.

5. Why Don't People Assume that Event Initiators are Causal Agents?

The results described in section 4.3 make it clear that affective/connotative dimensions underlying meanings of both nouns and verbs interact in accounting for causal attributions in sentences containing action verbs. Without contextual information, most action verbs elicit attributions to the sentence subject, reflecting the fact that the prototypical subject is the transmitter of force in the causal chain. However, once the identities of sentence participants are known, attributions vary depending upon their characteristics. In simple transitive English sentences such as the ones used in my experiments, why should perceivers attribute causality to the sentence object? Many theorists view responsibility, control, and volition as properties of prototypical sentence subjects. "Full affectedness appears to be the salient semantic feature for assignment as object, full control appears to be the salient semantic feature for assignment to the subject position" (Croft 1998: 88-89). Lakoff (1977) suggests that primary responsibility is most important for determining subjecthood; volition and control need not be present, but primary responsibility is always present. Dowty (1991:577) describes the properties associated with his agent proto-role as follows: "agent is volition + causation + sentience + movement or in some uses just volition + causation or just volition or causation alone." That is, even when agents do things accidentally or without awareness, they are still causal.

The data presented in this paper suggest that this is not always the case. Evidently, language users do not assume that an argument expressed as a grammatical subject must be a causal agent, as for example in (10a) where 'the elder,' who is viewed as more causal, is located in object position. As Langacker (1991:214) points out, "the objective properties of a situation do not mechanically determine the grammatical organization of a sentence or finite clause describing it." Nevertheless, it is common to profile the most prominent parts of a scene when describing it and this does not seem to be the case in (10a).

One answer may be that causality is not absolute, but is a matter of degree. Individuals may disagree as to how negative or positive a given identity is, how negative or positive a particular action is, and therefore how causal a particular participant is. The language must be constructed so that we can understand each other despite such disagreements. Furthermore, the language must allow us to describe events where identities behave in ways that contradict our expectations of how they should behave, as in (11b). Usually, the discourse surrounding a sentence does much of the work in supplying the context necessary for a listener to interpret the sentence.

A second answer may come from recent attempts to separate the notions of volition and control from that of agency. Croft (1994) argues that events can be construed in many ways and that the semantic notions of controller and affected are simply consequences of their positions within the causal chain of an event. The controller is the event participant that the speaker views as the starting point of an event and the affected is the one most concerned in the outcome, that is the endpoint of the event. (See Langacker 1991 for a similar position).

Recently, Van Valin and Wilkins (1996) argued that a new role is needed in semantic structure to explain such facts. They argue that 'agent' is a derivative notion which results from an interaction of morpho– syntactic, lexical, semantic and pragmatic factors. The more basic role deriving from verb semantics is 'effector,' roughly the dynamic participant doing something in an event. Nevertheless, speakers tend to treat effectors as agents unless there is information to the contrary (Holisky 1987).

Van Valin and Wilkins (1996) argue that agents are always composites; they are always also experiencers, effectors, themes etc. A typical agent contains a blend of entity-related and verb-related properties (very similar to the cluster of fourteen properties isolated by Lakoff (1977). VanValin and Wilkins claim that their fundamental insight is there are at least *two* competing hierarchies of properties which can be used to predict whether the referent of a particular NP is likely to be *conceived of or treated* as an agent in an action event. One dimension is essentially an animacy hierarchy. Being human implies being rational which implies that an entity is knowledgeable about the consequences of acts. Being rational implies intentionality which requires conscious acts of will and ability to plan. Being intentional implies being volitional, which is a property of entities which manifest nonconscious basic acts of will (such as a baby crying for milk). Consider sentences (13a) and (14a) from my experiment.

(13)   a.   The recluse hit the intruder.

       b.   The recluse accidentally hit the intruder.

(14)   a.   The intruder hit the recluse.

       b.   The intruder accidentally hit the recluse.

Both (13a) and (14a) can be modified by *accidentally* as indicated in (13b) and (14b), showing that there is no requirement that the act was intentional; this means that both subjects are effectors but neither are technically agents. However, given the tendency to treat effectors as agents, without additional context, (13b) is more reasonable than (14b). The semantics of 'intruder' is such that it suggests an identity who willfully, intentionally, and rationally does negative things such as hitting people. Agency is strongly implicated by the co-occurrence of this noun and the verb 'hit.' In my experiments, this is partly captured by the potency of the intruder and partly by the matching negative evaluation of the verb and the noun.

'Recluse' by contrast refers to an identity that is also considered to be negative, (less so than an 'intruder'), but who is low in potency, so may be considered less rational and less intentional. Why would a low potency individual purposefully hit a high potency individual? The default prediction is that someone else caused the act, i.e., that the recluse is non–agentive. In my data, the anomaly is captured partly by the lack of potency of the recluse and by the mismatch between a recluse and a negative physical act.

A second dimension suggested by Van Valin and Wilkins (1996) to be relevant to agency is an empathy/topicality hierarchy. The higher in the hierarchy, the more empathy an individual evokes. For example, an individual referred to in first person is not more animate than the person referred to in second person, but because one can be more sure of one's own volition, intent and rationality than another person's, we empathize with the individual referred to in the first person. One category in the Van Valin and Wilkins' hierarchy is 'referents of NPs referring to social/occupational status of adults.' Insights from Affect Control Theory presented in the current paper regarding evaluation and potency can give us information to further differentiate the social role category. For example, we presumably empathize more with positive, potent individuals than we do with negative, impotent ones.

6. Conclusions

Data from research on implicit verb causality suggest that that when nothing is known about the participants in simple, transitive events, lay judges assume that sentence subjects cause of the events. However, in more common circumstances, where social identities of event participants are known, their characteristics interact with those of the verb to produce attributions. Causality is generally attributed to whichever participant matches the evaluation of the verb and to the participant judged to be either the better agent or the better patient, based partially on the potency of the participants. Contrary to some traditional linguistic wisdom, this means that even in simple SVO sentences describing transitive events, such as 'X hits Y,' people do not always view the sentence subject as responsible for the action. This means that there are systematic semantic features of lexical items, independent of grammatical or thematic role, that language comprehenders use in assigning causality. If we are to take seriously the cognitive linguistics claim that the meaning of sentences depends upon our categorization and perception of the real world, then this necessitates an elaboration of the notion of causality in some grammars. I suggest that the empirical data presented in this paper support Van Valin's notions of a combined animacy and empathy hierarchy and Croft's notion of the controller as the starting point of an event. The first participant in an action event initiates the event, but does not necessarily cause it.

References

Au, Terry. 1986. A Verb is Worth a Thousand Words: The Causes and Consequences of Interpersonal Events Implied in Language. *Journal of Memory and Language* 25:104–122.

Brown, Roger and Deborah Fish. 1983. The Psychological Causality Implicit in Language. *Cognition* 14:237–273.

Corrigan, Roberta. 1988. Who Dun It? The Influence of Actor-Patient Animacy and Type of Verb in the Making of Causal Attributions. *Journal of Memory and Language* 27:447–465.

Corrigan, Roberta. 1992. The Relationship Between Causal Attributions and Judgments of the Typicality of Events Described by Sentences. *British Journal of Social Psychology* 31:351–368.

Corrigan, Roberta. 1993. Causal Attributions to States and Events Described by Different Classes of Verbs. *British Journal of Social Psychology* 32:335–348.

Corrigan, Roberta. 1998. Implicit Causality Is Not Solely in the Verb. Poster Presented at the American Psychological Society, Washington, D.C.

Croft, William. 1991. *Syntactic Categories and Grammatical Relations. The Cognitive Organization of Information*. Chicago: U. of Chicago Press.

Croft, William. 1993. Case Marking and the Semantics of Mental Verbs, in James Pustejovsky, ed. *Semantics and the Lexicon*. The Netherlands: Kluwer.

Croft, William, 1994. Voice: Beyond Control and Affectedness, in Barbara Fox and Paul Hopper, eds. *Voice. Form and Function*. Philadelphia: Benjamins.

Croft, William, 1998. The Structure of Events and the Structure of Language, in Michael Tomasello, ed., *The New Psychology of Language. Cognitive and Functional Approaches to Language Structure*. NJ: Erlbaum.

DeLancey, Scott, 1984. Notes on Agentivity and Causation. *Studies in Language* 8:181–213.

Dowty, David. 1991. Thematic Proto-Roles and Argument Selection. *Language* 67:3.547–619.

Fiedler, Klaus and Gun Semin. 1988. On the Causal Information Conveyed by Different Interpersonal Verbs: The Role of Implicit Sentence Context. *Social Cognition* 6:1.21–39.

Fillmore, Charles. 1977. The Case for Case Reopened, in Peter Cole and Jerrold Sadock, eds., *Syntax and Semantics, 8, Grammatical Relations*. New York: Academic Press.

Garvey, Katherine and Alfonso Caramazza. 1974. Implicit Causality in Verbs. *Linguistic Inquiry* 5:459–464.

Garvey, Katherine, Alfonso Caramazza, and Jack Yates. 1976. Factors Influencing Assignments of Pronoun Antecedents. *Cognition* 3:227–243.

Heise, David. 1992. Affect Control Theory and Impression Formation, in Elam Borgatta and Marie Borgatta, eds., *Encyclopedia of Sociology, Vol. 1*:12–17. New York: Macmillan.

Holisky, Dee Ann. 1987. The Case of the Intransitive Subject in Tsova-Tush (Batsbi). *Lingua* 71:103–132.

LaFrance, Marianne, Hiram Brownell, and Eugene Hahn. 1997. Interpersonal Verbs, Gender, and Implicit Causality. *Social Psychology Quarterly* 60:138–152.

Lakoff, George. 1977. Linguistic Gestalts. *Papers from the 13th Regional Meeting Chicago Linguistic Society*, 236–287.

Lakoff, George. 1987. *Women, Fire, and Dangerous Things. What Categories Reveal about the Mind.* Chicago: U. of Chicago Press.

Langacker, Ronald. 1991. *Concept, Image, and Symbol. The Cognitive Basis of Grammar.* Berlin: Mouton De Gruyter.

Lee, Ju Young and Joseph Kasof. 1993. Interpersonal Verbs and Interpersonal Experiences. *Journal of Social Psychology* 132:731–740.

Levin, B. 1993. *English Verb Classes and Alternations. A Preliminary Investigation.* Chicago: U. of Chicago Press.

Mackinnon, Neil. 1994. *Symbolic Interactionism as Affect Control.* Albany: SUNY Press.

McRae, Ken, Todd Ferretti, and Liane Amyote. 1997. Thematic Roles as Verb-Specific Concepts. *Language and Cognitive Processes* 12:2/3.137–176.

McKoon, Gail, Steven Greene, and Roger Ratcliffe. 1993. Discourse Models, Pronoun Resolution, and the Implicit Causality of Verbs. *Journal of Experimental Psychology* 19:5.1040–1052.

Osgood, Charles, William May, and Murray Miron. 1975. *Crosscultural Universals of Affective Meaning.* Urbana, Illinois: U. of Illinois Press.

Van Valin, Robert and Randy LaPolla.1997. *Syntax. Structure, Meaning and Function.* New York: Cambridge U. Press.

Van Valin, Robert and David Wilkins. 1996. The Case For 'Effector': Case Roles, Agents, and Agency Revisited, in Sandra Thompson and Masayoshi Shibatani, eds., *Grammatical Constructions: Their Form and Meaning.*

Vendler, Zeno. 1957[1967]. *Linguistics in Philosophy.* Ithaca: Cornell U. Press.

Vonk, Roos. 1995. Effects of Inconsistent Behaviors on Person Impressions: A Multidimensional Study. *Personality and Social Psychology Bulletin* 21:674–685.

The Cognitive Basis of Visual Evidentials

FERDINAND DE HAAN

University of New Mexico

1. Introduction[1]

Vision plays an important role, both in language and in the external world. Almost everything in our lives is vision-oriented and this in turn has led to the spread of vision-oriented words into other cognitive realms. For instance, the English verb *see* is used in such tags as *I see*, to denote that understanding has taken place (this understanding may or may not be based on visual evidence), and a saying like *seeing is believing* which underlines the importance of vision for absolute proof (see Matlock 1989 for a discussion of this metaphor).

In certain languages, vision forms a part of the evidential system. In these languages, it has been found desirable to have grammatical morphemes that denote that the action described in the sentence has been obtained visually. Surprisingly enough, it turns out that visual evidentials typically do not derive from vision words, such as the verb 'to see'. Rather, they tend to develop from demonstratives or tense/aspect markers. This paper gives a cognitive account for the deictic origin of visual evidentials. Some 160 languages in North and South America have been investigated for this study, as

[1] This paper developed from presentations given at the First Workshop on American Indian Languages, Santa Barbara, 1998, and at CSDL 4, Atlanta, 1998. I am grateful for the participants at the conference for helpful comments as well as Victor Golla for data and two anonymous referees for very helpful comments.

Conceptual and Discourse Factors in Linguistic Structure.
Alan Cienki, Barbara J. Luka and Michael B. Smith (eds.).
Copyright © 2001, CSLI Publications.

well as several languages from other parts of the world. The data of languages from North and South America are data from a project which aims to map the spread of evidentiality in the Americas, while the data of languages from other parts of the world come from the evidential literature.

This paper is built up as follows: in section 2 the possible definitions of visual evidentiality are discussed. Section 3 discusses those languages in which visual evidentials have a temporal deictic origin while section 4 examines those with spatial deictic origins. Section 5 looks at two minor grammaticalization processes, and section 6 gives a cognitive account for the grammaticalization processes.

2. Definitions

Before moving on to a discussion of the areas where visual evidentials occur, we need to define the precise focus of investigation. This study deals with those morphemes that show that the information contained in the speaker's utterance has been witnessed personally by the speaker; the speaker has *seen* the action described in the sentence.

Visual evidence is a form of *direct* evidence. Other direct evidentials include *auditory* evidentials which denote that the information was perceived by hearing the action involved, and *nonvisual* sensory evidence which denotes that the action was perceived by any of the senses except sight. Other languages do not make any sensory distinctions at all, and have one *sensory* evidential to denote all types of direct evidence.

In contrast, *indirect* evidence refers to information about actions or events which the speaker did not witness personally. Indirect evidence has two subtypes. The first consists of information which comes to the speaker from another source; it is generally called the *quotative, reportative,* or *hearsay* evidential. The other type of indirect evidence is *inference*. The speaker draws the conclusion that a certain action has occurred based on evidence available to him/her.

An example of a Visual[2] evidential is shown in sentence (1), from Maricopa (Yuman). By using the morpheme *-ʔyuu,* the speaker asserts that the fact that the subjects didn't win is known to him/her because he/she saw the action.

(1)   Waly-marsh-ma-*ʔyuu.*

        NEG-win.DU-NEG-VIS[3]

        '(I saw) They didn't win.'   (Gordon 1986:85)

---

[2] I will use the accepted convention that language-specific categories are written with a capital letter, and general categories are written entirely in small letters.

[3] The following abbreviations are used in this paper: ASP-aspectual marker; DET-determiner; DS-different subject; DU-dual; DUR-durative aspect; INF-inferential evidential; IPF-imperfective aspect; NEG-negation; NONVIS-nonvisual sensory evidential; OBJ-object case; PL-plural; PRES-present tense; PRF-perfective aspect; SG-singular; VIS-visual evidential; WIT-witnessed evidential.

This paper is limited to those evidentials that only denote visual evidence as opposed to other direct evidentials. Maricopa has another direct evidential, the Nonvisual Sensory evidential morpheme -ʔa, shown in (2). This evidential normally refers to auditory information but can refer to other sensory information, such as smell and taste, as well.

(2) ashvar-ʔa

    sing-NONVIS

    'He sang (I heard)'   (Gordon 1986:77)

Also excluded from the present discussion will be *general sensory* evidentials. These evidentials are fairly common among the world's languages. Unlike pure visual evidentials, this type can be found in many parts of the world. For instance, Southeastern Tepehuan (Totonacan, Willett 1991:162) has a particle *dyo* which can refer to all types of sensory information: visual, auditory, and other sensory evidence. Hixkaryana, a Southern Carib language (Derbyshire 1979:143), has grammaticalized the absence of an overt evidential as the marker for direct sensory evidence. In other words, zero is the marker for direct evidence in Hixkaryana. Such evidentials are disregarded for two reasons: first, these evidentials do not solely denote visual evidentiality and as such fall outside the scope of this paper; second, the exact status of such direct evidentials is still uncertain. In Hixkaryana, direct evidentiality has been grammaticalized by the absence of indirect evidentials, but this type of evidential marking has only been reported in a handful of languages. Many languages have overt morphemes for indirect evidentiality, but given the fact that detailed semantic information of evidential morphemes is on the whole absent in most grammatical descriptions, we cannot be sure whether direct evidentiality exist as a grammatical category if only indirect evidentials are mentioned in grammatical descriptions. Sometimes there is no grammaticalized direct evidential. For instance, Dutch uses the verb *moeten* 'must' for indirect evidentiality, but if the speaker chooses not to use this evidential, there is no entailment that the information has been obtained directly. For these reasons, direct evidentials have been disregarded in this study, unless, of course, they are purely visual evidentials. It must be mentioned, though, that the grammaticalization path of such evidentials may be similar to the paths described here, given that general direct evidentials have visual evidentiality as part of their meaning.

Finally, only *grammaticalized* visual evidentials will be considered here. Given that we are interested in the grammaticalization paths of visual evidentials, we need to exclude such constructions as 'I see that ...' which show no grammaticalization whatsoever and cannot tell us anything about visual evidentiality as a grammaticalized category. Criteria for grammaticalized evidentials can be found in De Haan 1997.[4]

Of the about 160 languages of North and South America, only some 10% have visual evidentials as defined in this section. Furthermore, most of these languages are confined to two geographical areas, California and the Vaupés River Region of the border area of Brazil and Colombia. In many ways, these areas are *Sprachbund* areas and visual evidentials are one feature of this Sprachbund (see De Haan 1999 for a fuller account of visual evidentiality as an areal feature).

3. Visual Evidentials from Tense and Aspect Markers

Tense and aspect markers are one of the major sources for visual evidentials. Among the languages of North and South America, they can be found in both areas where visual evidentiality is an areal feature. In this paper I will discuss three cases: the Pomo family, Wintu, and Tuyuca.

3.1 The Pomo Family

The Pomo family consists of a number of mutually unintelligible languages spoken in Northern California. The reflexes of the Proto-Pomo (PP) morpheme *-ya* are used in the modern languages as visual evidentials. This morpheme *-ya* is analyzed as a visual evidential in PP, according to Oswalt (1976:25). In addition, the PP morpheme *-a*, analyzed by Oswalt as the Factual or Indicative and used for general truths and actions in progress, is also used for visual evidence.

Oswalt's analysis is probably accurate, given the use of these PP reflexes as visual evidentials in many of the modern languages, but I believe that these morphemes originally denoted an aspectual opposition (perfective vs. imperfective), from which the notion of visual evidence developed. This reasoning is based on the fact that the two PP morphemes are in complementary distribution, based on Oswalt's description. PP *-a* is used for typical imperfective actions and events (general truths and actions in progress), while PP *-ya* is used for completed actions. This points to an original aspectual opposition of the two morphemes, which is lost in the modern languages. Also note that Oswalt 1976 does not reconstruct any tense or aspect morphemes, with the exception of the Future.

In most languages, only a reflex of PP *-ya* survived. This is the case, for instance, in Northern Pomo, where the reflex of PP *-ya* is *-ye*, and *-y* after a vowel. An example is:

(3)   kawi-nam mena-y

        child-DET cry-VIS

        'The child cried.'   (Caisse 1980:39)

---

[4] One of the criteria is that grammaticalized evidentials cannot be in the scope of a negation. See (12) and (13) below for the evidence from Maricopa.

As Caisse mentions, in certain cases -*ye* may be used without the implication that the speaker actually saw the action. In that case -*ye* is translated simply as a Past tense. The examples of Past tense -*ye* in Caisse 1980 are consistent with a Perfective aspect analysis of PP *-*ya*. In fact, in O'Connor 1992, the suffix -*ye* is consistently referred to as "perfective/past tense" although she called it a Visual evidential in an earlier work (O'Connor 1980).

The same situation holds in most of the other Pomoan languages, although it may not always be recognized as such. For instance, in Eastern Pomo (McLendon 1975), the morpheme -*ya* is glossed as the marker for the Indicative mode. The examples given in McLendon 1975 are more consistent with the hypothesis that -*ya* is a Visual evidential than a morpheme denoting Indicative mood.[5] Many examples in the grammar that seem, out of context, to be indicative in nature are used without -*ya*.

Kashaya Pomo possesses two Visual evidentials, -*wa* (from PP *-*a*) and -*ya*, used when the witnessed events are Imperfective and Perfective, respectively.

(4)   a.   qowaq-wa

            pack-VIS.IPF

            '(I just saw) He was packing.'

      b.   qowaq-ya

            pack-VIS.PRF

            '(I just saw) He packed.'   (Oswalt 1986:36)

On the basis of the data in (3) and (4), as well as similar data in other languages, the development of visual evidentiality in Pomo must have been the following: the PP aspectual morphemes *-*a* and *-*ya* acquired the interpretation that the action was witnessed visually. This interpretation took over completely in some languages, like Eastern Pomo (and this is why only one morpheme of the two PP morphemes survived), and in Kashaya the original aspectual meaning has been retained, hence the two visual evidentials. If the PP morphemes *-*a* and *-*ya* started out as visual evidentials, it would be hard to explain why there were two visual evidentials to begin with, and why they later acquired aspectual meanings.

Since the contention of this paper is that visual evidentials commonly derive from deictic morphemes (both temporal and spatial), it is necessary to relate aspect (not considered to be deictic in nature) to deixis. While aspect is not a deictic category, tense is and I believe that the reason why aspect morphemes develop into evidential morphemes is that there are no pure tense morphemes in those languages. In Pomo, tense and aspect are not distinguished (see the remarks on Northern Pomo above and the fact that there are no separate tense morphemes reconstructed for Proto Pomo) and in such

---

[5] I am grateful to Marianne Mithun (p.c.) for this observation.

cases, aspectual morphemes by virtue of their temporal component, can develop into visual evidentials.

3.2 Wintu -*bEy*

Wintu is a Penutian language spoken slightly to the north of the Pomoan area. In his 1984 grammar, Harvey Pitkin lists no less than three visual evidentials. They are shown in (5) below, as well as the lexical sources from which they derive. It turns out that these three morphemes relate to three different grammaticalization processes.

(5)   *Visual evidentials in Wintu (Pitkin 1984:146-8)*

    -*bEy*   'imperfective auxiliary verb'[6]

    -*ʔel*   'demonstrative copula'

    -*da*   '1st person, selfness'

This section deals with the morpheme -*bEy*, the others will be discussed in subsequent sections.

According to Pitkin, the morpheme -*bEy* (which becomes -*bi*(:) as surface form) derives from a lexical verb with the meaning 'to be in a lying position'. This verb is still in existence in the language (see (6a) below), and in this capacity it can take aspectual and evidential morphemes (as in (6b), where -*da* is the evidential morpheme). This morpheme is also used as Imperfective aspectual marker, as in (6a). In addition, it is used as a Visual evidential, which can be seen in (6c) below. However, (6c) also has a Progressive, Imperfective interpretation, showing that the aspectual interpretation is more basic. The Imperfective morpheme -*bi* in (6a) does not appear to have a Visual evidential interpretation, given the presence of the Inferential evidential morpheme -*re*.

(6)   a.   biya-bi-re:

        lie-IPF-INF[7]

        'I guess they are lying.'

    b.   ba: ʔi-bi:-da

        eat   be-IPF-1SG

        'I am eating.'   (Pitkin 1984:182)

    c.   kupa-be:

        chop.wood-VIS

        '(I see/have seen) he is chopping wood.'   (Pitkin 1984:183)

---

[6] The symbol /E/ is an underlying phoneme (Pitkin 1984:43-4).

[7] In all Wintu examples, the glosses are mine.

The development of -*bEy* in Wintu then appears to have been similar to the development of -*ya* in Pomo: from aspectual marker (in this case an Imperfective marker) to Visual evidential. As is the case with Pomo, Wintu has no separate tense morphemes, only aspectual morphemes, so that the development of an aspect morpheme to a visual evidential is not surprising.

3.3 Eastern Tucanoan: Tuyuca

The Eastern Tucanoan languages, spoken in the Vaupés River Region in the border area of Brazil and Colombia, are well-known for a proliferation of evidential morphemes. These languages have not only morphemes for Visual, Nonvisual, Inferential and Quotative evidentiality, but these morphemes also differ according to tense, person and gender. The best-described evidential system of Eastern Tucanoan languages is that of Tuyuca (Barnes 1984). The Visual evidential morphemes of Tuyuca are shown in (7) below, from Barnes (1984:258):

(7)   *The visual evidential paradigm in Tuyuca*

	past	present
3 sg. masc.	-*wi*	-*i*
3 sg. fem.	-*wo*	-*yo*
3 pl.	-*wa*	-*ya*
3 sg. inan., 1/2	-*wi*	-*a*

Unlike evidentials in many (if not most) other languages, evidentials in Tuyuca are obligatory. A speaker of Tuyuca must decide the appropriate level of evidence for every utterance. Given that evidential morphemes in Tuyuca also denote tense and person/gender (not commonly found outside the Tucanoan family), the origin of these morphemes must be an inflectional category, tense. Comparative evidence suggests that this hypothesis is true. Related Tucanoan languages are described as having tense morphemes. For instance, the Tuyuca Visual Past morphemes are cognate with the Remote Past morphemes in Tucano (West 1980) and the Regular Past in Carapana (Metzger 1981). Tuyuca has no nonevidential present or past tenses. It does have a nonevidential future tense, showing that original tense morphemes acquired evidential interpretations.

The Visual evidential in Tuyuca is also used for situations in which visual evidence does not play a role. These are 'timeless' events, such as 'two plus two equals four' (Barnes 1984:259). In most languages, sentences like these would be used without evidentials because the question of personally witnessing or not does not come up. But given that in Tuyuca evidentiality is obligatory, the Visual evidential is considered to be the most appropriate. This points to the conclusion that at some point in the history of Tuyuca, the visual evidential interpretation took over an original present tense (unmarked for evidence) and as a consequence of this development, some situations arose where the use of the Visual evidential is not really appropriate, but can be explained if we take the history of the Visual into account.

4. Visual Evidentials from Spatial Deictics

Given that temporal deictic morphemes are a common source for visual evidentials, it should come as no surprise that markers of spatial deixis, such as demonstratives and event locators, are also very common sources for visual evidentials. In this section I will discuss the cases of Wintu, Hupa, and Sanuma.

4.1 Wintu -ʔel

Besides a visual evidential derived from a temporal deictic source (see section 3.2 above), Wintu also possesses a Visual evidential derived from a spatial deictic source. The morpheme -ʔel (which has allomorphs -ʔele: and -ile:) derives from a dependent copula. It can never be the main verb of the sentence but is always dependent on the preceding verb. An example is shown in (8) below (-ile is an allomorph of -ʔel):

(8)   bo:s-ile

        sit-VIS

        '(I saw) them sitting there.'   (Pitkin 1984:176)

Pitkin (1984:175) proposes that the source of -ʔel is the (proximal) demonstrative root -ʔE and a derivational suffix -l and gives as paraphrase: 'See here, it is visibly true and actual.'

Pitkin argues that the difference in usage between -bEy and -ʔel is one that marks actions versus states (1984:148). When actions are observed visually, -bEy must be used, and -ʔel is used when states are seen. This is probably not a very rigorous division. Among the examples Pitkin gives of verbs that are used with -ʔel are such verbs as "go (south)" and "kill (a rattlesnake)" which are hardly verbs that denote states (1984:176).

No matter what the precise difference in usage between the visual evidentials in Wintu is, the Visual -ʔel is spatial in origin, since it places the speaker as witness close to the action described.

4.2 Pacific Coast Athabaskan: Hupa and Kato

The Pacific Coast Athabaskan languages Hupa and Kato are spoken in California in an area adjacent to Wintu. They differ from the other Athabaskan languages in that they have developed a full evidential system, including a visual evidential.

Both Hupa and Kato have a Visual evidential which Goddard (1911, 1912) transcribes as -e, but according to Victor Golla (p.c.) the Hupa morpheme at least is more accurately transcribed as -ye:y. An example of visual -e is shown in (9a), from Goddard (1911:124).

The origin of -*ye:y* is a deictic marker, and it is still used as such in Hupa and other Athabaskan languages. The deictic meaning can still be seen in sentences like those shown in (9b) and (c), due to Victor Golla (p.c.).

(9) a. *mowint'anne* 'he stuck to it (he saw)'

     b. *xahsya:-yey* 'it [sun, moon] rose right there'

     c. *xahsyay* 'it rose, came up'

This case is similar to the Wintu one: the speaker is in the same sphere as the action described and hence the development from a demonstrative to a visual evidential is not unexpected.

4.3 Sanuma

Sanuma is a Yanomami language spoken in Northwestern Brazil and Venezuela (Borgman 1990). Just as in the Eastern Tucanoan languages (section 3.3) evidentiality in Sanuma can be expressed as a portmanteau morpheme with tense, but from the study it appears that evidentiality is not an obligatory category in Sanuma, unlike in Tuyuca.

There are several visual evidentials in the language, depending on the tense of the statement, but all of them begin with the morpheme *ku*- or one of its allomorphs. In the Present tense, the location of the action must be included with *ku*-, which gives rise to such evidentials as *kule* 'near speaker', *kupoli* 'up above', and *kimakili* 'going away from speaker downriver' (see Borgman 1990:166-7 for a complete listing). An example is (10), from Borgman (1990:167):

(10) ala   a   lo-a   ku-poli

      macaw   3SG   perch-DUR   PRES.WIT-up.above

      'A macaw is perching up there.'

Although it is not discussed by Borgman, the most likely lexical source of *ku*- appears to be the verb *ku*- 'to be'. If this is correct, then the analysis of present tense visual evidence runs along the lines of "event A is happening and it is at location X", where location X is any point in three-dimensional space observable by the speaker. This analysis is especially attractive because the Visual evidential construction in Sanuma is then exactly parallel with the Wintu Visual morpheme -*ʔel* (section 4.1): both derive from the verb 'to be' plus a spatial deictic morpheme.

5. Other Sources for Visual Evidentials

In the previous sections the temporal and spatial deictic bases for visual evidentiality were discussed. These are not the only sources, however. In this section two other, apparently less common, sources are discussed, a first person singular morpheme, and morphemes deriving from the perception verb 'to see'.

5.1 First Person Singular Morpheme

A visual evidential deriving from the first person singular morpheme is found in (again) Wintu and Akha, a Lolo-Burmese language spoken in Southeastern Asia.

In Wintu, the suffix -*da* serves to indicate what is "... absolutely and reliably known to be true." (Pitkin 1984:137), see (6b) above for an example. The suffix -*da* serves to distinguish "self from non-self." (1984:136). This suffix is still used with a first person meaning as well, and as such it can combine with other evidential morphemes to denote first person, or "self-ness." Therefore, in Wintu the Visual evidential -*da* can only be used if the speaker is also the subject, i.e., if the speaker is a participant (and thus present) in the action.

This is not the case in Akha (Thurgood 1986). In Akha, the morpheme -*ŋa* serves as visual evidential but it is not restricted to first persons, as can be seen in the following example (1986:214):

(11) nɔ-màq   ajq-áŋ   dì-ŋá.

you-PL   he-OBJ   beat-VIS

'You (pl.) are beating him (I see it).'

The Visual evidential suffix -*ŋa* is identical with the Proto-Tibeto-Burman first singular pronoun *ŋa*. Thurgood (1986:217) gives two possibilities for the development from a first singular pronoun to an evidential suffix: either it is a reanalysis of an agreement marker or the Visual evidential originated from a separate clause consisting of -*ŋa* 'I' and a perception verb such as 'to see', from which the perception verb was lost.

Although Thurgood does not give evidence for either analysis (there presumably is no internal evidence to favor one analysis over the other), typological evidence suggests that the first one, reanalysis of an agreement marker, might be the correct one. Firstly, this development is similar to the Wintu case discussed above, and secondly, the clause reduction analysis is implausible: in a clause with a perception verb and a pronoun the salient part is obviously the perception verb and it would be implausible for this verb to disappear while maintaining the perception interpretation. Witness the very common development of quotatives from 'say'-verbs, in which the 'say'-verb is reanalyzed as quotative marker, and not the pronoun (see Harris and Campbell 1995).[8] Obviously the salient part in the quotative is the verb of saying, and this will not disappear. It would be the same with the development of the Visual evidential -*ŋa*: a perception verb would not easily dis-

---

[8] This development has taken place in many parts of the world. It has been attested in the Caucasian languages and certain Mixtecan languages, among others.

appear, while retaining the perception interpretation.[9] Given that visual evidentials do not appear to develop from perception verbs in most cases (see section 5.2 below), we can assume that there was no verb 'to see' to begin with.

For these reasons, it is assumed here that the Visual evidential -ŋa in Akha developed out of an old agreement marker and that this reanalysis is motivated by a desire to include the speaker in the sphere of action. The Akha case is similar to Wintu, but Akha has gone further to include those actions in which the speaker is not necessarily an active participant in the action.

5.2 The Verb 'to see'

The final source for visual evidentials is the perception verb 'to see.' Even though the verb 'to see' appears prima facie to be a good candidate for grammaticalization into a visual evidential, this is actually very uncommon. In my database there is only one clear example of a language which has taken this path, namely Maricopa, a Yuman language spoken in Arizona (Gordon 1986). The development of a visual evidential among the Yuman languages is unique to Maricopa; its closest relatives do not have a grammaticalized visual evidential. An example was shown in (1), repeated here as (12):

(12)   Waly-marsh-ma-ʔyuu.

      NEG-win.DU-NEG-VIS

      '(I saw) They didn't win.'   (Gordon 1986:85)

The Visual evidential morpheme -ʔyuu developed from the combination of two morphemes: -ʔ 'I' and -yuu 'see.' Although a first person morpheme is still present, it carries no syntactic weight: the first person is not the subject of (12). Another reason why we are dealing with a grammaticalized Visual evidential is that in (12) -ʔyuu is used without the obligatory aspectual morphemes. Witness (13), where the perception is negated instead of the act of winning. In this case, -yuu is a full verb and must take aspectual morphemes. Also, -ʔ 'I' is a separate morpheme in example (13).

(13)   Marsh-m   waly-ʔ-yuu-ma-k.

      win.DU-DS   NEG-1SG-see-NEG-ASP

      'I did not see them win.'   (Gordon 1986:85)

---

[9] The reanalysis of a perception verb into a visual evidential is precisely the analysis proposed for Maricopa, see 5.2 below.

6. The Cognitive Basis

In the previous sections a number of grammaticalization processes were discussed. For ease of reference, they are summarized in (14):

(14) a. Temporal deixis: tense/aspect markers

       b. Spatial deixis: demonstratives

       c. First person marker

       d. The verb 'to see.'

The first two processes, spatial and temporal deixis are obviously related. In both cases the deictic sphere is divided into two parts: witnessed by the speaker and unwitnessed by the speaker.

In the case of temporal deixis, the tenses that are available to form visual evidentials include the present and the recent past, and it will depend on the individual language exactly how the past tenses are divided. The Visual past evidentials of Tuyuca, for instance, are cognate with the Remote past morphemes of Tucano (see section 3.3), but this Remote past refers to those events that occurred more than three days before the moment of speech, so it includes events in time periods which the speaker may have witnessed. The cognate morphemes in Carapana are called the Regular past, which occupies a slot between the Immediate past and the Historic past, and it overlaps with the Tucano time period for the same morphemes.

The reason why aspectual morphemes can turn into visual evidentials is a lack of tense morphemes in the respective languages. From the grammatical descriptions of the Pomoan languages as well as Wintu it would appear that these languages lack pure tense morphemes. Then the aspectual morphemes can develop into visual evidentials because they show a time frame for the actions, which overlaps with the speaker's witness frame.

Spatial deixis in this case divides the world into visible and invisible events. In many languages, such a distinction exists in the demonstrative system or even in the personal pronoun system (see Anderson and Keenan 1985). When the action takes place in full view of the speaker, the demonstrative deixis markers that reflect the position of the speaker with respect to the action can then quite naturally develop into markers of visual evidence.

Visual evidentials are deictic extensions of the spatial and temporal morphemes discussed in sections 3 and 4. One of the functions of evidentiality in general is to mark the relation of the speaker with respect to the action he/she is describing (see e.g., the description of Wanka Quechua in Floyd 1997). In other words, evidentiality has a deictic component. The function of visual evidentiality is to place the speaker in the same deictic sphere as the action. Because this component overlaps with the function of spatial and temporal deictic morphemes, it is no wonder that visual evidentials develop from deictic morphemes. The visual evidential meaning is added to the other deictic meanings of the morpheme. Quite often the original meanings are retained. The evidential morphemes in Tuyuca, for instance, still have temporal deixis as part of their meaning and spatial deixis is still part of the meaning of Sanuma visual evidentials.

The development of first person morphemes into visual evidentials must also be seen as a type of deixis, in this case person deixis. This type of visual evidential is rarer than the first two types, but is attested in different parts of the world. The first person is obviously used to reflect the presence of the speaker, and the function of this path is then similar to the deictic paths discussed above: to place the speaker in the same sphere as the action.

In the case of the development of a first person evidential into a visual evidential the speaker presence is given directly by using the first person morpheme. Note that this morpheme does not necessarily carry any syntactic load when it is a visual evidential: example (11) from Akha shows that the change from agreement marker to evidential is complete; the first person is not a syntactic participant in the action described. In the other deictic processes speaker presence is inferentially given by describing a deictic space with both the action described and the speaker.

The final source for visual evidentials, the verb 'to see', is usually considered to be the prototypical source for a visual evidential (see Anderson 1986 and Matlock 1989 for such opinions). It appears to be quite natural so its relative rarity must be explained. After all, other evidential categories, such as quotatives, develop from corresponding verbs, like the verb 'to say' (see Harris and Campbell 1995 for this type of evidential). It is quite likely that verbs of seeing develop into other types of cognitive processes. Witness English *I see*, meaning *I understand*.

The difference between (14a)-(c) on the one hand, and (14d) on the other is one of *speaker participation*. In the first three cases the speaker is portrayed as being part of the action: he/she is placed in the same sphere (temporal or spatial) as the action. In the case of a 'see'-derivation, the speaker is portrayed as being an observer. Given that the act of seeing is not restricted, either physically or linguistically, to the speaker, a mere perception verb is not specific enough. The verb 'to see' will only develop into a visual evidential if the act of seeing is done by the speaker. So, the most relevant aspect of a visual evidential is the presence of the speaker and this fact is most often encoded in visual evidentials. Note that in the Maricopa case, the speaker is still present in the background: the visual evidential *-ʔyuu* is composed of the verb *-yuu* 'to see' and the first person morpheme *-ʔ* 'I'. Just as in the Akha case, the first person morpheme does not fulfill any syntactic role in the sentence.

References

Anderson, Lloyd B. 1986. Evidentials, Paths of Change, and Mental Maps: Typologically Regular Asymmetries, in Chafe and Nichols, eds., 273–312.

Anderson, Stephen R. and Edward L. Keenan. 1985. Deixis, in Timothy Shopen, ed., *Language Typology and Syntactic Description, Vol. III: Grammatical Categories and the Lexicon*. Cambridge: Cambridge University Press.

Barnes, Janet. 1984. Evidentials in the Tuyuca Verb. *International Journal of American Linguistics* 50:255–71.

Borgman, Donald M. 1990. Sanuma, in Derbyshire and Pullum, eds., 15–248.

Caisse, Michelle. 1980. Northern Pomo Verbal Suffixes, in Redden, ed., 39–47.

Chafe, Wallace and Johanna Nichols, eds. 1986. *Evidentiality: the Linguistic Coding of Epistemology*. Norwood, NJ: Ablex.

De Haan, Ferdinand 1997. *The Interaction of Modality and Negation: a Typological Study*. New York: Garland.

De Haan, Ferdinand. 1999. Visual Evidentiality and its Origins. Unpublished ms.

Derbyshire, Desmond C. 1979. *Hixkaryana*. Lingua Descriptive Studies, Amsterdam: North Holland Publishing Company.

Derbyshire, Desmond C., and Geoffrey K. Pullum, eds. 1990. *Handbook of Amazonian Languages, Volume 2*. Berlin: Mouton de Gruyter.

Floyd, Rick. 1997. *La estructura categorial de los evidenciales en el Quechua Wanka*. Lima, Peru: Instituto Lingüístico de Verano.

Goddard, Pliny E. 1911. Athapascan (Hupa). In Franz Boas, ed., *Handbook of American Indian Languages, Volume I*. Washington: GPO.

Goddard, Pliny E. 1912. *Elements of the Kato Language*. University of California Publications in American Archaeology and Ethnology 11.

Gordon, Lynn. 1986. The Development of Evidentials in Maricopa, in Chafe and Nichols, 75–88.

Harris, Alice, and Lyle Campbell. 1995. *Historical Syntax in Cross-linguistic Perspective*. Cambridge: Cambridge University Press.

Matlock, Teenie. 1989. Metaphor and the Grammaticalization of Evidentials. *BLS* 15:215–25.

McLendon, Sally. 1975. *A Grammar of Eastern Pomo*. Berkeley: University of California Press.

Metzger, Ronald G. 1981. *Gramatica Popular del Carapana*. Bogotá: Instituto Lingüístico de Verano.

O'Connor, Mary Catherine. 1980. Some Uses of Case-Markings in Northern Pomo. In Redden, ed., 48–58.

O'Connor, Mary Catherine. 1992. *Topics in Northern Pomo Grammar*. New York: Garland.

Oswalt, Robert L. 1976. Comparative Verb Morphology of Pomo, in Margaret Langdon and Shirley Silver, eds., *Hokan Studies*. The Hague: Mouton, 13–28.

Oswalt, Robert L. 1986. The Evidential System of Kashaya. In Chafe and Nichols, eds., 29–45.

Pitkin, Harvey. 1984. *Wintu Grammar*. Berkeley: University of California Press.

Redden, James E., ed., 1980. *Proceedings of the 1980 Hokan Languages Workshop*. Southern Illinois University Occasional Papers on Linguistics 9. Carbondale: SIU.

Thurgood, Graham. 1986. The Nature and Origins of the Akha Evidentials System. In Chafe and Nichols, eds., 214–222.

West, Birdie. 1980. *Gramatica Popular del Tucano*. Bogotá: Instituto Lingüístico de Verano.

Willett, Thomas L. 1988. A Cross-Linguistic Survey of the Grammaticization of Evidentiality. *Studies in Language* 12:51–97.

Willett, Thomas L. 1991. *A Reference Grammar of Southeastern Tepehuan*. Dallas: Summer Institute of Linguistics.

The Processing of Fixed Expressions During Sentence Comprehension

DIETER HILLERT AND DAVID SWINNEY[1]
University of California, San Diego

1. Fixed Expressions—Issues of Representation and Processing

Understanding language involves recognition and access to not only individual words, but also to a vast array of fixed expressions—idioms, collocations, proverbs, common quotations, names, titles, slogans, song lyrics, etc. The purpose of the present paper is to examine the question of how fixed expressions—particularly those with non-literal interpretations—are understood during on-line sentence comprehension. The work we present examines cases of both truly fixed expressions and those which are deemed somewhat more malleable but still 'idiomatic', with a focus on the processing of these expressions in a language that has a highly productive (active) use of word collocation, particularly for compounds—German. We begin by outlining some general assumptions and issues underlying our work.

To begin with, there is no clear ground upon which to firmly establish definitions of what constitutes a purely 'literal' vs. 'figurative' (non-literal) expression. Such definition ultimately awaits a monolithic (universal and correct) theory of semantics/syntax. Similarly, distinguishing what are

---

[1] The authors gratefully acknowledge support from the grant NIH DC02984 to the second author for the work reported herein. Correspondence to dhillert@ucsd.edu or to dswinney@ucsd.edu.

truly fixed expressions vs. expressions with some productive features vs. expressions that are highly productive and malleable is equally problematic, and awaits a universally descriptive theory of language. However, the cases we deal with in the research presented below do not fall on the grey areas of any such descriptive generalizations—we use cases for which there will be wide agreement (backed by empirical data) as to the degree of non-literal and fixedness of interpretation, and we take such clear cases to be important end points in developing a processing theory of figurative expressions. Thus, while we acknowledge the ongoing tension between approaches that hold that 'literal' and 'metaphoric/figurative' processes are different processing *types* vs. simply different endpoints on a single *continuum* of processing, (see, e.g., Clark 1978; Gibbs 1984; Lehrer 1974; Newmeyer 1972; Weinreich 1967 for variations on such approaches) the work we present is intended to be independent of either viewpoint (although it is designed to illuminate the debate).

Similarly, while much literature has debated the degree of (de)compositionality (or, 'frozenness') inherent in idioms (see, e.g., Frase, 1974; Gibbs and Nayak 1989; Heringer 1976), we accept the problem of heterogeneity among 'non-literal' expressions with regard to current linguistic compositional theory—our approach is independent of (but, again, may shed light on) the resolution of such issues.

One traditional way in which non-literal (figurative) expressions have been treated is as merely one of a heterogeneous bundle of pragmatic phenomenon that are stored and computed outside of 'standard language processing' per se (see, e.g., Katz & Fodor 1963). This view of metaphoric processing has been extended by some theoreticians to include figurative expressions that have become fixed forms (idioms) in the language. Other approaches have assumed such fixed-form expressions to have a representation all their own (whether as part of the language system or not; e.g., Bobrow & Bell 1973). Still other approaches have assumed that fixed-form expressions, whether literal or figurative in interpretation, are simply lexical entries precisely like those assumed for standard literal interpretation of individual words (see, e.g., Di Sciullo & Williams 1987; Swinney & Cutler 1979). Our work is designed to examine certain aspects of this issue.

Finally, in its simplest description, a fixed figurative expression (for simplicity, the term "idiom" will be used hereafter to refer to such an expression) is a string of words for which the interpretation is not (entirely) derived from the individual meanings of the words comprising the string (even if there can be seen some historical linkage of the literal words to the overall expression). Further, this non-literal interpretation has become 'fixed' in the language by use. Thus, the idiom "trip the light fantastic" (meaning, roughly, "to dance") has little relationship to the current individual meanings of the words in that phrase. The work we present in this paper concerns word compounds that have idiomatic meaning. The work will be focused on idiomatic compounds in German, a language that, in contrast to English, has a highly productive use of compounding in natural language. Thus, the study of these forms in German provides a strong laboratory for examining the operation of a processing device that must deal with both highly literal and highly non-literal compounding of words on a regular basis. We note here that, as in all idioms, an idiom compound's meaning may be: a) entirely independent from the 'literal' meanings of the individual words in the compound, or b) partially related to one of the 'literal' meanings of the compound via either structural or semantic analysis, or c) entirely ambiguous—having both a 'literal' and a 'figurative' meaning.

Consider, for example, the English compound "redhead". This has the structurally decomposable literal meaning involving a head that is red in color (perhaps from sunburn or dye), the partially decomposable meaning of "having hair that is red", and the non-decomposable figurative meaning of "hot tempered"—a meaning derivable only by 'knowledge' of personality features stereotypically associated with persons who have red hair. The latter meaning has come to be 'fixed' by use—and is thus idiomatic. Consider also the English compound "horse-laugh". With the exception of the small class of individuals who deal closely with horses (and who might attribute the human descriptor of laughter to a horse) there is no literal (decomposable or otherwise) interpretation of this compound. Yet the fixed idiom is easily understood to mean a loud annoying (braying) laugh by a human. Overall, we are not primarily concerned here with the compositional origins of a metaphoric derivation of these fixed forms, but we note that it is clear that no single concept of (de)composition will easily work in describing interpretation for such a variety of forms (see, e.g., Lehnert 1986). Relatedly, we want to note that neither representation nor processing of putatively compositional lexical concepts necessarily induces more computational costs than non-decompositional ones (see, e.g., Fodor, Fodor, & Garrett 1975; Fodor, Garrett, Walker, & Parkes 1980), and thus measures of processing *load*, per se, will not be sufficient to differentiate processing models concerning such entities. It will, rather, take direct evidence about the activation (or lack thereof) of various non-literal and literal meanings of individual (and joint) elements in the compounds—and the time-course of their activations—to distinguish among such models. The present work is focused on providing an analysis of the computational processes involved in the interpretation of fixed compound expressions during sentence processing, using on-line measures that are sensitive to the temporal constraints of sentence processing, and which reveal activation of individual words and concepts during such processing.

2. Idiom Processing Accounts

There are two broadly differing accounts of idiom processing, accounts that might best be distinguished as 'literal-meaning-dependent' vs. 'literal-meaning-independent' models. The former all hold that access to idiomatic meanings is, in one way or another, tied to an attempted literal analysis of the items comprising the idiom. In some approaches, this takes the form of a claim that the perceiver accesses first the literal meaning(s) of the words the idiom is composed of before s/he accesses the non-literal (idiomatic) meaning (e.g., Clark & Lucy 1975; Fraser 1970; Weinreich 1967). In a related approach, it is assumed that there is a separate 'idiom list' (perhaps outside of the lexicon) which will be accessed when the processing of a literal interpretation fails (e.g., Bobrow & Bell 1973). All approaches within this model essentially assert a form of two-stage serial access/processing in which the idiomatic interpretation is achieved only in the second stage. In some cases this two-stage processes is viewed as cascaded (somewhat temporally overlapping), but in all such models, some temporal distinctions between initial literal analysis and later idiomatic analysis all hold. In this approach, idioms are treated much as non-fixed figurative language forms would be.

There are also several types of literal-meaning-independent hypotheses about idiom processing that have been proposed. The lexical representation hypothesis (LRH) holds that idiomatic and literal meanings of words and word compounds are simultaneously activated upon encountering the idiom (see, e.g., Swinney & Cutler 1979). In this, idioms are simply large (multi-segment) words stored in the lexicon much as meaning is stored for any word. Given that the lexical ambiguity literature provides strong evidence that all meanings associated with a word are accessed upon encountering the 'form' of the word (e.g., Ahrens 1998; Seidenberg, Tanenhaus, Leiman and Bienkowski 1982; Swinney 1979; among others), the idiom meaning is accessed along with the other meanings of words—based on complete identification of the form of the word.

In a somewhat different but related view, the "direct access hypothesis" holds that linguistic analysis can be completely bypassed if the perceiver immediately recognizes the relevant expression as an idiom (Gibbs 1980; 1984; 1986). This approach does not specify whether this is considered to be lexical access or not, and it has variants in which semantic and syntactic aspects of idiom use can be considered in the access process. The latter are "idiom decomposition approaches" in which a perceiver analyzes decomposable idioms by accessing first the figurative meaning of parts of the idioms. For example, in interpreting the idiom "pop the question" the perceiver would access the figurative meanings of "pop" (suddenly utter) and "the question" (marriage proposal) and interpret the entire idiom from these (e.g., Gibbs, Nayak, & Cutting 1989).

Overall, both off-line as well as on-line processing evidence has tended to support the literal-meaning-independent accounts over the literal-meaning-dependent approaches, largely via evidence that access to the idiomatic meaning takes either about the same time as (or is even faster than) access to the literal counterpart of the expression (e.g., Gibbs 1980; 1986; Ortony, Schallert, Reynolds & Antos 1978; Swinney & Cutler 1979). (Note, this is a considerably different model than the evidence about non-idiomatic figurative language processing supports—but that is not the issue of relevance here.) Clearly, such evidence is highly dependent on a clear understanding of the experimental methods applied to studies of idiom processing, and we examine such concerns below. However, overall, there is considerable evidence that idiomatic meanings are not made available any less rapidly than literal interpretations of these words, a fact that can only be taken as support for the literal-meaning-independent models.

For example, Gibbs et al. (1989) have examined processing for three types of idioms (normal, abnormally decomposable idioms and non-decomposable idioms) in a reaction time study. The example "pop the question" is considered to be a normal decomposable idiom as each part contributes to the overall meaning of the idiom; in contrast, "to carry a torch" would be an abnormal decomposable idiom because only one part ("torch") would express a figurative relationship ("warm feelings"); and, independent from etymological considerations, the parts of non-decomposable idioms appear not to contribute the idiomatic meaning directly at all (e.g., "to chew the fat"). Exemplars of these idiom types were presented visually to subjects who were asked to verify (acceptable/ unacceptable judgments) such phrases, along with their literal counterparts (e.g., "ask the question", "light the torch"). It was found that decomposable (normal and abnormal) idioms were verified faster than their literal counterparts, thus leading the authors to support a literal-meaning-independent model in which idioms do not need to be analyzed into their literal readings. In this study, it was found that the non-decomposable idioms were verified significantly slower than their literal control phrases. This and similar findings have often been argued to demonstrate that subjects would perform a compositional analysis on the idiomatic word strings to determine their figurative meaning, and their attempt (and inability) to do so causes slower processing. However, such an interpretation of these interesting results may not have sufficiently considered critical methodological aspects of the task used. For example, the idiomatic phrases that are used in these studies are presented in isolation, out of sentential context. After seeing a large number of items which are compositional (two-thirds of the experimental materials and all of the matched controls) and being required to make a conscious decision about each of them, it appears highly likely that subjects will tend toward a conscious 'compositional analysis' mode of evaluating these short phrases. Such conscious processing, however, is most likely to take place only subsequent to actual unconscious comprehension of the phrases. Thus, it may simply be that finding something unusual (e.g., the few non-decomposable items) in this list causes the conscious processing and analysis of these expressions to 'hiccup' (so to speak), and make for longer conscious decisions. In general, isolated phrase verification techniques of this type can lead to many specialized strategies that are not used in normal language understanding, a point which leaves unanswered the question of how such materials are processed during normal language comprehension. We strongly feel that the existing evidence suggests that more sensitive tasks—particularly those which do not cause conscious introspection about the stimulus materials in question—need to be utilized in order to provide stable answers to these fundamental questions underlying sentence comprehension. (For more detailed arguments and evidence concerning methodology see: Nicol, Fodor, Swinney 1994; Fodor 1995; Nicol & Swinney 1989; Swinney 1981.)

There are a few studies that applied sensitive and non-consciously introspective on-line paradigms to the examination of how idiomatic phrases are processed during sentence comprehension (see, e.g., Cacciari & Tabossi 1988; Colombo 1993; 1998; Swinney 1981; Tabossi & Zardon 1993; 1995; Titone & Connine 1994). Most of these have used a cross-modal-lexical-priming methodology (CMLP); Swinney, Onifer, Prather & Hirshkowitz 1979; Swinney 1979; Swinney 1981) in which subjects listening to spoken sentences (or larger discourse units). The sentences contained idioms, and at selected points while the idiom is being heard, a visual 'target' is displayed to which subjects make a binary decision (usually: word/non-word decision task) or 'name' it as fast as possible. The visual target is a word that is associatively related to either a part of the idiom (e.g., a literal word occurring in the idiomatic word string) or to the figurative meaning of the idiom overall. (Necessarily, the target may also be a 'control' word which is unrelated to any part of the idiom, but matches to the 'associated' word on all other grounds—a priori (isolated) reaction time, frequency, concreteness, category, etc.; if the task involves a lexical decision, a non-word letter string may be displayed; see for related issues Borsky & Shapiro 1998; Hillert 1997). Decision reaction times to 'classify' the visual target (word/non-word) or 'name' the visual target are recorded. When priming (speeded responses to the associated word vs. the control word) is found, it is taken as evidence that the 'associated material' in the idiom has been accessed and is available to 'prime' the decision made to the target word. Such priming, where found, constitutes prima facia evidence for access and activation of various aspects of the phrase comprising the idiom in the sentence. Even with use of these techniques, however, there is disagreement over the nature of the process by which idioms are comprehended.

Swinney (1981) for example, used the CMLP paradigm to examine access to idiomatic meanings in sentence contexts, probing at the offset of the first word and last word of a 'grammatical idiomatic phrase' (one with both literal and idiomatic interpretations) that occurred in the middle of a sentence. Consider, for example, the phrase "kick the bucket". Swinney found that target words related to the literal meaning of the first word ("kick") were primed at the offset of that word but not at the offset of the last word in the idiom ("bucket"). Further, he found priming for the overall idiomatic meaning ("die") at the offset of the idiom phrase (at "bucket"), but not at the offset of "kick". It was argued from this that literal meanings of idioms are always accessed along with idiomatic meanings (at least for 'grammatical' idioms). This evidence was also argued to demonstrate that the cohort model of lexical access proposed by Marslen-Wilson and Tyler (1976) is not, at the least, comprehensive, in that it does not accurately describe access to lexicalized idiom meanings. (Under the cohort model the entire idiomatic word meaning ("die") should have been accessed from the initial consonant-vowel cluster of "/ki.../" (in "kick").)

In fact, Titone and Connine (1994) interpreted the above finding as evidence against the LRH for idioms because of the failure to find priming for the idiom meaning at the offset of the *first* word of the idiom phrase. Their reasoning however, hinges on a belief that the cohort model of lexical access is correct (namely, that all meanings for all words having an initial consonant-vowel cluster will be accessed when that cluster is heard), a prediction that has not been universally supported in the literature for simple words, much less for multi-segmental words such as idioms. In fact, the Swinney (1981) evidence stands against the cohort model as an overall account of lexical access. The issue here really is one of what constitutes the basis for lexical access—the first consonant cluster, the initial syllable (e.g., Foss and Swinney 1973) the first stressed syllable (e.g., Cutler & Norris 1988), the entire form of the word (Swinney 1981), or the basic orthographic syllable (Taft and Forster 1975). The answer is simply not definitively known at this time. Certainly, however, the Swinney data do not in any way stand against the notion that idioms are stored and accessed as words from the lexicon; the data, however, do not tell precisely how lexical access takes place, and thus do not directly support the LRH (see, however, work by Swinney & Cutler 1979). The data do suggest that, at least for grammatical idioms, a literal analysis is attempted along with whatever constitutes idiomatic processing.

Cacciari and Tabossi (1988; see also Cacciari & Glucksberg 1991; Titone & Connine 1994) have proposed a "configuration model" of idiom processing, which holds that idiom meaning is not a separate lexical entry but is meaning 'associated with a particular configuration of the words', a meaning which is accessed only when the perceiver encounters an "idiom key" in a phrase. An idiom key is a portion of an idiom that allows access to this idiomatic meaning. Consider, for example, the idiom "kick the bucket" The idiom interpretation of this phrase is more frequent than that for its literal counterpart, and thus, it is argued that hearing the initial part of the phrase ("kick the...") will more likely lead to an association and completion with the word "bucket" than (for example) with the word "ball". This idiom key / configuration model is clearly a type of literal-meaning-dependent model, but one which holds as a central tenant the assumption that language processing takes place via use of associative prediction.

Cacciari and Tabossi (1988), for example, used a modified CMP (cross modal priming) task to examine online access to predictable idiomatic phrases in Italian. "Predictable" in this case means that the first words of the idiom indicate/suggest the figurative meaning. In an initial study, they probed for activation of words related to the idiomatic and literal meaning of the idiom at the offset of the idiomatic phrase (PP, probe point; e.g., "Il ragazzo pensava che suo fratello fosse nato con la camicia." ^PP; gloss: "The boy believed that his brother was born with the shirt"; tr. "The boy believed that his brother was born with a silver spoon in his mouth"). Cacciari and Tabossi reported that they found priming only for the idiomatic meaning but not for the literal meaning at the end of sentence probe point. In interpreting these data, we want to emphasize that the test point in this study was at the end of the sentence/trial, a point that is usually avoided in most CMP studies precisely because of sentential/trial 'wrap-up', 'reconsideration' and 'conscious interpretation' effects that come in at this point. (See e.g., discussions in Hillert & Swinney 2000; Swinney 1981; Swinney, Nicol, Love, & Hald 1999; Balogh, Zurif, Prather, Swinney, & Finkel 1998 on many of these issues). Overall, ignoring any other experimentally-related concerns, we note that the effect of priming between literal and control probes reached a significance level of p <.08, but the possibility of a Type II error cannot be discounted. Thus, although it stands against 'configurational' hypothesis, it appears that the literal meanings are likely activated in these material conditions, thus supporting the LRH. In a second study involving low-predictable idioms Cacciari and Tabossi report significant priming only for the literal meaning of the idiom, although, again, a strong trend (p <.09) for significance of the idiomatic meaning was effectively discounted. Prudence suggests that such a strong trend should not be dismissed lightly. A third study which had a 300 ms delay between offset of the idiom and the probe found priming for both literal and idiomatic meanings. Thus, it appears that all meanings of the idioms—literal or figurative—were eventually accessed in these studies, thus supporting a multiple-access hypothesis in some form (e.g., LRH). The question remains, however, as to the precise time course of the availability of each of the literal and idiomatic interpretations during sentence comprehension.

In addition to the lack of robust evidence about the nature of the operations involved in the processing of idioms, a number of important overarching issues remain that are of concern. For example, the existing studies of sensitive, on-line examinations of idiom processing have all taken place only on a limited number of languages. For example, English and Italian are hardly representative of the range of language structures and processes that a universal theory of figurative language (even fixed figurative language) processing needs to consider. Further, the range of idiomatic structures that have been examined is extremely limited—limited enough that significant generalizations may easily be missed, even if all of the data would be in agreement. In what follows, we describe new evidence that is intended to move in a direction to correct these holes in the empirical literature.

3. On-line Examination of Idiom Compounds in German

Languages significantly differ with respect to the degree of lexical composition. For example, English and Chinese prefer single words to compounded words while German tends to use (and create) compounds of great length and complexity with high frequency. Although in Standard European Languages (SEL) 80-90 percent of nominal compounds contain only two-elements, German has a relatively high percentage of compounds that consist of more than two elements. For example, the complex compound "Tonnentaschenfederkernmatratzenladenverkaufspreis" (discovered in a German furniture store) can be relatively easily parsed by a native speaker. The individual parts of this compound are: Tonnen-taschen-feder-kern-matratzen-laden-verkaufs-preis; gloss: Tons-bags-feather-pit-mattress-shop-selling-price). At least in SEL it is a general rule that the second element of a nominal compound (head) dominates the first element (as it typically does in English, e.g., "shrimpboat" is a type of boat). In the German example "Bienenhonig" (bee-honey) the second element "-honig" can be analyzed as the head and the first element "Biene-" as the modifier/subject (honey produced by bees); conversely, in "Honigbiene" (honey-bee) the second element "-biene" is the head and the first element "Honig-" is the descriptor/modifier (bees of a type that produce honey). Sometimes adult speakers actively use/create novel compounds in a metaphoric sense and apply a 'literal' compositional strategy (e.g., "Peter sucht sich Wortblumen für den Strauß seiner Rede"; gloss: Peter is looking for word-flowers for the bouquet of his speech). Similarly, children often create new words to describe an object for which they have not yet acquired an existing word (e.g., "Wolkenwasser" (clouds-water) instead of "Regen" (rain)), and second language speakers actively (de)compose foreign words to create (understand) new meanings which results sometimes in funny constructions (e.g., "cloud scraper" (German: "Wolkenkratzer") instead of "sky scraper").

Again, a very large number of compounds with idiomatic meanings exist in German. For these, a speaker typically cannot apply a decompositional strategy to understand the idiomatic meaning. As with most phrasal idioms some idiomatic compounds assign only an idiomatic meaning but no literal meaning. For example, "Lampenfieber" (gloss: lamp-fever; "stage-fright") has no literal counterpart. However, "Eselsohren" (literal: "donkey's ears"; idiomatic: "dog's ear") does have a literal counterpart ("donkey's ears" are real things). The range of idiom compounds is enormous—and they represent a particularly vexing problem for models of language processing in a highly compound-productive language such as German to account for. It is precisely in this domain, however, that we feel we can most profitably examine the time course and nature of idiom processing.

The initial work we report here examines the LRH by measuring the time course of access to the literal and idiomatic meaning of German nominal compounds during spoken sentence comprehension. The CMLP paradigm was employed throughout. In an initial study, we examined ambiguous compounds (compounds with both a literal and an idiomatic interpretation) such as "Bienenstich" (literal: "bee-sting"; idiomatic meaning: "a particular cake") in a sentence context biased toward the idiomatic interpretation, as shown in (1).

(1)   Zu Weihnachten backte die Mutter stets einen *Bienenstich* ^ PP und
         einen Stollen.

         (At Christmas baked the Mother always a "bee-sting" and a fruit
         loaf.)

Probe words related to the idiomatic meaning of the compound (related: KUCHEN/cake; control: KANZEL/pulpit) and to the literal meaning of the compound's head (related: HONIG/honey; control: ANKER/anchor) appeared at the offset of the idiomatic compound in the figuratively biased sentence.[2] Mean reaction times for 50 native (German) speakers (who saw only a single probe with the sentence for each exemplar) can be seen in Table 1. The priming effect for both the idiomatic-related target (p <.01) and the literal-related target (p <.01) strongly support the argument that both the literal and idiomatic interpretations of these ambiguous idioms were accessed in this study, even in the presence of a context biased only toward the (more frequent) idiomatic interpretation.

Table 1. Priming patterns (mean difference of reaction time to control-related probes) of ambiguous idiomatic compounds in figuratively biased sentence contexts.

Idiomatic Meaning	87 ms
Literal Meaning	48 ms

A second study, which used the same procedures and methods as the first experiment, was run to examine a dramatically stronger case—that of the processing of idiomatic compounds which only have idiomatic interpretations (idioms without literal interpretation) such as "Lackaffe" (gloss: "lac-monkey"; someone who shows off). These idioms have fixed meanings and are frequently used in everyday German conversation. In this study, such idiomatic compounds were presented in a neutral sentence context.

(2)   Hans war nach der Ansicht der meisten Mitschüler ein Lackaffe ^PP
         im aus gesprochenen Sinne.

         (Hans was after the view of the most class mates a "lac-monkey" in a
         decisive sense.)

---

[2] We used a display time of 300 ms, a zero interstimulus-interval (0-ISI) and an intertrial-interval of 2000 ms). Because of space limitations, we discuss in the present context only a part of the conditions examined (see for further details Hillert & Swinney 2000).

For example, in (2) we probed for the activation of the idiomatic meaning (related: EITEL/vain; control: BUNT/colorful) and for the activation of the literal meaning of the head noun (related: BAUM/tree; control: SAMT/velvet) at the offset of the idiom compound. As in the previous study, this experiment was designed so that no subject hears/sees more than one probe/experimental word with any exemplar sentence. The mean reaction times of fifty native German speakers to the idiomatic meaning and to the literal meaning of the compounds' head in the neutral context condition can be seen in Table 2. We found significant priming for idiomatic (p <.0001) and literal (p <.05) interpretations in the neutral context with these 'idiom-only-interpretation' compounds. These results seem to strongly support the interpretation that the literal meaning of the head noun of these exclusively idiomatic compounds was accessed when the idiom was heard. This was so in spite of the fact that there was no possible literal interpretation for this compound. These data argue therefore strongly for the LRH, at least in the processing of German compounds.

Table 2. Priming patterns (mean difference of reaction time to control–related probes) for exclusively idiomatic compounds in a neutral sentence context.

Idiomatic Meaning	70 ms
Literal Meaning	67 ms

The outcome of both experiments together demonstrate that both idiomatic meaning and literal meanings of words comprising idiom compounds in German appear to be immediately activated when the idiom is heard during sentence comprehension. This strongly suggests that fixed meaning phrases act in much the same way as do lexical ambiguities—all meanings associated with the form of the word(s) are accessed automatically and exhaustively.

4. Conclusions

The research presented here, combined with prior work in the literature, suggests strongly that fixed form expressions are processed in a manner consistent with the literal-meaning-independent general models of idiom processing. Moreover, they support a 'multiple-form-driven-access' version of such models (all meanings—both idiom and literal—are accessed). The evidence we present does not demonstrate any particular support for an idiom key or configurational role in such access, and it is completely consistent with an account that holds that fixed idiomatic meanings are lexically stored (LRH). The current evidence provides no basis for speculation about a (de)compositional procedure involved in such access, but we note that we only examined one particular idiom type in our work—compounds). Finally, there is no evidence in our work supportive of an anticipatory-predictive process in the comprehension of idiom strings (such a process would have allowed only the idiomatic interpretation to be accessed in a figuratively biased sentence context). The present work supports the LHR, that is, lexical access (whether of 'literal' or fixed 'idiomatic' meanings) is a strictly form-driven process.

References

Ahrens, K.V. 1998. Lexical Ambiguity Resolution: Languages, Tasks, and Timing, in D. Hillert, ed., *Sentence Processing: A Crosslinguistic Perspective, Syntax and Semantics 31*. San Diego, CA: Academic Press.

Balogh, J., E. Zurif, P. Prather, D. Swinney, and L. Finkel. 1998. End-of-Sentence Effects in Real-time Language Processing: A New Perspective on Blumstein et al.'s Findings. *Brain and Language* 61:169–182.

Bobrow, S. & S. Bell. 1973. On Catching on to Idiomatic Expressions. *Memory & Cognition* 1:343–346.

Borsky, S., & L. P. Shapiro. 1998. Context-independent sentence processing. In D. Hillert, ed., *Syntax and Semantics 31, Sentence Processing: A Crosslinguistic Perspective*. San Diego: Academic Press.

Cacciari, C. & S. Glucksberg. 1991. Understanding Idiomatic Expressions: The Contribution of Word Meanings.. in G. Simpson, ed., *Understanding Word and Sentence*. Amsterdam: North Holland.

Cacciari, C. & P. Tabossi. 1988. The Comprehension of Idioms. *Journal of Language and Memory* 27:668–683.

Clark, H. 1978. Inferring What is Meant, in W. J. M. Levelt & G. B. Flores d'Arcais , eds., *Studies in the Perception of Language*. Chichester, UK: Wiley.

Clark, H. & P. Lucy. 1975. Understanding What is Meant from What is Said: A Study on Conversationally Conveyed Requests. *Journal of Verbal Learning and Verbal Behavior* 14:56–72.

Colombo, L. 1993. The comprehension of ambiguous idioms in context, in C. Cacciari & P. Tabossi, eds., *Idioms, Processing, Structure and Interpretation. Hillsdale,* NJ: Lawrence Erlbaum.

Colombo, L. 1998. Role of Context in the Comprehension of Ambiguous Italian Idioms, in D. Hillert, ed., *Syntaxt and Semantics, 31, Sentence Processing: A Crosslinguistic Perspective*. San Diego: Academic Press.

Cutler, A. & D. Norris. 1988. The Role of Strong Syllables in Segmentation for Lexical Access. *Journal of Experimental Psychology: Human Perception and Performance* 14:113–121.

Di Sciullo, A.M. & E. Williams. 1987. *On the Definition of Words*. Cambridge, MA: MIT press.

Fodor, J. A., J. D. Fodor, and M. Garrett. 1975 The Psychological Unreality of Semantic Respresentation. *Linguistic Inquiry* 6:515–531.

Fodor, J. A., M. Garrett, E. Walker, & C. Parkes. 1980 Against Definitions. *Cognition* 8:263–367.

Fodor, J. D. 1995. Comprehending Sentence Structure, in L.R. Gleitman, & M. Liberman, eds., *An Invitation to Cognitive Science, Language, Vol. 1*. Cambridge, MA: MIT Press.

Foss, D. J., and D. A. Swinney. 1973. On the Psychological Reality of the Phoneme: Perception, Identification and Consciousness. *Journal of Verbal Learning and Verbal Behavior* 12:246–257.

Fraser, B. 1970. Idioms with a Transformational Grammar. *Foundations of Language* 6:1. 22–42.

Fraser, B. 1974. *The Verb-Particle Combination in English*. Tokyo: Taishukan.

Gibbs, R. 1980. Spilling the Beans on Understanding and Memory for Idioms in Conversation. *Memory & Cognition* 8:449–456.

Gibbs, R. 1986. Skating on Thin Ice: Literal Meaning and Understanding Idioms in Conversation. *Discourse Processes* 9:17–30.

Gibbs, R. 1984. Literal Meaning and Psychological Theory. *Cognitive Science* 8:275–304.

Gibbs, R. W., & N. P. Nayak. 1989. Psycholinguistic Studies on the Syntactic Behavior of Idioms. *Cognitive Psychology* 21:100–138.

Gibbs, R., P. Nayak & C. Cutting. 1989. How to Kick the Bucket and not Decompose Analyzability and Idiom Processing. *Journal of Memory and Language* 28:576–593.

Gibbs, R.W. & N. P. Nayak. 1989. Psycholinguistic Studies on the Syntactic Behavior of Idioms. *Cognitive Psychology* 21:100–138.

Heringer, J. 1976. Idioms and Lexicalization in English, in J.P. Kimball, ed., *Syntax and Semantics, vol. 9: The Grammar of Causative Constructions*. New York: Academic Press.

Hillert, D. & D. A. Swinney. 2000. Access to Idiomatic Meanings during Online Sentence Processing. (ms. submitted.)

Hillert, D. 1997. Language in Time: Lexical and Structural Ambiguity Resolution, in M. Stamenov, ed., *Approaches to Language and Consciousness*. Amsterdam & Philadelphia: John Benjamins.

Katz, J. J. and J. A. Fodor. 1963. The Structure of a Semantic Theory. *Language* 39:170–210.

Lehnert, W. G. 1986. The Analysis of Nominal Compounds. *VS* 44/45:155–180.

Lehrer, A. 1974. *Semantic Fields and Lexical Structure*. Amsterdam: North Holland.

Marslen-Wilson, W. D. 1976. Linguistic Descriptions and the Psychological Assumption is the Study of Sentence Perception, in R. J. Wales and E. C. T. Walker, eds., *New Approaches to Language Mechanisms*. Amsterdam: North - Holland.

Newmeyer, F., 1972. The Insertion of Idioms, in *Papers from the Eighth Regional Meeting.* Chicago: Chicago Linguistic Society, 294–302.

Nicol, J., & D. Swinney. 1989. The Role of Structure in Coreference Assignment during Sentence Comprehension. *Journal of Psycholinguistic Research* 18:5–24.

Nicol, J., J.D. Fodor, & D. Swinney. 1994. Using Cross-Modal Lexical Decision Tasks to Investigate Sentence Processing. *Journal of Experimental Psychology: Learning, Memory, and Cognition* 20:5.1229–1238.

Ortony, A., D. Schallert, R. Reynolds, & S. Antos. 1978. Interpreting Metaphors and Idioms: Some Effects of Context on Comprehension. *Journal of Verbal Learning and Verbal Behavior* 17:465–478.

Seidenberg, M., M. Tanenhaus, J. Leiman, & M. Bienkowski. 1982. Automatic Access of the Meanings of Ambiguous Words in Context: Some Limitations of Knowledge-based Processing. *Cognitive Psychology* 14:4.489–537.

Swinney, D. & A. Cutler. 1979. The Access and Processing of Idiomatic Expressions. *Journal of Verbal Learning and Verbal Behavior* 18:523–534.

Swinney, D. 1979. Lexical Access during Sentence Comprehension: (Re)consideration of Context Effects. *Journal of Verbal Learning and Verbal Behavior* 18:645–660.

Swinney, D. and A. Cutler. 1979. The Access and Processing of Idiomatic Expressions. *Journal of Verbal Learning and Verbal Behavior* 18:523–534.

Swinney, D., J. Nicol., T. Love, & L. Hald. 1999. Methodological Issues in the On-Line Study of Language Processing, in R. Schwartz, ed., *Childhood Language Disorders*, N.Y.: Erlbaum.

Swinney, D., W. Onifer, P. Prather, and M. Hirshkowitz. 1979. Semantic Facilitation across Sensory Modalities in the Processing of Individual Words and Sentences. *Memory and Cognition* 7:3.54–178.

Swinney, D.A. 1981. Lexical Processing during Sentence Comprehension: Effects of Higher Order Constraints and Implications for Representation, in T. Myers, J. Laver & J. Anderson, eds., *The Cognitive Representation of Speech.* Amsterdam: North Holland.

Tabossi, P. & F. Zardon. 1993. The Activation of Idiomatic Meaning in Spoken Language Comprehension, in C. Cacciari & P. Tabossi, eds., *Idioms, Processing, Structure and Interpretation.* Hillsdale, NJ: Lawrence Erlbaum.

Tabossi, P. & F. Zardon. 1995. The Activation of Idiomatic Meaning, in M. Everaert, E. van der Linden, A. Schenk, & R. Schreuder, eds., *Idioms. Structural and Psychological Perspectives.* Hillsdale, NJ: Lawrence Erlbaum.

Taft, M., and K. I. Forster. 1975. Lexical Storage and Retrieval of Prefixed Words. *Journal of Verbal Learning and Verbal Behavior* 14:638–647.

Titone, D. A. & C. M. Connine. 1994. Comprehension of Idiomatic Expressions: Effects of Predictability and Literality. *Journal of Experimental Psychology: Learning, Memory and Cognition* 20:1126–1138.

Weinreich, U. 1967. Problems in the Analysis of Idioms, in J. Puhvel, ed., *Proceedings of the Summer 1966 Linguistics Forum at UCLA*. Berkeley: University of California Press, vol. 11:23–81.

Constructional Grounding: On the Relation between Deictic and Existential *there*-Constructions in Acquisition

CHRISTOPHER JOHNSON

University of California, Berkeley and
International Computer Science Institute

1. Introduction

A striking property of language is the prevalence of pairs of conventional signs that serve distinct but related functions and that are identical or nearly identical in form. This phenomenon includes but goes beyond the traditional lexical-semantic concept of polysemy, occurring with more abstract phrasal and clausal signs, or *constructions*, as well (see, e.g., Goldberg 1995; Michaelis 1994).

Such relations between signs are widely assumed to have just two types of explanation: the diachronic and the synchronic. In a diachronic explanation, two signs are shown to be derived historically from the same source. Often one is found to be an extension from what may be considered an earlier form of the other. In a synchronic explanation, the relation between two signs is assumed to be represented in some way in the system of knowledge internalized by contemporary adult speakers. It might take the form of a linguistic rule or a principled conceptual relation such as a metaphor. While synchronic and diachronic accounts are compatible and may apply simultaneously to the same phenomenon (see, e.g., Sweetser 1990), they represent

Conceptual and Discourse Factors in Linguistic Structure.
Alan Cienki, Barbara J. Luka and Michael B. Smith (eds.).
Copyright © 2001, CSLI Publications.

two distinct theoretical ideas. Taken together, they are commonly assumed to exhaustively explain relations between signs.

The purpose of this paper is to discuss the possibility of a third type of explanation for relations between signs in a language. Termed *constructional grounding* (see Johnson 1999), it arises from general tendencies in the dynamic processes by which children acquire a language. Constructional grounding maintains that children may use one sign as a model for another in the learning process, based on utterances that exemplify key properties of both. As a consequence, one sign may "motivate" another not by means of some property of the system eventually mastered by the child, but rather by playing a pivotal role in the process by which the child constructs this system. This view is compatible with both synchronic and diachronic explanations, but is not reducible to either. Rather, it adds a new dimension to our understanding of the way in which one sign can be "based on" another. As we will see, this dimension makes it easier to explain how diachronic and synchronic processes might interact and reinforce one another.

2. What is Constructional Grounding?

Constructional grounding is the use of occurrences of one construction (the *source construction*) as the starting point in the acquisition of another construction (the *target construction*). That is, utterances construed as instances of the source construction, together with contextual information associated with those utterances, serve as the domain of generalization in the formation of the initial representation of the target construction—what is here called the *target proto-construction*.

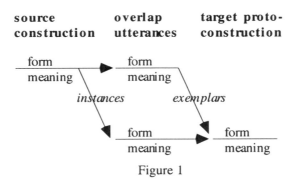

Figure 1

Figure 1 schematically represents the basic properties of constructional grounding. In this diagram, the source construction and the target proto-construction are represented as form-meaning pairs surrounded by boxes with bold lines (to indicate that they are treated as conventional units by the learner). Utterances are represented as form-meaning pairs in plain boxes. The dotted line between these boxes is meant to suggest an arbitrary number of utterances presented to the child over time. The arrows represent two things about the utterances: first, that they are treated by the child as *instances* of the source construction, which, it is assumed, the child has already learned, and second, that they are used by the child as *exemplars* of the most important properties of the target construction, which the child needs to figure out. The target proto-construction—the child's initial hypothesis about the form and meaning of the target construction—is represented as a generalization over the overlap utterances.

3. What Makes Constructional Grounding Possible?

Constructional grounding depends on two enabling factors. First is a significant overlap between two constructions which makes it possible for an instance of one, in the right context and in the absence of perfect knowledge of adult grammar, to be mistaken for an instance of the other. Second is the existence of *overlap contexts*, which are utterance contexts in which either a source construction or its corresponding target construction could be felicitously used. In such contexts, a use of the source construction often has pragmatic properties that resemble the conventional semantic-pragmatic properties of the target construction. Conversely, a use of the target construction can often reasonably be mistaken, especially by someone with incomplete knowledge of that construction (such as a very young child), for an instance of the source construction. Utterances occurring in such situations that exhibit important formal and semantic-pragmatic properties of both the source and the target construction shall be referred to as *overlap utterances*.

In some cases overlap utterances can actually be simultaneously construed, even from the adult point of view, as instances of either the source construction or the target construction. Below are some sentences that, in combination with appropriate contexts, characterize possible overlap utterances involving different pairs of constructions:

(1) Let's see what's in the box.

      source form: **see NP**(headless relative)
      source meaning: 'Let's see the things in the box'

      target form: **see S**(interrogative clause)
      target meaning: 'Let's determine what's in the box'

(2) What are you doing in my room?

      source form: (Wh-question)
      source meaning: 'What activity are you engaged in in my room?'

      target form: **what <u>be</u> NP doing PRED?**
      target meaning: 'How come you're in my room?'

(3) I made a mistake.

      source form: **make**(full verb) **NP**(head: mistake)

source meaning: 'I created a physical flaw'

target form: **make**(support verb) **NP**(head: mistake)
target meaning: 'I did something incorrectly'

All the above sentences are ambiguous. However, this ambiguity is *harmonious*, in the sense of Norvig (1988). While normal ambiguity is an obstacle to semantic interpretation, harmonious ambiguity need not be, because it involves meanings that are compatible with one another. For each of these sentences it is possible to imagine contexts in which the two possible meanings can co-exist and in fact reinforce one another. (1) might be uttered by an adult about to show a child the contexts of a box. In this context, the child's visual experience of the contents would correspond exactly to the child's finding out what the box contains. Grady & Johnson (2000) characterize overlap scenarios like this as *primary scenes* consisting of sensorimotor and subjective *subscenes*. Such primary scenes are the types of experience that give rise to what Grady (1997) calls *primary metaphor*. In (2), an answer to the question about what activity the addressee is engaged in in the room might provide an answer to the other question expressed by this form, which can be paraphrased as 'How come you're in my room?' (see Kay & Fillmore 1999 on the "What's X doing Y?" construction). (3) might be uttered by an adult who is pointing to a stray mark on a drawing; the fact that this mark is a *mistake* would imply that the adult *made a mistake* in putting it there.

Johnson (1997b; 1999) argues that sentences such as (1) occur frequently in children's earliest input involving the verb *see*, helping children learn the mental sense of the word (as in *I see what you mean*) on the basis of visual situations. Similarly, Johnson (1997a; 1999) argues that sentences such as (2) help children reanalyze Wh-questions to derive the properties of the semi-idiomatic "What's X doing Y?" construction. (3) suggests how the properties of the support verb *make* might be derived from certain uses of *make* that the child takes as instances of the full verb.

4. Why Does Constructional Grounding Happen?

Assuming for a moment that constructional grounding is a real phenomenon, why should it happen? The answer to this question is not simple; it must address both why there are constructions in a language that are related to one another in the appropriate way, and, given such relations, why they should have the specific consequences that they do for the acquisition of that language.

Let us ignore for a moment the former issue and focus on the question of acquisition. It is assumed here that the main challenge faced by a young child in learning constructions is the correct identification of linguistically encoded meanings, the identification of the formal parameters that encode meanings, and the correct pairing of meanings with sets of formal parameters. Certain types of meaning are easier to identify than others because they can be suggested by non-verbal cues understood even by prelinguistic learners (e.g. direction of gaze). The easiest constructions to learn are those with simple forms whose meanings can be so cued in the spatiotemporal contexts in which the forms are uttered. Constructions are more difficult to learn either when their forms or meanings are difficult to identify or when their meanings are difficult to cue in the context of utterance, and therefore difficult to associate with one particular set of formal parameters rather than another.

If we examine pairs of constructions that exhibit significant overlap, we usually find a strong asymmetry corresponding to this hypothesized difference in acquisitional difficulty. Typically source constructions occur with perceptual cues that a child can use to identify an appropriate meaning in context, and target constructions do not. For example, visual uses of the verb *see* are often accompanied by demonstrative gestures and other signals telling the child where to direct his or her gaze or indicating that the speaker's visual experience is relevant. The mental use of the verb *see*, on the other hand, typically lacks such cues.

The claim of constructional grounding is that overlap utterances provide optimal conditions for children to learn target constructions by leveraging the relatively transparent, contextually-cued interpretations of source constructions. Since a source construction is likely to be learned first, a child is likely to pass through a stage when he or she knows a source construction but not its corresponding target construction. At this stage, overlap utterances are likely to be interpreted by the child as instances of the source, whether or not they are intended that way by adults, because they formally resemble the source and because a source interpretation is supported by context. At the same time, a source interpretation often gives rise to a pragmatic inference that is closely related to, or even identical to, the conventional meaning of the target construction. This situation can be represented graphically in the following way:

Source experiences Target experiences

Overlap experiences

Figure 2

The circle on the left represents the contexts in which the source construction would be appropriate. It is bold to indicate that these contexts typically provide the child with clues about the appropriate interpretation of the source construction. The circle on the right represents contexts in which the target construction would be appropriate. It is not bold, because such contexts typically lack the intersubjective cues that characterize source contexts. Overlap contexts, represented by the intersection of these two circles, have the properties of both source and target contexts. They support and provide cues to source interpretations, but they also support target interpretations.

These conditions suggest that the child can "freeze" the analysis assigned to the overlap utterances regarded as instances of the source construction, make minor adjustments to this analysis on the basis of the new implied target interpretation, and then attribute the resulting structure and meaning to a the new target proto-construction. After this, the child is in a good position to interpret any formal differences between the source and target construction as a marker of the difference in interpretation.

This general learning strategy, it is argued, might be simpler than trying to extract the form and meaning of the target construction from the full set of its uses. In fact, for certain target constructions, such as the "What's X doing Y?" construction, overlap uses are the most likely starting point for the child because they occur earlier and are far more frequent in the child's input than are unambiguous uses of the target (Johnson 1997a).

5. Deictic and Existential *there*-Constructions

As an example of constructional grounding, this paper examines the relation between English deictic and existential *there*-constructions, discussed in detail in Lakoff (1987). In Lakoff's analysis, deictics and existentials each comprise a radial category of distinct but related constructions, and these radial categories are related to one another in complex ways. It is beyond the scope of this paper to examine all the different types of deictics and existentials. Rather, I will focus on central deictics and central existentials. Central deictics are the prototypical deictics associated with basic situations of pointing out, and are the first type to be produced by children. Central existentials are the ones that most closely resemble central deictics. Lakoff claims central existentials are based on central deictics. This claim, it is argued here, seems to be true. However, this is not necessarily a fact about how these constructions should best be described in the adult language, but rather about how the deictic construction serves as a model for the existential early in the acquisition process.

The central deictic construction licenses sentences with the following structure: a deictic locative (*here* or *there*) is followed by a basic locative or motion verb (e.g. *be, sit, stand, go*), followed by an NP, followed by an optional Predicate expression (which Lakoff refers to as the *final phrase*).

(4)   a.   There's your mother.

        b.   Here's Sam.

        c.   There sits Harry.

        d.   There goes the dog down the street.

        e.   There's the dog running around.

The function of this construction is to call an addressee's attention to some object or situation in the immediate perceptually-accessible context of utterance.

The central existential construction licenses sentences with the following form: the word *there* (not a deictic locative) serves as the grammatical subject of the verb *be*, followed by an indefinite NP followed optionally by a Predicate expression. The function of the construction is to inform an addressee of the existence of some entity or situation, and/or to introduce that entity or situation into the current discourse:

(5)   a.   There's beer. (in answer to: What do we have to drink?)

      b.   There's a dog in the yard.

      c.   There's a person in the corner with a funny hat on.

6. Minimal Differences and Neutralizing Contexts

As Lakoff points out, certain deictics and existentials differ minimally from one another:

(6)   a.   THERE'S a new MERCEDES across the street. (deictic)

      b.   There's a new MERCEDES across the street. (existential)

When (6a) is read as a single utterance—not, for example, as the two utterances that would be written *There's a new Mercedes! Across the street!*—it is distinguishable from the existential in (6b) by the stress on *there*. An utterance like (6b), with the vowel of *there* reduced, would not under normal circumstances be interpreted by an adult as a deictic. However, the initial *there* of a deictic may have varying degrees of stress depending on the context in which it is used. If several deictics are produced in succession, for example, the non-initial ones can have unstressed *there*:

(7)   a.   THERE'S a DOG!

      b.   There's a CAT!

      c.   There's a PIG!

In a discourse about a perceptually present situation, utterances of this form can even be accompanied by pointing gestures:

(8)   What animals are there in the picture? Well...

      a.   There's a dog, and

      b.   there's a cat, and

      c.   there's a pig...

Both of these conditions are typical of input heard by children. Child-directed speech is full or repetition, as in examples (7a-c), and it is typically about the here-and-now, as in examples (8a-c). This fact, it is argued below, is relevant to the acquisition of the existential construction, and the role that the deictic construction may play in this process.

7. The Grounding of Central Existentials in Central Deictics

Despite the differences between deictics and existentials, the central deictic and central existential constructions overlap significantly in superficial form:

Deictic form:	*there* BE/GO/etc. NP (Pred)
Existential form:	*there* BE NP (Pred)
Shared form:	*there* BE NP (Pred)

In addition, they overlap in meaning. The NP in deictic expressions may be either definite (as in all the examples in (4)) or indefinite. When it is indefinite (as in the examples in (7)), the construction typically serves the existential-like function of informing an addressee of the existence of an object or situation and introducing it into the discourse. Sentences like (9) involve an additional type of overlap between deictics and existentials:

(9)   There's a lake over there.

Even when used and interpreted as a deictic (i.e. with stress on the initial *there*), (9) would have the characteristic pragmatic force of the existential construction, since the NP is indefinite. When used as an existential (i.e., without stress on the initial *there*), (9) would still have a deictic meaning (due to the final deictic locative) and could be accompanied by a pointing gesture. While adults may be able to distinguish the deictic and existential interpretations on the basis of the vowel of the initial *there*, such utterances provide young language learners with scant evidence for a difference between the constructions, especially since the earlier-learned deictic construction allows variable stress on *there*.

Assuming children learn the deictic construction before they learn the existential, it seems likely that utterances such as (9), even when intended as existentials by adults, would first be interpreted by children as deictics. Such utterances, in fact, provide an opportunity for children to ground the existential in the deictic, since they present the basic meaning and structure of the existential in a context that can easily be associated with the already-mastered deictic. Recalling Figure 2, we can represent this situation graphically as follows:

Pointing-out situations   Existence-informing situations

Overlap situations:
Informing of existence
by pointing out.

Figure 3

8. Child Language Data

This section presents child language data supporting the claim that children base the central existential construction on the central deictic.

8.1 Predictions

If indeed children base the existential construction initially on their experiences with overlap utterances construed as deictics, the following things should be true:

1. Children must learn deictics before existentials.
2. Children should be exposed to and produce numerous overlap utterances before producing obvious existentials.

8.2 Data Sources

To find data bearing on these predictions, I examined the following corpora from the CHILDES archive (see MacWhinney 1995):

Brown corpus (Brown 1973)
child: Adam
age range: 2;3 - 4;10

Clark corpus (Clark 1982)
child: Shem
age range: 2;2 - 3;2

Sachs corpus (Sachs 1983)
child: Naomi
age range: 1;1 - 5;1

8.3 Utterances by the Children

Table 1 shows the stages exhibited by all three children in their uses of *there*-constructions. In confirmation of the first prediction above, they all begin using *there* as a deictic locative (Stage 1). Some initially use it only in clause-final position, but eventually all start using it in the clause-initial position characteristic of the deictic construction. At this stage (Stage 2), utterances are difficult to classify as deictic or existential, since deictics with indefinite NPs can serve an existence-informing function as well as a pointing-out function. However, what is striking about these utterances is that none are unmistakably existential in meaning — all could plausibly be analyzed as deictics. For that reason they can be considered overlap utterances. Since they so strongly resemble deictics and allow deictic interpretations, it is not unreasonable to assume that they are deictics from the children's point of view, since no independent evidence for mastery of the existential appears at this stage for any of the children. Finally, at Stage 3, the children produce existentials with properties that are incompatible with a deictic meaning. These provide the first convincing evidence that the children have truly mastered the existential construction.

Table 1: Stages in Deictic Uses Leading to Existentials

Stage 1: *there* used as a deictic locative in initial and final position

There lion.	Adam 2;4.15
You standing in there.	Naomi 2;2.0
Tower right there.	Shem 2;2.16

Stage 2: overlap deictics (with indefinite NPs and final phrases)

There factory right there.	Adam 2;6.17
There's one for you.	Adam 2;9.18
There's a lollipop right there.	Naomi 2;4.30
There's cup for Mom.	Naomi 2;5.8
There's a radio over there.	Shem 2;2.16
There's somebody going the scales.	Shem 2;3.8

Stage 3: first existentials incompatible with deictic interpretation

Where there's a heel?	Adam 3;2.9
Are there more down there?	Adam 3;4.18
There was a big kangaroo.	Naomi 2;9.9

Tables 2-4 show, for each child, selected uses of *there*-constructions, focusing on overlap uses (in boldface), leading up to the first clear existentials (underlined). The existentials are characterized by the presence of some property that is incompatible with deictic semantics: embedding, negation, etc. Notice that the second prediction is borne out: all three children produce overlap utterances before producing unmistakable existentials.

Table 2: Selected Utterances by Adam Leading to First Existentials

There factory right there.	**2;6.17**
There Jiminy Cricket there.	2;6.17
There's one for you.	**2;9.18**
There another one.	**3;0.25**
<u>Where there's a heel?</u>	<u>3;2.9</u>
There's some meat in there.	**3;2.9**
There's another snake.	**3;4.1**
<u>Are there more down in there?</u>	<u>3;4.18</u>

Table 3: Selected Utterances by Naomi Leading to First Existentials

There some for Mommy.	**2;0.18**
There's a lollipop right there.	**2;4.30**
There is Susie right there.	2;5.8
There's cup for Mom.	**2;5.8**
There's a fox in the box.	**2;5.8**
And there's more electricity.	**2;7.16**
There's some more books xx.	**2;8.14**
<u>There was a big kangaroo.</u>	<u>2;9.9</u>
<u>There's not enough room.</u>	<u>2;11.13</u>
<u>...because there's two Erics.</u>	<u>3;3.27</u>
<u>Sometimes there's three Erics.</u>	<u>3;3.27</u>

Table 4: Selected Utterances by Shem Leading to First Existentials

There's a radio over there!	**2;2.16**
There's food by the 'frigerator.	**2;3.2**
There's somebody...going the scales.	**2;3.8**
Outside outside there's blocks.	**2;4.4**
<u>There wind anymore?</u>	<u>2;4.25</u>
<u>There no wind anymore?</u>	<u>2;4.25</u>
There something in there.	**2;4.25**
<u>There's no workies.</u>	<u>2;5.16</u>
There is a hole to go in and out.	**2;5.23**
There's paint up there.	**2;5.30**
There's tennis racquet there.	**2;6.6**
There's an apple on there.	**2;6.27/8**
There's a palm tree here.	**2;6.27/8**
There's a snake there.	**2;6.27/8**
There is two.	**2;7.10**
<u>There is no mouth.</u>	<u>2;7.18</u>

These data support the constructional grounding analysis of the relation between deictics and existentials in child language, suggesting that children use the existence-informing function served by overlap utterances to form their first hypotheses about the existential construction. Recalling Figure 1, we can represent the process they might go through in the following way:

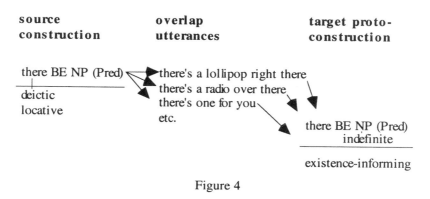

Figure 4

The value of this learning strategy lies in the way it allows children to associate a relatively abstract constructional meaning with a specific, familiar constructional form. By treating overlap utterances as deictics, children are able to activate a constructional form that they have already learned and readily assign an interpretation to it. Happily, this interpretation often implies the new constructional meaning that children need to master---that of the existential.

9. The Significance of Constructional Grounding

Part of the value of constructional grounding is that it allows us to reconcile the notion of motivation with the fact that constructions have arbitrary properties. In the scenario sketched out above, it is both the case that the deictic motivates the existential in the acquisition process, and that the existential has properties which may have nothing to do with the deictic. These properties, it is hypothesized, are learned only after the child has taken advantage of the motivating properties of the deictic construction.

This kind of motivation differs from that normally discussed in cognitive linguistics and in fact in all kinds of synchronic studies. As a matter of course it is assumed that motivation, if it exists at all, is to be captured as a property of a static synchronic system. In cases in which two constructions are closely parallel but also have incompatible properties, this assumption only leaves a few choices: (1) The shared properties can be extracted from the two constructions and attributed to some abstract construction that is never instantiated independently. (2) The constructions can be related by some principle that accounts for the ways in which they differ. (3) The constructions can be treated as two distinct and arbitrary form-meaning pairings whose resemblance is "purely historical" (or simply coincidental). Choices (1) and (2) treat the relation between constructions as a synchronic fact, and choice (3) treats it as a historical relic.

Constructional grounding differs from all these choices, allowing us to avoid making an either/or decision between a synchronic and a diachronic explanation. Note that the process of constructional grounding, as it has been described, closely resembles the process of reanalysis which leads to new signs historically (see, e.g., Traugott 1988). That is, source constructions are analogous to historically prior ones, overlap contexts to those contexts in which constructions are reanalyzed, and target constructions to the constructions that result from historical change. It is likely that all the constructions that are related by constructional grounding are also related through historical reanalysis. The conditions that would naturally result from reanalysis would also be perfect for constructional grounding.

To see this point, consider the historical scenario: Speakers assign a new meaning to a construction as it is instantiated in a particular context. Once this new construction is conventionalized, the first generation to use it would be likely to use it in contexts similar to the ones it started out in—that is, in contexts in which it closely resembles or overlaps with the construction from which it emerged (which we would expect to still be in existence). Thus, they would be likely to reproduce overlap utterances for the benefit of the following generation. These learners would be likely to use these overlap utterances to learn the new construction, associating the new construction with the one from which it emerged, and so on. New properties might be added to either construction over time, but these properties could be the result of pressures on adult-to-adult communication and not be prevalent in child-directed speech. Constructional grounding could in that case continue to relate constructions even after they have diverged from one another historically.

References

Brown, Roger. 1973. *A First Language: The Early Stages*. Dordrecht: Kluwer.

Clark, Eve V. 1982. The Young Word Maker: A Case Study of Lexical Innovation in the Child's Lexicon, in E. Wanner and L. R. Gleitman, eds., *Language Acquisition: The State of the Art*. Cambridge University Press.

Grady, Joseph. 1997. *Foundations of Meaning: Primary Metaphor and Primary Scenes*. Doctoral dissertation, Linguistics, University of California, Berkeley.

Grady, Joseph and Christopher Johnson. 2000. Converging Evidence for the Notions of Subscene and Primary Scene. *Proceedings of the 23rd Annual Meeting of the Berkeley Linguistics Society*. Berkeley, CA: Berkeley Linguistics Society.

Johnson, Christopher. 1997a. The Acquisition of the "What's X doing Y?" Construction, in E. Hughes, M. Hughes, and A. Greenhill, eds., *Proceedings of the 21ˢᵗ Annual Boston University Conference on Language Development, Vol. 2.* Somerville, MA: Cascadilla Press.

Johnson, Christopher. 1997b. Learnability in the Acquisition of Multiple Senses: Source Reconsidered. *Proceedings of the 22ⁿᵈ Annual Meeting of the Berkeley Linguistics Society.* Berkeley, CA: Berkeley Linguistics Society.

Johnson, Christopher. 1999a. *Metaphor vs. Conflation in the Acquisition of Polysemy: The Case of* see, in M. K. Hiraga, C. Sinha, and S. Wilcox, eds., *Cultural, Typological and Psychological Perspectives in Cognitive Linguistics.* Amsterdam: Benjamins.

Johnson, Christopher. 1999b. *Constructional Grounding: The Role of Interpretational Overlap in Lexical and Constructional Acquisition.* Doctoral dissertation, Linguistics, University of California, Berkeley.

Kay, Paul and Charles J. Fillmore. 1999. Grammatical Constructions and Linguistic Generalizations: The *What's X doing Y?* Construction. *Language* 75:1.1–33.

Lakoff, George. 1987. *Women, Fire, and Dangerous Things: What Categories Reveal about the Mind.* Chicago: University of Chicago Press.

Lakoff, George and Mark Johnson. 1980. *Metaphors We Live By.* Chicago: University of Chicago Press.

MacWhinney, Brian. 1995. *The CHILDES Project: Tools for Analyzing Talk.* Hillsdale, NJ: Erlbaum.

Michaelis, Laura A. 1994. A Case of Constructional Polysemy in Latin. *Studies in Language* 18:45–70.

Norvig, Peter. 1988. Interpretation under Ambiguity. *Proceedings of the 14ᵗʰ Annual Meeting of the Berkeley Linguistics Society.* Berkeley Linguistics Society.

Rosch, Eleanor. 1978. Human Categorization, in N. Warren, ed., *Studies in Cross-Cultural Psychology* 1:4.1–49.

Sachs, J. 1983. Talking about the There and Then: The Emergence of Displaced Reference in Parent-Child Discourse, in K. E. Nelson, ed., *Children's Language, Vol. 4.* Hillsdale, NJ: Erlbaum.

Sweetser, Eve E. 1990. *From Etymology to Pragmatics: Metaphorical and Cultural Aspects of Semantic Structure.* Cambridge Studies in Linguistics 54. Cambridge University Press.

Traugott, Elizabeth C. 1988. Pragmatic Strengthening and Grammaticalization. *Proceedings of the 14ᵗʰ Annual Meeting of the Berkeley Linguistics Society.*

What WH Means

RONALD W. LANGACKER

University of California, San Diego

A basic claim of *cognitive grammar* is that lexicon, morphology, and syntax form a continuum consisting solely of assemblies of *symbolic structures* (pairings between semantic and phonological structures). It follows that all valid grammatical constructs, and especially grammatical morphemes, must be attributed some kind of semantic value. Over the years, meanings have been proposed and justified for numerous grammatical morphemes (see, for example, Langacker 1987a; 1988; 1990; 1991; 1992; 1993). One of the hardest cases is the English WH formative. This paper is a first attempt to elucidate its conceptual structure using the descriptive apparatus of cognitive semantics.

Let me start with some basic observations that an adequate characterization ought to accommodate. The first is the banal observation that WH occurs in both question words and relative pronouns. The inventories of question words and relative pronouns are by no means identical, nor can question and relative constructions be fully assimilated to one another (e.g. relative pronouns prepose obligatorily, question words only optionally). Yet the number of elements having both relative and interrogative functions—*who, whom, whose, which, when, where, why*—strongly suggests a connection, as does the intuition that both questions and relatives involve selection from a range of alternatives. Thus, while I would not claim that WH has precisely the same meaning in questions and in relatives, the two senses must at least be related.

Reinforcing this conclusion is the second observation, namely that question and relative constructions each have a secondary use in which they display the other's primary meaning. On the one hand, an interrogative

Conceptual and Discourse Factors in Linguistic Structure.
Alan Cienki, Barbara J. Luka and Michael B. Smith (eds.).
Copyright © 2001, CSLI Publications.

clause can be used as a "free relative" that refers to a clausal participant, as in (1).

(1)   a.   Who steals my purse steals trash.

      b.   What he bought her is quite inexpensive.

      c.   Where they live is still largely unpopulated.

On the other hand, a relative clause construction can have the semantic value of a "concealed question", as in (2).

(2)   a.   They wouldn't tell me the person who did it.

      b.   We need to find out the place where they keep the explosives.

      c.   I don't know the time when their plane is due in.

A revealing semantic description of WH should explain the ease of this interchange.

A third observation is that there is in addition a non-trivial parallelism between WH words and demonstratives, which also involve selection from a range of alternatives. Pairs of WH and TH forms include the following: *what/that, when/then, where/there, whence/thence, whither/thither*. They are not very numerous, even including the archaisms, and of course *what* and *that* are less alike phonetically than orthographically. Still, the similarities cannot be wholly accidental. And once again we can find corroborating evidence.

Demonstratives have a range of values or uses. Here it is sufficient to make the global distinction between a "strong" use and a "weak" use. A "strong" use is exemplified in (3a). Here a demonstrative—often stressed, and typically accompanied by a pointing gesture—can be solely and directly responsible for singling out the intended referent. By contrast, a "weak" use is unstressed and is not accompanied by physical pointing. As seen in (3b), it is essentially anaphoric, merely referring to a unique element already established in the current discourse situation.

(3)   a.   I want THIS one, not THAT one.   [strong demonstrative]

      b.   He bought a fancy new Porsche. This car impressed everybody.
                                            [weak demonstrative]

There is a basic similarity between strong demonstratives and question words: in a direct question, the question word indicates a request to single out the proper referent, which is just what a strong demonstrative does. (In fact, the answer can take the form of a demonstrative accompanied by a pointing gesture: *Where is it? There.*) There is likewise an obvious resemblance between weak demonstratives and relative pronouns, in that both are anaphoric.

These relationships are summarized in Table 1. Elements in the same row share a component of form, while those in the same column are comparable in function.

	Active singling out	Anaphora
TH	strong demonstratives	weak demonstratives
WH	question words	relative pronouns

Table 1

What all these elements appear to have in common is some general notion of selecting from a range of alternatives. To characterize this common conceptual basis, we first need a notation for a range of alternatives. The one in Figure 1(a) is adopted. I will assume for present purposes that the alternatives are always *things* (as the term is abstractly used in cognitive grammar (Langacker 1987b)), so they are given as circles. To this we add the notion of *mental contact*, for which a dashed arrow is used, as in Figure 1(b). To establish mental contact with some entity is to single it out for individual conscious awareness. Selecting from a range of alternatives involves establishing mental contact with one particular alternative, as shown in Figure 1(c).

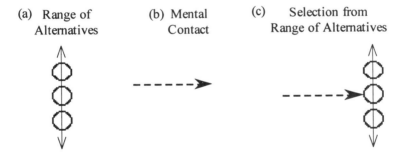

Figure 1

A number of additional notions are needed to characterize and distinguish the elements in Table 1. One of these is *profiling*. An expression can be thought of as an instruction to evoke some array of conceptual content—called its conceptual *base*—and to focus attention on some particular substructure within it. This focused substructure—the *profile*—is the entity the expression is construed as designating (i.e. its referent within the evoked conceptualization). For instance, the expressions *husband* and *wife* have the same conceptual base, namely the conception of a marriage relationship involving a male and a female. As shown in Figure 2, they differ semantically by virtue of profiling—referring to—different substructures within it.

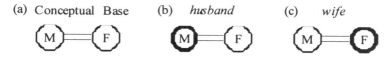

Figure 2

Another relevant notion is what I call the *current discourse space* (CDS): the mental space comprising those elements and relations construed as being shared by the speaker and hearer as a basis for communication at a given moment in the flow of discourse. The current discourse space figures, for example, in the characterization of personal pronouns (for a cognitive grammar description, see van Hoek 1995; 1997; Langacker 1996; 1998). A pronoun refocuses attention on a thing that is already salient in the CDS by virtue of having previously been singled out by the speaker and hearer. In Figure 3, the dotted correspondence line indicates that the two circles stand for the same referent. The dashed arrows represent two episodes of the speaker and hearer establishing mental contact with this referent: a prior episode, making it salient in the CDS, and the current episode serving to refocus attention on it as the pronoun's profile.

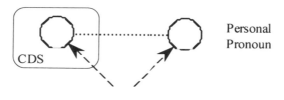

Figure 3

We need one additional notion, namely that of a *reference point relationship* (Langacker 1993). This is a matter of *sequenced mental access*, i.e. of mentally accessing one entity *via* another, which must therefore have some kind of salience or conceptual priority that makes it readily accessible. Establishing mental contact with this more accessible *reference point* (R) enables the conceptualizer to make mental contact with a *target* (T), as shown in Figure 4. A reference point's *dominion* (D) is the set of potential targets that can be accessed through it.

(a) Possessive Construction   (b) Topic Construction

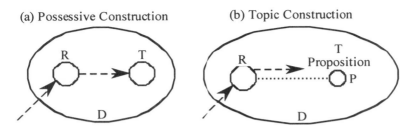

Figure 4

Reference point relationships have myriad linguistic manifestations, involving different kinds of entities as well as different dimensions and levels of language structure. In *metonymy*, an expression's usual referent (its profile) functions as a reference point providing mental access to its intended referent. Van Hoek (1995; 1997) successfully analyzes *pronouns* as targets in the dominion of their antecedents. I have argued elsewhere (1993; 1995) that *possessive constructions* are revealingly characterized in terms of a reference point relation between two things, as seen in Figure 4(a); at the most schematic level, a possessor is a reference point and a possessed entity is a target in its dominion. I have also suggested that a *topic construction* consists of a reference point relationship between a thing and a proposition, as shown in Figure 4(b). A topic's dominion is the domain of knowledge it evokes, and the target is a proposition interpreted with respect to that domain.

Observe that Figure 4(b) includes a thing labeled P, for *pivot*. The pivot in a topic construction is the element within the target proposition that corresponds to the topic. Whether it is central or peripheral to the target proposition, the pivot is the point of contact with the topic and is thus responsible for the coherence of integrating the proposition in the topic's dominion. In (4a), for example, the topic is *that damn cat of yours* and the corresponding pivot is *it*. Note further that the topic and pivot functions are sometimes manifested by a single nominal element. Thus in (4b), preposing indicates that the nominal *that cat* functions as clause-level topic, but it simultaneously serves as pivot by virtue of being the clausal direct object.

(4)   a.   *That damn cat of yours*, I found *it* in my garbage can again.

      b.   *That cat* I really dislike.

The relevance of topic constructions is that a topic-like relationship between a thing and a proposition figures in the characterization of WH forms. Both question words and relative pronouns are integral parts of clauses, and their role in the proposition expressed by the interrogative or relative clause is an inherent and critical aspect of their semantic value. The function of an interrogative or relative clause construction is precisely to single out some entity on the basis of its participation in the clausal relationship. Observe, moreover, that question words and relative pronouns are normally clause-initial, yet directly instantiate a clausal role—e.g. direct object, as in (5)—that would otherwise be expressed by a non-initial element. In this respect they are quite analogous to the preposed topic *that cat* in (4b).

(5)   a.   I wonder [*what* she bought at the auction].

       b.   The urn [*which* she bought at the auction] was full of ashes.

I am *not* claiming that a question word or a relative pronoun is a discourse topic. I am merely suggesting that they are *like* a (clause-internal) topic by virtue of serving as reference point providing mental access to a proposition in which they have some role. In the case of a discourse topic, as in (4), the topic is characterized and its reference determined independently of its role in the target proposition. In fact, the interpretation of the associated clause depends on the topic's identity, which thus has a certain conceptual priority. By contrast, question words and relative pronouns belong to a lower level of organization and their reference is not determined independently of the clause in which they appear. Apart from direct questions (which I will treat as special adaptations), interrogative and relative clauses are subordinate, whereas discourse topics are primarily a main-clause phenomenon. And while I do want to say that question words and relative pronouns have referents, they certainly do not pick out and independently identify a specific, actual individual (as the topics do in (4)). In (5a), the only identification of *what* stems from its role in the interrogative clause, which in that sense might be regarded as conceptually prior. Likewise, *which* in (5b) has no identified referent when considered in isolation. Its role in the relative clause affords a partial characterization, and at a higher level of organization it is specified as being coreferential to the head noun. Yet this is still quite different from a topic nominal, whose reference is established on the basis of its own internal specifications.

It would thus appear that one facet of the characterization of WH resides in selection from a range of alternatives specifically on the basis of participation in a process (eventually identified as the process profiled by the clause in which it appears). This notion is sketched in Figure 5, which can be recognized as a combination of Figures 1(c) and 4(b). WH marks a point of access to the proposition expressed by a clause, and this alternative is itself selected for access precisely because it figures in the proposition. In other words, WH directs attention to an entity whose only distinguishing property is its role as reference point for a clausal proposition.

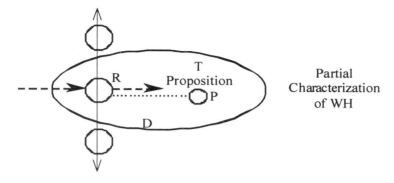

Figure 5

To what extent is the proposition expressed by the clause exclusive to the entity selected by WH? Is that entity the only one (in the range of alternatives being considered) to have that proposition in its dominion? Question words and relative pronouns evidently differ in this regard. With a question, there is some expectation that the answer will specify all the individuals who play the appropriate role in the clausal process. If speaker A poses the question in (6), the response of speaker B is less than fully cooperative if B knows that the urn is only one of several items the subject purchased.

(6)   A: What did she buy?   B: She bought an urn full of ashes.

Such exclusiveness is not however characteristic of WH in relatives. It might at first appear to be; (7a) carries the implication that the student selected on the basis of having cheated on the test is the only one who did so.

(7)   a.   {The/That} student who cheated on the test is here to see you.

       b.   {A/Some} student who cheated on the test is here to see you.

Yet there is no such implication in (7b). The exclusiveness observed in (7a) is actually a function of the contextual uniqueness conveyed by the definite determiner on the head noun. There is of course a presumption that the proposition expressed by the relative is to some extent *distinctive* for members of the class evoked by the head. The examples in (8), where this is not the case, are a bit peculiar:

(8)   a.   ?a rabbit which had a neck

       b.   ?some person who was a human

But this is probably just because no evident communicative function is served by specifying a universally shared property.

We can now attempt to characterize the various elements listed in Table 1. The diagrammatic representations in Figure 6 are offered as a first approximation. In each case the profiled entity is a thing, which is further specified as being selected from a range of alternatives, as well as serving as reference point for a proposition found in its dominion. However the four elements differ in regard to the salience and importance of these further specifications. While serving as point of access to a proposition is essential to question words and relative pronouns, for demonstratives it is non-central and perhaps extrinsic. Similarly, selection from a range of alternatives is central and salient for strong demonstratives and for question words, but fades into the background with weak demonstratives and relative pronouns. These two distinctions, along orthogonal dimensions, produce the array in Table 1.

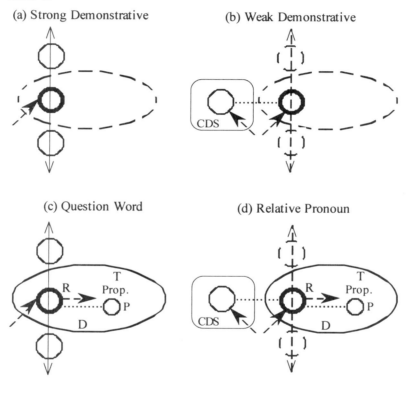

(a) Strong Demonstrative   (b) Weak Demonstrative

(c) Question Word   (d) Relative Pronoun

Figure 6

Let us consider these elements in turn. As shown in Figure 6(a), a strong demonstrative actively singles out one particular thing from a range of evident alternatives. The singling out is often effected by a physical pointing gesture, and phonologically the demonstrative commonly bears focus accent or is at least fully stressed:

(9) a. Give me THAT [☞] one.

   b. THIS car is much sportier than THAT one over there.

   c. Thát dress is much nicer than the others you showed me.

Physical pointing, focus accent, and unreduced stress are all in line with the notion of actively singling out the profiled entity. Contrastive uses, like (9b), explicit comparisons, as in (9c), and the deictic proximal/distal contrast all reflect the centrality of selecting from a range of alternatives. Now there is always some reason for singling out a particular alternative—we do not just point and say *THAT one* for the sheer hell of it. Rather, we single something out in order to say something about it, i.e. to indicate its role in some kind of proposition. For this reason schematic reference to a proposition in the profile's dominion is included in diagram 6(a). We have seen, however, that the profile is singled out (e.g. by pointing) independently of its role in the proposition, which is therefore backgrounded and non-essential to its characterization.

Since a weak demonstrative is basically anaphoric, Figure 6(b) is essentially equivalent to Figure 3, representing a personal pronoun. The profile's status as reference point for a proposition is once again backgrounded, and it is singled out independently of its role in that proposition. The notion of the profile being selected from a range of alternatives is also non-salient. In fact, the demonstrative's anaphoric nature implies that the referent has already been selected, hence is prominent and uniquely identifiable in the current discourse space. It is thus a matter of refocusing attention on an entity already singled out. We can reasonably think of an anaphoric demonstrative as pointing to its referent in the context of the discourse itself (rather than the external circumstances to which the discourse pertains).

Let us turn next to relative pronouns, sketched in Figure 6(d). A relative pronoun is analogous to a weak demonstrative, except that the profile's role in a proposition is salient and essential. Within the relative clause itself, the profile is selected and identified solely by virtue of its role in the proposition expressed. As for a relative pronoun's anaphoric function, the current discourse space is locally construed, being identified as the nominal element that the clause modifies. The referent of this nominal is the salient entity already in the CDS that the relative pronoun profiles and thus establishes once more as a focus of attention. This focusing occurs in the context of a clausal proposition, which is accessed via the focused element.

It is worth pointing out the common co-occurrence of strong demonstratives with modifying clauses containing relative pronouns. The combination *that...[which...]* seems especially well entrenched and is usually more natural than alternatives involving other options for the relative clause:

(10) That urn {which/?that/??∅} she bought is quite ugly.

I suggest that this particular use of the strong demonstrative is one that does exploit the latent reference point function of its profile, which is thus singled out by virtue of its role in the clausal process (rather than independently of it). In the overall nominal construction, the proposition evoked by the demonstrative is put in correspondence with the one inherent in the characterization of the relative pronoun. Likewise, their profiles correspond to one another, since each corresponds to the thing profiled by the head noun.

Strong demonstratives take on a similar value when used in response to questions:

(11)   A: Which urn did she just buy?   B: THAT [☞] one.

Here the latent proposition in the dominion of the demonstrative's profile is equated with the one inherent in the characterization of the question word. Although the profiled entity is singled out and identified independently (e.g. by pointing), its role in the interrogative clause provides the basis for selecting it from a range of alternatives and the reason for putting it in focus. We see, then, that the backgrounded proposition associated with a strong demonstrative has the potential to be specifically evoked and exploited as part of higher-level constructions in grammar and discourse.

Finally, we come to question words, diagrammed in Figure 6(c). Alone among the elements in Table 1, question words render salient both the role of their profile in a clausal proposition and also its selection from a range of alternatives. The former property accounts for their overlap with relative pronouns, and the latter for their parallelism with demonstratives. In a question-answer sequence like (11), both the question word and the demonstrative single out their profile from a range of alternatives on the basis of its participation in the process designated by the interrogative clause. However, participation in this process is the sole basis for characterizing the question word's referent, whereas the demonstrative identifies the referent on independent grounds. In other words, the question word relies on participation in the process for both *selecting* and *describing* its profile. By contrast, the demonstrative *selects* its profile on that basis but *describes* it independently.

I should note that the diagrams in Figure 6, as they stand, do not fully capture this distinction. In particular, diagram (a) does not directly represent the deictic character of a strong demonstrative, its ability to describe and identify its referent through a physical act of pointing or an abstract analog of pointing (notably the proximal/distal contrast). There is also an aspect of diagram (c) that needs elaboration and adjustment. In its present form, this depiction of the WH component of question words is a bit too similar to the one given for relative pronouns in diagram (d). A relative pronoun refers anaphorically to the referent of its head, but a question word does not profile a specific individual.

Another way to see this problem is by observing the ambiguity of the sentences in (12):

(12)   a.   Tell me what Janet told you.

        b.   I can't believe what Janet told me.

    c.   What Janet said is important.

These are ambiguous between an interrogative and a free relative reading. On the interrogative reading, for example, (12b) indicates that the speaker is incredulous that Janet said what she said, while on the free relative reading the speaker simply disbelieves Janet's statement. Similarly, (12c) may indicate that Janet's statement was important (the free relative interpretation), but it can also refer to the importance of determining what it was that she might have said (the interrogative interpretation). There is nothing in Figure 6(c) which captures this distinction.

    I suggest that Figure 6(c) is appropriate for the question words that appear in free relatives. In this use a question word is in fact like a relative pronoun in that it has a specific referent. This referent is simply not identified or characterized other than by its role in the clausal proposition. It is therefore non-anaphoric, and the clause occurs without a nominal head. The clause can however be regarded as a relative clause, in that it constitutes a nominal expression which profiles one of its participants. In a free relative, the full expression adopts as its profile the thing designated by the question word (rather than the process designated by the verb), which makes it nominal despite its clause-like internal structure (it is one kind of "headless relative"). It can therefore function as a subject or object, as seen in (12).

    What about the interrogative interpretation of these clauses? On the interrogative reading they still apparently have a nominal character, since they still function as main-clause subject or object. Moreover, the thing they profile is still the entity designated by the question word. The difference, I suggest, is a matter of what that entity is. The contrast between the free relative and the interrogative variants of WH pertains to the notion of choosing from a range of alternatives: it comes down to whether profiling is conferred on the *entity chosen* or on the *path of choice*. As seen in Figure 6(c), the entity chosen participates directly in the clausal process (it corresponds to the pivot, P); the profiling of that entity is what makes the free relative a kind of relative clause construction. However, the path of choice leading to that entity is not per se a participant in the clausal process. An interrogative clause is therefore not a relative clause construction, since the profile of WH and of the overall expression—namely, the path of choice—is not itself a clausal participant.

    What, then, does it mean to say that the interrogative variant of WH profiles a *path of choice*? I take this notion to be one facet of the conceptualizations evoked by verbs like *choose, select,* and *opt for*. It seems evident that the meaning of a verb like *choose* incorporates the notion of selecting from a range of alternatives. As shown in Figure 7(a), it profiles an act in which the trajector establishes mental contact with a particular entity, the landmark, when other entities could just as well have been singled out in this fashion. At some point in the trajector's mental activity, an array of alternative potential paths of mental access present themselves, one of which is followed to the exclusion of others (the potential paths not actually taken are depicted without arrow heads). I am not necessarily claiming that the spatial metaphor of following a path is anything more than an analytical convenience. Nor am I claiming that the full meaning of *choose*, or of any other such verb, is incorporated in the interrogative sense of WH. I am merely suggesting that, in a suitably abstracted form, a pivotal conceptual component shared by such verbs also figures crucially in the meaning of the WH formative.

(a) *choose*   (b) *choice₁*

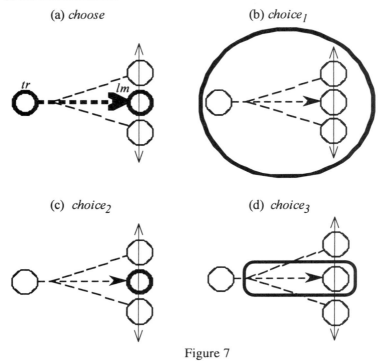

(c) *choice₂*   (d) *choice₃*

Figure 7

Whereas the verb *choose* profiles a process consisting in the trajector's mental action, the derived noun *choice* has three distinct senses obtained by profiling different things involved in that process. The senses diagrammed in Figure 7(b)-(d) are respectively exemplified in (13a-c):

(13)   a.   She only needed a few seconds to make her choice.   [choice₁]

       b.   Her choice turned out to be a competent manager.   [choice₂]

       c.   Her choice is still a secret.   [choice₃]

Choice₁ profiles an event of choosing, i.e. an abstract thing derived by the conceptual reification of an instance of the process *choose*. *Choice₂* profiles the entity chosen, corresponding to the landmark of the process. *Choice₃* profiles the path of choice, which leads to the entity chosen but nevertheless has to be distinguished from it. The thing profiled by *choice₂* may be a physical entity (e.g. a manager), but in any case it exists independently of the act of choosing. By contrast, the thing profiled by *choice₃* inheres in the act of choosing and is necessarily abstract. It represents the conceptual reification of the trajector's course of mental activity viewed in relation to other alternatives.

The distinction between *choice₂* and *choice₃* is reflected in the ambiguity of sentences like (14):

(14)   *We were amazed by her choice for the post.*   [*choice₂* or *choice₃*]

This can either mean that the person chosen amazed us, or else that we were amazed by the fact that she chose the person she did rather than someone else. That this is a true ambiguity is demonstrated by the contrast in (15):

(15)   a.   We were amazed by *her choice. He* impressed us.   [choice₂]

      b.   We were amazed by *her choice. It* impressed us.   [choice₃]

The pronoun *he* refers to the person chosen, while *it* refers to the path of choice.

The semantic distinction between *choice₂* and *choice₃* is directly analogous to the contrast between the free relative and interrogative interpretations of sentences like those in (12). The difference between the free relative and interrogative senses of WH is thus captured by the two profiling options shown in Figures 7(c)-(d). By adopting these alternate profiles, we obtain for WH the two meanings sketched in Figure 8.

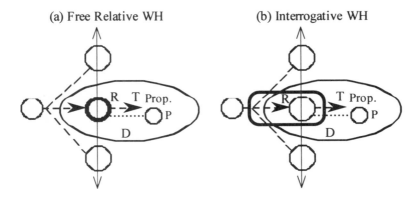

(a) Free Relative WH   (b) Interrogative WH

Figure 8

This analysis accounts straightforwardly for the alternate choice of pronouns in (16):

(16)   a.   *Who(ever) marries her* will have a better wife than *he* deserves.

      b.   We discovered *who stole the money*, and we all found *it* disturbing.

In (16a), the free relative *who(ever)* profiles an individual implicitly selected from a range of alternatives, so the pronoun *he* is appropriate for anaphoric reference. On the other hand, the pronoun *it* occurs in (16b) even though *who* supposedly refers to a person. The proposed analysis explains this by claiming that the interrogative WH (as well as the overall interrogative expression, such as *who stole the money*) designates the path of choice, not the entity chosen by following that path. Although the interrogative *who* does indicate that the entity chosen is a person, it is the path that is profiled rather than the person per se.

Note further that in (16a) the person designated by *who(ever)* participates directly in the clausal process (as the trajector of *marry*). We see this diagrammatically in Figure 8(a), where the profile of WH is itself identified as the pivot for the proposition in its dominion. This configuration—where the profile of a nominal expression is identified as a participant in a clause it contains or comprises—is what makes the free relative a type of relative clause construction. On the other hand, the referent of *who* in (16b) is not a person as such but rather one (arbitrary) path chosen from an array of potential paths each leading to a person. Examination of Figure 8(b) reveals that the profile of WH does not itself participate directly in the clausal process. The interrogative WH profiles an abstract entity, a path of choice, but the individual responsible for stealing the money must be a person. The slight disjunction between the profile of WH and the pivot within the interrogative clause implies that this is not a relative clause construction.

The analysis does however make evident the nature of the affinity between interrogative constructions and relative clause constructions with relative pronouns. As seen in Figure 8, the difference between an interrogative and a free relative reduces to whether profiling falls on the entity chosen or on the path leading to that entity. This is a simple and natural instance of *metonymy*, which in general is just a matter of imposing alternate profiles on the same conceptual base. A comparable metonymy at the level of the head noun (or in the trajector/landmark alignment of the main-clause predicate) accounts for "concealed questions," exemplified in (2).

The proposed analysis also extends naturally to interrogative clauses with *whether*:

(17)   a.   I couldn't determine whether he was telling the truth.

      b.   Whether the bull market will continue through the election could affect its outcome.

Whether is directly analogous to the other question words, sketched in Figure 8(b), except that the entity chosen is not a participant in the clausal proposition, but is rather that proposition itself. It is selected from a range of alternative propositions, typically limited to the one expressed by the clause as well as its negation. Since the interrogative WH profiles the path of choice, an abstract thing, both *whether* and the full subordinate expression are nominal in character, even though the clause *whether* combines with is relational (designating a process). The clause thus nominalized by *whether* can function as either the subject or object in the main clause, as seen in (17). It can also function as the object of a preposition and be referred to anaphorically by the pronoun *it*:

(18)　a.　They argued about whether they could afford a new car.

　　　b.　*Whether she gets the award* is less important than she thinks *it* is.

Moreover, since the entity chosen is a process and not a thing, the analysis correctly predicts that *whether* expressions should lack a free relative interpretation:

(19)　*Whether she got the award surprised me.*

I should conclude by emphasizing the limited nature of what has been attempted here. The discussion was largely confined to elucidating the meaning of WH in English. How much will carry over to other languages remains to be determined. For instance, the relationship between question words and relative pronouns is certainly not universal. Different issues arise, say, in languages where question words are instead based on indefinite pronouns. Even for English, the characterization of WH is only one facet of the overall analysis of relative and interrogative clauses. The proposed semantic value is best understood in the context of a comprehensive description of question words and relative pronouns, the clauses containing them, and interrogative and relative clause constructions as integrated wholes. While I have alluded to various aspects of an overall description, I cannot claim to have worked one out in full detail. Still, I hope to have demonstrated that a characterization along the lines suggested is revealing in regard to both the meaning of WH and its grammatical behavior. Moreover, it requires no theoretical devices or descriptive notions that have not already been advanced and justified on independent grounds. I am sure it is only a first approximation to the meaning of WH, but I have some confidence that it will set the stage for a closer approximation.

References

Langacker, Ronald W. 1987a. *Foundations of Cognitive Grammar*, vol. 1, *Theoretical Prerequisites*. Stanford: Stanford University Press.

Langacker, Ronald W. 1987b. Nouns and Verbs. *Language* 63:53–94.

Langacker, Ronald W. 1988. Autonomy, Agreement, and Cognitive Grammar, in Diane Brentari, Gary Larson, and Lynn MacLeod, eds., *Agreement in Grammatical Theory*, 147–180. Chicago: Chicago Linguistic Society.

Langacker, Ronald W. 1990. *Concept, Image, and Symbol: The Cognitive Basis of Grammar*. Berlin and New York: Mouton de Gruyter. Cognitive Linguistics Research 1.

Langacker, Ronald W. 1991. *Foundations of Cognitive Grammar*, vol. 2, *Descriptive Application*. Stanford: Stanford University Press.

Langacker, Ronald W. 1992. The Symbolic Nature of Cognitive Grammar: The Meaning of *of* and of *of*-Periphrasis, in Martin Pütz, ed., *Thirty Years of Linguistic Evolution: Studies in Honour of René Dirven on the Occasion of his Sixtieth Birthday*, 483–502. Philadelphia and Amsterdam: John Benjamins.

Langacker, Ronald W. 1993. Reference-Point Constructions. *Cognitive Linguistics* 4:1–38.

Langacker, Ronald W. 1995. Possession and Possessive Constructions, in John R. Taylor and Robert E. MacLaury, eds., *Language and the Cognitive Construal of the World*, 51–79. Berlin and New York: Mouton de Gruyter. Trends in Linguistics Studies and Monographs 82.

Langacker, Ronald W. 1996. Conceptual Grouping and Pronominal Anaphora, in Barbara Fox, ed., *Studies in Anaphora*, 333-378. Amsterdam and Philadelphia: John Benjamins. Typological Studies in Language 33.

Langacker, Ronald W. 1998. Grounding, Coding, and Discourse. LAUD Linguistic Agency.

van Hoek, Karen. 1995. Conceptual Reference Points: A Cognitive Grammar Account of Pronominal Anaphora Constraints. *Language* 71:310–340.

van Hoek, Karen. 1997. *Anaphora and Conceptual Structure*. Chicago and London: University of Chicago Press.

Deixis and the FRONT/BACK Opposition in Temporal Metaphors*

KEVIN EZRA MOORE
San Jose State University

1. Introduction

Scholars have long noted that two opposite directions of motion are involved in temporal metaphors (cf. H. Clark 1973; Fleischman 1982; Lakoff and Johnson 1980; McTaggart 1993/1927; Traugott 1975 and references therein). One type construes temporal experience in terms of a person metaphorically moving toward the future. This type is called Moving Ego, and is exemplified in (1a) below. (Note that the meaning of the word *ahead* involves the assumption that its reference point is associated with a mover in some scenario, even if the mover is temporarily at rest (cf. Fillmore 1997/1971:45). In *Atlanta is ahead*, Atlanta is the figure (F), or entity whose location is being determined, and the speaker's (changing) location is the reference point (RP) relative to which the location of the figure is determined.)

(1) a. *I hope we get a chance to meet in the weeks ahead.* (Moving Ego)

* I heartily thank these people for their help: I. Bâ, B. Bergen, H. Clark, K. Diop, M. Emanation, J. Grady, Y. Hasegawa, Y. Hirose, C. Johnson, J. Jóob, K. Kinjo, G. Lakoff, L. Niang, K. H. Ohara, J. Patent, P. K. Radetzky, D. Slobin, P. A. Sow, E. Sweetser, E. Traugott, and two anonymous reviewers. The issues in this paper are also treated in Moore 2000. Author's email: moore@socrates.berkeley.edu

Conceptual and Discourse Factors in Linguistic Structure.
Alan Cienki, Barbara J. Luka and Michael Smith (eds.).

153

There are also metaphors that construe points or periods of time as moving with respect to a person (whom I'll call *Ego*). These are Moving Time metaphors, as in (1b) below.

(1)   b.   *I hope we get a chance to meet in the <u>coming</u> weeks.* (Moving Time)

This paper proposes that what has previously been analyzed as a single Moving Time metaphor is actually two metaphors. This has implications for how linguists understand metaphorical mappings and what may be crosslinguistically valid about them. The investigation is situated in the theory of conceptual metaphor following Lakoff and Johnson 1980, 1999; Grady 1997; Yu 1998 and others.

A metaphor in this theory involves correspondences between concepts in different domains. Such correspondences, called *metaphorical mappings*, enable people to talk and think about one kind of experience in terms of another. For example, in the conceptual metaphor UNDERSTANDING AS SEEING, *seeing* corresponds to, or *maps onto*, understanding. By means of this metaphor we can talk about experiences of understanding almost as if they were experiences of seeing and say things like *I <u>see</u> what you mean, That's a <u>clear</u> argument,* or *That reasoning is <u>opaque</u>.* The correspondences involved in this metaphorical mapping are summarized in Table 1 below. The domain from which vocabulary and conceptual structure are taken is called the Source domain, and the domain which is being construed in terms of the Source domain is called the Target domain. Elements of the Source domain are said to map onto ("→") elements of the Target.

Table 1: The UNDERSTANDING AS SEEING mapping.

SOURCE DOMAIN		TARGET DOMAIN
Person who sees	→	Person who understands
Thing seen	→	Thing understood
Aids to seeing	→	Aids to understanding
Impediments to seeing	→	Impediments to understanding

In this paper, we are concerned with the Moving Ego and Moving Time metaphors exemplified in (1), whose mappings are given below.

Table 2: The Moving Ego mapping. (Cf. Lakoff and Johnson 1999.)

SOURCE		TARGET
Ego's "here " (RP).	→	Ego's "now" (RP).
The region in front of Ego.	→	Ego's future.
The region behind Ego.	→	Ego's past.
A location on Ego's path (F).	→	A point or period of time (F).
Ego's arrival at a location.	→	The occurrence of a point or period of time.

The *Ego-centered* Moving Time metaphor in Table 3 below is essentially the same as what is usually called simply Moving Time.

Table 3: The Ego-entered Moving Time mapping. (Cf. Lakoff 1993; Lakoff and Johnson 1999.)

SOURCE		TARGET
Ego's "here " (RP).	→	Ego's "now" (RP).
A moving thing (F).	→	A point or period of time (F).
(Other moving things.)	→	(Other points or periods of time.)
The arrival of a thing at Ego's location.	→	The occurrence of a point or period of time.

2. The Problem: Deixis and Semantic Extension

The facts that I'll be using to argue about metaphor have to do with deixis, which involves linguistic forms that depend crucially on the situation in which they are uttered for their interpretation (Fillmore 1997/1971 and many others). (Research on the relationship between deixis and conceptual metaphor has been done by Bergen and Plauché, this volume; E. Clark 1974; Emanatian 1992; Lakoff 1987; Radden 1996; and Taub 1996.)

I will assume that the deictic properties of a linguistic form will be relevant to how that form undergoes semantic extension, including metaphorical mapping (Bergen and Plauché, this volume). Take for example the sentences in (2a-b) below (Bergen and Plauché, this volume; Lakoff 1987), in which the metaphorical meanings of the words *here* and *there* are related in a principled way to the nonmetaphorical physical-space meanings of the words *here* and *there*:

(2) a. *Here's the opportunity we've been waiting for.*

   b. *There goes our last hope.*

Here in (2a) indicates something that is metaphorically (about to be) in the same place as the speaker. *There* in (2b), on one reading, has to do with an event that is metaphorically not in the same place as the speaker. The contrast between these metaphorical uses of *here* and *there* is thus analogous to what is found in their spatial uses. There is however no metaphorical analogue to locative contrast in the case of existential *there* (2e), which is presumably semantically extended from deictic *there* (2d), (C. Johnson, this volume; Lakoff 1987). (Capitalization in the examples indicates stress.)

(2) c. *HERE's something we can plug the hole with.* (Deictic)

   d. *THERE's something we can plug the hole with.* (Deictic)

   e. *There must be something we can plug the hole with.* (Existential)

The failure of existential *there* to contrast with *here* can be explained if existential *there* involves a mapping of location onto existence (cf. Lakoff 1987). This mapping allows a two-way contrast between existence and non-existence—*there is* vs. *there isn't*. Metaphorically, this contrast corresponds to being located vs. not being located, but the mapping of location *per se* onto existence *per se* does not provide for a distinction between different locations. My assumption is thus that if a deictic expression-type extends semantically, we should be able to give an account of what deixis has to do with the extended meaning. This assumption is consistent with what is known about conceptual metaphor[1]: It has been found that the structure of a Target-domain concept does not differ arbitrarily from that of the Source-domain concept that maps onto it; cf. the invariance principle (e.g., Lakoff 1990, 1993; Turner 1991). We now turn to the specific problem at hand.

Note the deictic contrast between (3a) and (3b) below: In actual discourse, the reference point relative to which the temporal location of *the coming weeks* is understood in (3a) would be Ego's "now." By contrast, the reference point of *the following weeks* in (3b) would have already been established in the context at the moment of speech. While it is possible to use the lexeme *come* deictically to establish "now" as the reference point of a predication, such a deictic use is not available for the lexeme *follow*.

(3)   a.   *I hope we get a chance to meet in the <u>coming</u> weeks.*

        b.   *I hope we get a chance to meet in the <u>following</u> weeks.*

Examples like (3b) are analyzed as instances of Moving Time because they share with (3a) the properties that moving entities map onto points or periods of time, and that entities farther in the direction of motion map onto earlier times. However, despite the similarities, I am arguing that (3a) and (3b) instantiate different (though compatible) mappings.

It has been previously assumed (e.g., Lakoff 1993; Lakoff and Johnson 1999) that the temporal meaning of *follow* in sentences like (3b) is entailed by a mapping like the Ego-centered Moving Time mapping in Table 3. The idea is that times are conceptualized in this mapping as objects that are moving towards Ego—who is facing the future—in such a way that "If time 2 follows time 1, then time 2 is in the future relative to time 1" (Lakoff 1993; cf. Lakoff and Johnson 1999:142-3). This way of integrating *follow* expressions into the Moving Time metaphor accounts correctly for the sequential semantics of *follow* expressions, and of expressions with FRONT or BACK. (Hereafter, these expressions will be referred to collectively as FRONT/BACK expressions.) But this way of integrating FRONT/BACK expressions into the Moving Time metaphor does not account for the fact, observed by Elizabeth Traugott in 1975, that Moving Time FRONT/BACK expressions do not necessarily have anything to do with the deictically rele-

---

[1] Radden 1996 provides evidence involving the verbs *go* and *come* that the assumption is reasonable.

vant concepts *past, present,* or *future.* For example, in order to understand *Dessert follows dinner,* the speaker/hearer does not have to conceptualize dessert as being in the future from the point of view of dinner. *Dessert follows dinner* states a temporal relationship between dinner and dessert that is independent of any particular speech time or point of view.

On Lakoff and Johnson's analysis, it is reasonable to suppose that "The observer's [i.e. *Ego's*][2] location serves as a reference point for the words *preceding* and *following.* Thus the preceding day is in the past and the following day is in the future" (1999:143). However, what serves as a reference point for temporal uses of *following* is a metaphorically moving entity, not Ego's location. This moving entity maps onto a contextually determined time, not onto "now" as experienced by Ego. This is true even if this reference point coincides with the moment of speech, as in (3c) below.[3]

(3)   c.   *This week I'm busy, but I hope we get a chance to meet in the <u>following</u> week.*

In accordance with the nondeictic character of the word *following* observed in (3b) above, *the following week* (i.e. the figure) in (3c) is construed as metaphorically following a particular week (the reference week); it is not construed as following Ego's "now." One indication of this is the fact that Ego's "now" is not construed as metaphorically moving towards a region that corresponds to an earlier time, whereas the mapping of the *follow* relation onto two times by the Moving Time metaphor entails that both times are construed as metaphorically moving in a direction that corresponds to 'earlier'. This analysis is consistent with the Source-domain semantics of *follow,* which denotes a relationship between two moving things in which the figure does not necessarily move relative to the reference point, as in a sentence like *Fido followed Harry down the road.* Contrast this with the semantics of *come,* which denotes a relationship between a moving thing and Ego's location, in which the thing necessarily moves relative to the location, as in a sentence like *Grandma's coming. Come* but not *follow* inherently denotes this kind of dynamic relationship between figure and reference point. Since the reference point of *follow* is not a static location, Ego's location should not be analyzed as the reference point of *follow.*

Let us now turn to a comparison of Moving Ego and Moving Time uses of FRONT/BACK expressions. This comparison will help me make the point that FRONT/BACK Moving Time expressions have no particular tendency to be used deictically.

3. The FRONT/BACK Opposition

Some languages, for example Wolof (Niger-Congo, West Africa), use nouns meaning FRONT or BACK to name temporal relations that are understood according to the Moving Ego metaphor. (On uses of the word *gannaaw*

---

[2] Words in square brackets inside quoted material are my comments.
[3] The seeds of this observation are due to H. Clark 1973 and Traugott 1975.

'back' in Wolof, see Robert 1997.) Moving Ego uses of the Wolof words for 'front' and 'back' are exemplified below. In these uses 'front' is associated with future and 'back' with past. I include a literal translation of the examples in double quotes and an idiomatic English translation in single quotes.[4]

(4) a. *kanam* 'face, front, ahead':

    xaaral   *ba*   *ci*   <u>*kanam*</u>.

    wait:IMPERATIVE TO.THE.POINT.OF LOCPREP <u>ahead</u>

    "Wait until at <u>ahead</u>." 'Wait until <u>later</u>.' (i.e., "later from *now*.")

  b. *gannaaw* 'back':

    bind *nañ*   *ko*   *ci*   *fan yale ci*   <u>*gannaaw*</u>.

    write PERF.3PL 3OBJ LOCPREP day those LOCPREP <u>back</u>

    "They wrote it in those days in <u>back</u>." 'They wrote it a while <u>ago</u>.' (i.e., a while *back*.)

Crucially, Moving Ego uses of *kanam* 'front' and *gannaaw* 'back' tend very strongly to be deictically anchored, as in the examples above.

    Words for FRONT and BACK are appropriately used in Moving Time metaphors because moving things can be talked about has having fronts on the side that is in their direction of motion and backs on the other side (Fillmore 1971/1997). The Japanese nouns *mae* 'front' and *ato* 'space behind a moving entity' are used in accordance with the Moving Time metaphor (Ohara 1991). (Cf. also Hasegawa 1993 on the Moving Time metaphor in Japanese.) For expository purposes, I consistently gloss *mae* as 'front', and *ato* as 'behind', even though the interpretation of the word in the example in question may be temporal rather than spatial.

(5) a. *mae* 'front, ahead' (spatial and temporal example):

    taroo *ga*   *nageta booru wa* *dan* *ga*   *nageta booru yori*

    Taroo NOM threw ball   TOP Dan NOM threw ball   from

    <u>*mae*</u> *ni*   *otita*.

    <u>front</u> LOC fell

    'The ball that Taroo threw fell {<u>ahead of/before</u>} the ball that Dan threw.' (This sentence is ambiguous between a spatial and temporal interpretation. Thanks to Yukio Hirose.)

---

[4] The following abbreviations are used in the glosses of this and subsequent examples. 3 'third person'; ACC 'accusative'; GEN 'genitive'; LOC 'locative'; LOCPREP 'locative preposition'; NOM 'nominative'; OBJ 'object'; PERF 'perfect'; PL 'plural'; TE "verb connector"; TOP 'topic'.

    b. *ato* 'space behind a moving entity':

       syokuzi no   <u>*ato*</u>   *de*   *ha*   *o*   *migaita*

       meal   GEN <u>behind</u> LOC teeth ACC brushed

       "<u>Behind</u> a meal, [I] brushed my teeth." '<u>After</u> a meal, [I] brushed my teeth.' (Thanks to Katsuya Kinjo.)

It is ordinary in Japanese to use *mae* and *ato* without deictic anchoring to talk about sequence. This is similar to the case of English *before* and *after*, which are historically derived from words for 'in front' and 'behind' respectively. (Unlike *follow*, *mae* and *ato* also occur comfortably with deictic anchoring.)

    The generalization I wish to focus on here is that FRONT/BACK Moving Ego expressions have a very strong tendency to be deictically anchored while FRONT/BACK Moving Time expressions have no such tendency. Thus, from a standpoint of deictic considerations, Ego-centered Moving Time has more in common with Moving Ego than it does with FRONT/BACK Moving Time. For example, (1a) and (3a) pick out certain weeks as figure relative to Ego's "now" as reference point, and are rough paraphrases of each other, whereas (3b) picks out the figural weeks relative to some contextually established time and does not necessarily paraphrase the (a) examples (These examples are repeated from above):

(1)   a.   *I hope we get a chance to meet in the weeks <u>ahead</u>.* (Moving Ego)

(3)   a.   *I hope we get a chance to meet in the <u>coming</u> weeks.* (Ego-centered Moving Time)

       b.   *I hope we get a chance to meet in the <u>following</u> weeks.*

       (FRONT/BACK Moving Time)

In discussing correlations between deictic facts and expression type, I will say that the FRONT/BACK Moving Time metaphor is deictically neutral.

4. A Proposed Additional Moving Time Mapping

I propose that the metaphor underlying FRONT/BACK Moving Time expressions is the one depicted in Table 4 below.

Table 4: The FRONT/BACK Moving Time mapping. (Cf. Svorou 1988.) Example: Dessert follows dinner.

SOURCE		TARGET
Moving things.	$\rightarrow$	Points or periods of time.
A thing farther in the direction of motion.	$\rightarrow$	An earlier point or period of time.
A thing less far in the direction of motion.	$\rightarrow$	A later point or period of time.

The essential point on which the FRONT/BACK Moving Time mapping in Table 4 contrasts with the Moving Ego and Ego-centered Moving Time mappings in tables 2 and 3 is that in Table 4, the viewpoint from which motion is observed is not part of the mapping. This correctly predicts that FRONT/BACK Moving Time metaphors denote sequential relations independently of viewpoint. This is a prediction that the Ego-centered mapping in Table 3 does not necessarily make. Before discussing the experiential grounding of the FRONT/BACK Moving Time metaphor, let us discuss a prediction that follows from the mapping in Table 4.

5. FRONT/BACK Expressions and Deixis Crosslinguistically

The mapping in Table 4 predicts a crosslinguistic tendency concerning expressions that mean 'earlier' or 'later' and also FRONT or BACK (or that are derived from expressions meaning FRONT or BACK) and do not require deictic anchoring, i.e., expressions like Japanese *mae* 'front, before', *ato* 'behind, later', or English *before/after*. The prediction is given in (6) below.

(6) a. If a FRONT or BACK expression means (or develops into an expression that means) 'earlier than' or 'later than' and is neutral vis à vis deictic anchoring, FRONT will tend to correspond to 'earlier than' and BACK will tend to correspond to 'later than' (as would be expected if the expressions were motivated by the FRONT/BACK Moving Time metaphor).

b. If a language has an expression which goes counter to the tendency in (a), the more common expression in that language will conform to the tendency.

The reasoning here is based on the assumption that the mappings *FRONT* → *later than* and *BACK* → *earlier than*—the opposite of those involved in the prediction—are experientially grounded in a correlation between Ego's bodily orientation and the order in which Ego encounters entities on a path (Moving Ego), and that this experiential grounding would result in expressions that tend to be deictically anchored. By the same token, expressions which are neutral vis à vis deixis should stem from an experiential grounding and metaphor that do not involve deixis, such as the FRONT/BACK Moving Time metaphor (FRONT — *earlier than*; BACK → *later than*).[5]

The prediction in (6a) is born out by the overwhelming majority of the data of which I am aware. Haspelmath 1997 provides two kinds of evidence that conform to the prediction and no counterexamples. The first kind of evidence involves expressions that synchronically express not only what Haspelmath calls the *anterior* or *posterior* [temporal] semantic functions but also the spatial relations 'in front' or 'behind'. Essentially, *anterior* means

---

[5] I am not claiming that all the expressions are necessarily metaphorical synchronically.

'before' and *posterior* means 'after'. Haspelmath (p. 43) points out that expressions which encode the anterior or posterior function do not depend on deictic anchoring. Haspelmath provides twenty-five anterior/posterior expressions that conform to the prediction; i.e., expressions in which 'front' corresponds to 'earlier than' or 'back' to 'later than'.

The second kind of evidence that Haspelmath provides involves adpositions, which relate figures to reference points regardless of whether or not the reference point is deictically anchored. In addition to data gathered from Haspelmath 1997, data was gathered from Heine et al. 1993, and Svorou 1988. Taken together, these three sources provide thirty-two adpositions that conform to the prediction in (6a). With the addition of the twenty-five expressions from Haspelmath 1997 already mentioned, there is a total of fifty-seven expressions from these three sources, representing a variety of languages, that conform to the prediction, and no counterexamples.

I am aware of two counterexamples to (6a) and none to (6b). One counterexample, from Spanish, is *Del quince para atras hay boletos, pero del quince para adelante, no hay* 'There are tickets available before the fifteenth [lit: "from the fifteenth back"], but not after [lit: "from the fifteenth forward"]'. The other is from Hausa and appears in a 1998 paper by Bernard Caron: *Bà à san àbîn dà ya fàru à gàban rân nan ba.* 'It is not known what happened after that day.' (lit. "in front of"). Spanish has the more usual words *antes* and *despues*, which conform to the prediction; and 'later than' is also expressed in Hausa by the word *baayan* 'behind', which conforms to the prediction: According to Caron, *baayan* 'behind' is more common in Hausa as a way of saying 'after' than *gàban* 'in front of'. (Cf. also Haspelmath 1997:57.)

In summary, the hypothesis that deictically neutral FRONT/BACK expressions with the meanings 'earlier than' or 'later than' are structured by the FRONT/BACK Moving Time metaphor strongly predicts the robust crosslinguistic tendency in these expressions for 'front' to be associated with 'earlier' and 'back' with 'later'. It has been suggested elsewhere that this FRONT=EARLIER/BACK=LATER pairing is due to Moving Time (e.g. Haspelmath 1997). However, in the absence of my hypothesis, we would lack a convincing argument for why the expressions in question should be structured by Moving Time rather than Moving Ego, since Moving Time as previously formulated (= Ego-centered Moving Time) employs Ego as a reference point in essentially the same way as the Moving Ego metaphor does.

6. Experiential Groundings

Since Lakoff and Johnson 1980, experiential groundings have been central to the theory of conceptual metaphor. Joseph Grady (1997) has refocused attention on experiential grounding. Grady emphasizes the importance of cases in which the Source- and Target-domain concepts of a given metaphor can be analyzed as arising from a single scene that is pervasive in experience. The approach that I take here relies heavily on Grady's work, and that of Grady and C. Johnson 1997.

Here is an account of the experiential grounding of the Ego-centered Moving Time metaphor: Someone is moving toward Ego's location, and there is a correlation between Ego's experience of the person's motion and her experience of the time that elapses while the person is moving towards her. When the person arrives where Ego is, Ego experiences that arrival not only as the culmination of a motion event, but also as the occurrence of a previously expected moment of arrival. This scenario thus has salient spatial and temporal dimensions that correlate in experience. Moreover, Ego's location plays a central role as the reference point and the locus of point-of-view relative to which motion events are understood. The Ego-centered Moving Time metaphor thus structures linguistic forms that depict temporal experience as grounded in Ego's "now." These are expressions like *Christmas is coming* and *Christmas is here*. (Cf. Grady 1997, Section 4.3.)

The FRONT/BACK Moving Time mapping in Table 4 has a very different, but equally plausible, experiential grounding. According to Grady 1997, and as exemplified for the Ego-centered mapping above, an experiential grounding should be recurrent in ordinary experience, noteworthy in that people tend to care about the type of experience in question, and it should involve a salient experiential correlation between the Source-domain and Target-domain concepts involved in the metaphor. (Cf. also Lakoff and Johnson 1980.)

The grounding for the FRONT/BACK Moving Time metaphor was originally proposed by Svorou 1988, and hinted at independently by Heine, Claudi, and Hünnemeyer (1991a:66; 1991b). It consists of a scenario in which two or more entities (typically people or animals) are going somewhere. In this scenario, the entity that is *in front* arrives *first*, and the entity that is *behind* arrives *later*. Events of sequential arrival are common, and relevant to people's goals and intentions, for example when competition for resources is involved. Thus, the proposed grounding satisfies Grady's criteria mentioned above.

In this grounding scenario, there is a correlation in experience between position on a path of motion—which can be described with FRONT/BACK expressions—and the order in which events of arrival occur. An example of such a scenario would be a scene that could be described by example (7) below. In example (7), there is a metonymic relation in which position on path stands for sequence of arrival. This metonymy is evidence for the proposed experiential grounding because it demonstrates the salience of the Source-domain concept (which has to do with position) and the Target-domain concept (which has to do with sequence) in a single experience.[6]

---

[6] This raises questions about the notion of *domain*, but space (not to mention time!) does not permit me to deal with them here. On relationships between metaphor and metonymy see Grady 1999, Kövecses and Radden 1998, Moore 2000, authors in Panther and Radden 1999.

That is, (7) simultaneously has a spatial and a temporal interpretation (cf. Emanatian 1992; C. Johnson 1999; Norvig 1988), which are entirely compatible with each other. The two interpretations are: i) 'Pat was ahead (in front) of Kim when Pat got to the office'; and ii) 'Pat got to the office earlier than Kim'. This is a metonymy rather than a metaphor because it involves one aspect of a scenario (the 'ahead/in-front of' relation) standing for another aspect of the same scenario (the 'earlier than' relation). This metonymy highlights a correlation of the sort that has been recognized since Lakoff and Johnson 1980 as relevant to the experiential grounding of metaphor. Cf. also Lakoff and Johnson's (1980) discussion of *experiential gestalts*.

(7)   *Pat got to the office ahead of Kim.*

The next example, from Japanese, is parallel to the previous one, in that the 'ahead/in-front of' relation can be construed as standing metonymically for the 'earlier than' relation. Thus, the metonymic relation just discussed with respect to English in connection with example (7) is plausible for Japanese speakers as well, although not all speakers consulted got a spatial interpretation in addition to the more conventional temporal one. (The variation is indicated by the percent sign in the translation.)

(8)   *pam wa   kim no   mae ni   haitte   itta*

        Pam TOP Kim GEN front DAT enter:TE went

        'Pam went in {before/%ahead of} Kim.'

The above discussion shows that the experiential groundings motivating the two Moving Time metaphors are distinct. The claim that Ego-centered Moving Time and FRONT/BACK Moving Time are different metaphors can be summarized now with an example that focuses on the distinct Target-domain concepts of the two metaphors, comparing the sentence *Christmas is coming* with *New Year's follows Christmas*. In the case of *Christmas is coming* the Target-domain concept involves the expectation that a point or period of time will occur and the feeling that this time is getting more and more immanent. This use of the word *coming* is structured by the Ego-centered Moving Time metaphor. In the case of *New Year's follows Christmas*, the Target-domain concept involves the knowledge that two points or periods of time routinely occur in sequence. This use of *follow* is structured by the FRONT/BACK Moving Time metaphor.

7. Implications for a Theory of Conceptual Metaphor

The theoretical implications of this work have to do with the importance of identifying particular grounding scenarios and the mappings that arise from them, as opposed to an emphasis on the idea that a metaphor is a relationship between domains. This method involving grounding scenarios is

For a recent discussion of the problem of domains in metaphor theory see Engberg-Pedersen 1999; there is some discussion in Moore 2000.

adapted from Grady 1997, and Grady and C. Johnson 1997. My "grounding scenarios" are more or less equivalent to their *primary scenes*.

Consider the notion of *direction of metaphorical motion* in the contrast between Moving Time and Moving Ego metaphors, which is an issue that has received a lot of attention in the literature (e.g. Fleischman 1982). The focus on direction of motion is evident, for example, in Lakoff and Johnson's suggestion that Moving Time and Moving Ego (= *Moving Observer*) are figure-ground reversals of one another (1999:149). The analysis I have presented here shows that FRONT/BACK Moving Time is not a figure-ground reversal of Moving Ego, because the two metaphors involve different kinds of Source-domain relations: In FRONT/BACK Moving Time the relation is between two moving things; in Moving Ego, the relation is between a mover and a location. When the phenomenon being investigated is treated in terms of a mapping from the *domain* of motion to the *domain* of time, the "figure-ground" generalization seems natural because it is natural to think that there is something called *time* that can be construed as either static or moving. However, the current analysis shows that the metaphorical direction of motion of Moving Time has a different (though presumably related) motivation for each kind of Moving Time metaphor. Moreover, on the current analysis, it is not important to identify a concept or domain called *time*.

However, the assumption that there is something called *time* that is philosophically and linguistically relevant is common in the literature (cf. for example Lakoff and Johnson 1999, McTaggart 1993/1927). Lakoff and Johnson (1999) provide an insightful analysis in which they claim that, for English speakers at least, "Time is not conceptualized on its own terms, but rather is conceptualized in significant part metaphorically and metonymically" (ibid: 137). They show that there is a complex variety of literal, metonymic, and metaphoric ways that temporal concepts are structured, and thus that there are various valid construals of time, not all of which are necessarily consistent with each other.

But what I want to call attention to is the implicit assumption, conveyed for example by the way the word *time* is used above, that there is a single entity *time* (that can be construed in a variety of ways). Moreover, it is sometimes assumed that experiences of time essentially involve experiences of "now." Thus, for example, in characterizing the metaphor system for time in English, Lakoff and Johnson (ibid: 140) hypothesize that "The most basic metaphor for time has an observer at the present who is facing toward the future, with the past behind the observer."

What I am claiming is that there is at least one other, equally basic, kind of temporal understanding. This understanding is not based on a salient experience of "now," but rather on an experience of sequence of the sort that I have claimed is involved in the experiential grounding of the FRONT/BACK Moving Time metaphor.

Since there are at least two equally basic kinds of temporal experience that temporal concepts can be based on, it is probably best not to assume that there is a single entity *time* that is fundamental in human conceptual systems. It may be that a tacit assumption that there was a single, fundamental, (Ego-centered) phenomenon *time* obscured the distinction between the Ego-centered and the FRONT/BACK versions of the Moving Time metaphor. Thus, we must be cautious of how our assumptions about the nature of reality can affect our analyses of thought and language.

7.1 Crosslinguistic Validity and a Theory of Metaphor

The superordinate notions *space* and *time* seem to be culturally constructed to a greater degree than the more specific spatial and temporal concepts focused on in this paper. For example, Levinson (1996) supposes that "Probably few languages have lexicalized the abstract superordinate concept 'space' itself in the way that the European ones have (although for the contrary assumption see [Goddard and Wierzbicka 1994])." In support of his opinion, Levinson cites Tzeltal, Guugu Yimithirr, and Arrernte. To these languages can be added Wolof, which also lacks a way of talking about a superordinate concept *time* with native vocabulary. Thus we would not expect metaphorical mappings based on the concepts *space* and *time* to be widespread crosslinguistically. (See Alverson 1994 for the contrary opinion.) Of course, it is well known that many languages have ways of talking about time in terms of space (cf. Heine, Claudi, and Hünnemeyer 1991a). But this last sentence is a generalization expressed in English using English concepts; it does not describe any particular metaphorical mapping. While it is inevitable that we will frame our analyses in our own native concepts, we need to focus attention on exactly what kinds of spatial experiences map onto which kinds of temporal experience in order to understand how and why people tend crosslinguistically to talk about temporal experience with spatial vocabulary.

References

Alverson, Hoyt. 1994. *Semantics and Experience: Universal Metaphors of Time in English, Mandarin, Hindi, and Sesotho*. Baltimore: The Johns Hopkins University Press.

Bergen, Benjamin and Madelaine Plauché. This volume. Voilà *voilà*: Extensions of Deictic Constructions in French.

Caron, Bernard. 1998. From Body to Space and Time: Hausa *gaba* and *baya*. Manuscript. INALCO-LLACAN (MEUDON - FRANCE).

Clark, Eve. 1974. Normal States and Evaluative Viewpoints. *Language* 50:316–332.

Clark, Herbert. 1973. Space, Time, Semantics, and the Child, in T. E. Moore, ed., *Cognitive Development and The Acquisition of Language*. New York: Academic Press.

Emanatian, Michele. 1992. Chagga 'Come' and 'Go': Metaphor and The Development of Tense-Aspect. *Studies in Language* 16:1.1–33.

Engberg-Pedersen, Elisabeth. 1999. Space and Time, in Jens Allwood and Peter Gärdenfors, eds., *Cognitive Semantics: Meaning and Cognition*, 131–152. Amsterdam: John Benjamins.

Fillmore, Charles. 1997/1971. *Lectures on deixis.* Stanford: CSLI Publications.

Fleischman, Suzanne. 1982. The Past and The Future: Are They *Coming* or *Going?* in M. Macaulay, O. Gensler et al., eds., *Proceedings of The Eighth Annual Meeting of The Berkeley Linguistics Society*, 322–334.

Goddard, C. and A. Wierzbicka, eds. 1994. *Semantic and Lexical Universals.* Amsterdam: Benjamins.

Grady, Joseph. 1997. *Foundations of Meaning: Primary Metaphors and Primary Scenes.* Doctoral dissertation, University of California at Berkeley.

Grady, Joseph. 1999. A Typology of Motivation for Conceptual Metaphor: Correlation vs. Resemblance, in Raymond Gibbs and Gerard Steen, eds., *Metaphor in Cognitive Linguistics.* Amsterdam: John Benjamins.

Grady, Joseph and Christopher Johnson. 1997. Converging Evidence for The Notions of *Subscene* and *Primary Scene*, in M. Juge and J. Moxley, eds., *Proceedings of The Twenty-Third Annual Meeting of the Berkeley Linguistics Society.*

Hasegawa, Yoko. 1993. Prototype Semantics: A Case Study of TE K-/IK- Constructions in Japanese. *Language and Communication* 13:1.45–65.

Haspelmath, Martin. 1997. *From Space to Time: Temporal Adverbials in The World's Languages.* München: Lincom Europa.

Heine, Bernd, Ulrike Claudi and Friederike Hünnemeyer. 1991a. *Grammaticalization.* Chicago: The University of Chicago Press.

Heine, Bernd, Ulrike Claudi and Friederike Hünnemeyer. 1991b. From Cognition to Grammar: Evidence from African Languages, in Elizabeth Traugott and Bernd Heine, eds., *Approaches to Grammaticalization.* Amsterdam: John Benjamins (2 Volumes).

Heine, Bernd, Tom Guldemann, Christa Kilian-Hatz, Donald A. Lessau, Heinz Roberg, Mathias Schladt and Thomas Stolz. 1993. *Conceptual Shift: A Lexicon of Grammaticalization Processes in African Languages.* [AAP 34/35 Cologne: Universität zu Köln].

Johnson, Christopher. This volume. Constructional Grounding: On the Relation between Deictic and Existential *there*-Constructions in Acquisition.

Johnson, Christopher. 1999. Metaphor vs. Conflation in The Acquisition of Polysemy: The Case of *see,* in Masako Hiraga, Chris Sinha and Sherman Wilcox, eds., *Cultural, Typological, and Psychological Perspectives in Cognitive Linguistics.* Amsterdam: Benjamins.

Kövecses, Zoltán and Günter Radden. 1998. Metonymy: Developing a Cognitive Linguistic View. *Cognitive Linguistics* 9:1.37–77.

Lakoff, George. 1987. *Women, Fire, and Dangerous Things: What Categories Reveal about The Mind.* Chicago: The University of Chicago Press.

Lakoff, George. 1990. The Invariance Hypothesis: Is Abstract Reason Based on Image Schemas? *Cognitive Linguistics* 1:39–74.

Lakoff, George. 1993. The Contemporary Theory of Metaphor, in A. Ortony, ed., *Metaphor and Thought*. Cambridge: Cambridge University Press. [Second Edition]

Lakoff, George and Mark Johnson. 1980. *Metaphors We Live By*. Chicago: University of Chicago Press.

Lakoff, George and Mark Johnson. 1999. *Philosophy in The Flesh: The Embodied Mind and Its Challenge to Western Thought*. New York: Basic Books.

Levinson, Stephen. 1996. Language and Space. *Annual Review of Anthropology* 25. 353–82.

McTaggart, J.M.E. 1993/1927. The Unreality of Time, in Robin Le Poidevin and Murray MacBeath, eds., *The Philosophy of Time*. Oxford: Oxford University Press.

Moore, Kevin. 2000. *Spatial Experience and Temporal Metaphors in Wolof: Point of View, Conceptual Mapping, and Linguistic Practice*. Doctoral dissertation, University of California at Berkeley.

Norvig, Peter. 1988. Interpretation under Ambiguity, in S. Axmaker, A. Jaisser and H. Singmaster, eds., *Proceedings of The Fourteenth Annual Meeting of The Berkeley Linguistics Society*.

Ohara, Kyoko (Kyoko Hirose Ohara). 1991. Extensions of MAE and SAKI from Space to Time. UC Berkeley: Unpublished.

Panther, Klaus-Uwe and Günter Radden, eds. 1999. *Metonymy in Language and Thought*. Amsterdam: John Benjamins.

Radden, Günter. 1996. Motion Metaphorized: The Case of *Coming* and *Going*, in E. Casad, ed., *Cognitive Linguistics in The Redwoods*. Berlin: Mouton

Robert, Stéphane. 1997. From Body to Argumentation: Grammaticalization as A Fractal Property of Language (The Case of Wolof *ginnaaw*), in A. Bailey, K. Moore and J. Moxley, eds., *Proceedings of The Twenty-Third Annual Meeting of the Berkeley Linguistics Society: Special session on Syntax and Semantics in Africa*.

Svorou, Soteria. 1988. *The Experiential Basis of The Grammar of Space: Evidence from The Languages of The World*. Doctoral dissertation, State University of New York at Buffalo.

Taub, Sarah. 1996. How Productive Are Metaphors? A Close Look at The Participation of A Few Verbs in The STATES ARE LOCATIONS Metaphor (and Others), in Adele Goldberg, ed., *Conceptual Structure, Discourse, and Language*. Palo Alto, CA: CSLI Publications.

Traugott, Elizabeth. 1975. Spatial Expressions of Tense and Temporal Sequencing: A Contribution to The Study of Semantic Fields. *Semiotica* 15: 3.207–230. Berlin: Mouton Publishers.

Turner, Mark. 1991. *Reading Minds: The Study of English in The Age of Cognitive Science*. Princeton: Princeton University Press.

Yu, Ning. 1998. *The Contemporary Theory of Metaphor: A Perspective From Chinese*. Amsterdam: Benjamins.

Linking Early Linguistic and Conceptual Capacities: The Role of Theory of Mind

ANNA PAPAFRAGOU
University of Pennsylvania

1. Introduction[*]

The relationship between language and thought has resurfaced as a vibrant and hotly debated topic in recent research in linguistics, psychology and philosophy of mind. Especially within developmental cognitive science, much experimental and theoretical work has started looking at interrelations between purely linguistic and broader conceptual contributions to the child's growing mental capacities (for an overview of the issues, see Carruthers and Boucher 1998).

One area which seems to set a particularly promising research agenda in linking early language and thought is the ability to attribute to oneself and to others mental representations. This ability, variously referred to as "folk psychology" or "Theory of Mind" (ToM), is responsible for the fact that (normal adult) humans explain people's observable behavior on the basis of underlying mental states such as beliefs, desires, intentions, doubts, ideas,

[*] I wish to thank Kent Bach, Tonia Bleam, Nancy Budwig, Eve Clark, Lila Gleitman, Alison Gopnik, Alan Leslie, Marilyn Shatz, Dan Slobin, Neil Smith, Ursula Stephany, Eve Sweetser, Jill de Villiers, Deirdre Wilson and the two anonymous referees for comments on various aspects of this work. This paper was originally written while the author was at the University of California at Berkeley.

Conceptual and Discourse Factors in Linguistic Structure.
Alan Cienki, Barbara J. Luka and Michael B. Smith (eds.).
Copyright © 2001, CSLI Publications.

and so on. There is by now evidence that the capacity to mentalize is crucial for various early achievements in language acquisition; such achievements include learning the meaning of words (Bloom 1999; Tomasello, Strosberg and Akhtar 1996; Baldwin 1991), grasping opaque reference (de Villiers and Fitneva forthcoming), or mastering communicative skills (Siegal 1996). Recently, several commentators have started exploring the possibility that, inversely, language development may have a causal effect on ToM development (for an overview, see de Villiers 1999).

My primary goal in this paper is to contribute to the growing body of work which suggests that central semantic and pragmatic aspects of language acquisition presuppose ToM development. I focus on two linguistic phenomena, modality and evidentiality, and argue that they implicate sophisticated aspects of ToM. My secondary goal is to address the question of whether language development can affect ToM development and to offer some reasons for being sceptical towards proposals which accept linguistic determinism. Here is how I propose to proceed. In section 2, I start out by presenting some aspects of ToM which will serve as the cognitive backdrop for the linguistic data. In section 3, I present specific arguments to show that both epistemic modals and evidentials involve thoughts about beliefs and that, consequently, their acquisition presupposes advanced ToM abilities. In sections 4 and 5, I critically discuss possible effects of language on ToM and implications for broader issues in the language-thought debate.

2. Developments in ToM

Much current work has shown that children from an early age construe others as having mental states that underlie behavior. For instance, it has been convincingly demonstrated that even 2-year-olds can distinguish between accidental and intentional actions (Tomasello and Kruger 1992), and are sensitive to social cues such as eye gaze in detecting ostensive stimuli (Baldwin 1993). For present purposes, I will concentrate on some more sophisticated aspects of folk psychology (sometimes referred to as "representational theory of mind"; Gopnik and Wellman 1994; Leslie, forthcoming). These mostly involve the ability to appreciate that people stand in different and variable informational relations to the world—hence beliefs can vary, they may occasionally be false, and they are often modified or updated as new evidence becomes available.[1]

The most widely studied aspect of such advanced ToM capacities is false belief understanding. In one of the standard false-belief tests (Wimmer and Perner 1983), a child is shown a character—Maxi, in the original ver-

---

[1] The term "theory" in what follows is not used literally (as in, e.g., Gopnik and Wellman 1994), but only implies a commitment to theory-*like* structures required to represent knowledge in different domains, such as naive biology, naive physics, or naive psychology.

sion—who hides an object in some place and goes away. In his absence, the object is moved to a different location. Maxi comes back. The child is now asked to predict where Maxi will look for the hidden object. In order to answer correctly, the child has to realize that Maxi holds a false belief—that is, he/she has to contrast his/her own understanding of the situation with that of Maxi. This necessitates a more complex step than simply representing the state of affairs in the world: it requires the representation of someone else's (false) representation of reality. In a variation of the "unseen displacement" task, the "unexpected contents" task (Perner, Leekam and Wimmer 1987), the child is shown a familiar container, such as a Smarties box, and is asked to predict the contents of the box. Contrary to expectation, it turns out that the box contains pencils. The child is next asked what a friend who has just come in will think is in the box. Again a correct reply relies on the child's ability to understand false belief in someone else.

It appears that children standardly fail false belief tasks before the age of 4;0 or 5;0. That is, most 3-year-olds respond to both the above tasks on the basis of their own (correct) beliefs. The conclusion that children around the age of 4;0 develop a better understanding of how the mind works is further evidenced by their performance in several related tests. For instance, in the "unexpected contents" experiment, when 3-year-olds are asked what they initially thought was in the box, they reply "pencils" not "candy"; by contrast, children after 4;0 can accurately remember their own previous false beliefs (Gopnik and Slaughter 1991). In a similar way, children after 4;0 begin to appreciate the distinction between appearance and reality (Flavell 1986); for instance, they realise that something may look like a rock but is in reality a sponge.

Even though the period around 4;0-5;0 years has attracted a lot of experimental attention, it is interesting to see what precedes and follows this stage in terms of folk psychological development. Three-year-olds can already draw the distinction between real and mental entities, such as a real and an imagined cookie (Wellman and Estes 1986). They also seem to know more about how desires work than about how beliefs do: for instance, unlike memory of previous false beliefs, 3-year-olds are able to remember their own earlier desires (Gopnik and Slaughter 1991). Moreover, children of this age can reason not only about desires but also about beliefs in order to predict an individual's behavior, provided these beliefs do not contradict the child's beliefs (Wellman and Bartsch 1988). Furthermore, three-year-olds show some appreciation of the link between perception and knowledge. Even though children can show objects to others and then hide them by 2;0, only after 3;0 do they understand that one who looks into a box gets to know what's in the box, and one who doesn't look doesn't know (Hogrefe, Wimmer and Perner 1986).

Still, there are many things that lie beyond the grasp of children of this age. Only after 5;0 years do children understand that people may acquire different information from the same perceptual experience depending on their previous knowledge (Taylor 1988). By 5;0, they can also remember how they found out about a certain fact (i.e. the sources of their information; O'Neill and Gopnik 1991), as well as link specific types of knowledge with the appropriate type of sensory modality (e.g. texture and touching, color and seeing; O'Neill and Astington 1990). After 5;0, children's understanding of the mind progresses in many domains: in knowledge about the mind and brain, in knowledge related to social concepts, such as responsibility and commitment, which depend on multiple embeddings of mental states, etc.

There is some evidence that these developments in folk psychology are reflected in early language. For instance, it has been shown that the uses of mental verbs such as *know, think* and *remember* become more stable and reliable after the third birthday (Shatz, Wellman and Silber 1983). In the next section, I introduce two further classes of linguistic data and argue that they are directly related to sophisticated understanding of the mind.[2]

3. Two Linguistic Case Studies

3.1 Modality

The linguistics literature standardly draws a distinction between *deontic* modality (which deals with obligation, permission, etc.) and *epistemic* modality (which involves inference from known premises). To illustrate, *may, must, should* and *have to* in the examples in (1a)–(4a) express deontic modality, while the same verbs in the examples in (1b)-(4b) are interpreted epistemically:

(1) a. The candidates may leave the room now.

     b. You may be wondering why I disappeared.

(2) a. She must find a way to help her son.

     b. You must be tired.

(3) a. After such a scandal, the mayor should resign.

     b. Looking for "Hamlet"? It should be on the top shelf.

---

[2] It should be noted that the interpretation of the empirical findings on ToM is surrounded by considerable theoretical disagreement. Some researchers take the wide-ranging changes in children's responses in ToM tasks around age 4;0 as evidence for conceptual change (Gopnik and Wellman 1994; Perner 1991); others consider them the result of improvement of independent performance factors (Fodor 1992; Leslie 2000). I take it for granted that, regardless of how theories of ToM turn out, they will have to account for the fact that semantic and pragmatic aspects of language crucially rely on our commonsense knowledge of the mind.

(4)   a.   The authorities have to stop hooliganism.

       b.   You have to be right; you are the expert.

Other non-epistemic modal meanings involve ability (e.g. *can*), intention (e.g. *will*), and so on; for ease of exposition, I am going to group them together with deontic meanings under *root* modality.

According to cross-linguistic longitudinal studies, epistemic modality lags behind root modality in language acquisition. Since in a variety of languages certain modal expressions are capable of communicating either epistemic or root modality on different occasions (cf. the examples in (1)-(4) above), this practically means that such modal terms are initially confined to root interpretations, while their epistemic interpretations are acquired later on.

To take the example of English, the first modals to appear are *can* and *will*, which are first used between 1;10 and 2;6 to communicate ability/permission and "intention"/volition respectively (Shatz and Wilcox 1991; Wells 1979). Later on, *will* extends from volition to prediction and tends to refer to events which lie beyond the child's control, or belong to the distant future. At this stage, *gonna* takes over the space of events in the near future or events that the child can control (Shepherd 1982; Gee and Savasir 1985). By 3;0, *hafta, needta* and *wanna* have appeared with root meanings in child language (Gerhardt 1991). *Could* emerges later than *can* and is used much less frequently for ability and permission; similarly, *may* is used for permission much less frequently than *can* (Wells 1979). *Should, must* and *had better* have root interpretations which are present before 3;6. Epistemic interpretations, by contrast, first appear after 2;6 and have negligible frequencies till about the fourth year, or even later (Kuczaj 1977). Uses of *must* to convey certainty have not yet stabilised at 5;0 years, while the use of modal adverbs and adjectives such as *possibly, necessarily, it is possible/necessary that*, etc. still progresses between 6;0 and 12;0 years (Wells 1985; Perkins 1983).[3]

Similar acquisitional patterns have been observed for other languages:

(a) *German*. According to research reported in Stephany (1993), *wollen* ('will') and *können* ('can') appear before *müssen* ('must') and *sollen* ('should'),and root interpretations generally precede epistemic ones.

(b) *French*. Between the ages of 2;0 and 4;0, root modal utterances are the first to appear and far more frequent than epistemic utterances in Bassano's (1996) study. The first reliable spontaneous epistemic productions

---

[3] For more extensive reviews, see Stephany (1986), Shatz and Wilcox (1991), Papafragou (2000).

appear at 2;3. Until 4;0, there is a steady developmental progression in epistemic interpretations with a sharp increase after 2;8.

(c) *Modern Greek.* The verbs *boro* ('can/may') and *prepi* ('must') are restricted to conveying root modality in children's speech (Stephany 1986; although the main expressions of root modality in early child data are the uses of the subjunctive to convey wish, promise, permission, etc. as well as the imperative). Some epistemic uses of *bori* ('may') are noted after 3;9.

(d) *Polish.* Expressions of root modality in Polish appear before 2;0. Their use becomes more frequent during the third year to communicate obligation/root possibility and prohibition/permission. Epistemic uses of modal verbs appear later, although some epistemic modal particles emerge around 2;0—*chyba* ('probably'), *na pewno* ('for sure'; Smoczynska 1993).

(e) *Antiguan Creole.* Shepherd (1982) reports on uses of modals between 3;2 and 5;0 in this English-based creole spoken in the West Indies. *Mosa* ('must'), which is used exclusively in epistemic environments in adult language, appears initially with deontic meaning; its epistemic interpretation emerges after 5;0. *Go(n)* ('going to') is the form most children used earliest for volition, followed by *kyan* ('can') for ability and permission. Both are in use by 3;0, while *hafu* ('have to') and *mos* ('must') are used for obligation by 3;5. Epistemic uses of *hafu* occur even later.

(f) *Korean.* In the speech of three children time-sampled between roughly 1;8 and 3;0/4;0 years by Choi (1995), there are scarce occurrences of epistemic modal auxiliaries. Of the five epistemic modal auxiliaries in the adult system, only *-na pwa* (indicating inference) appears productively (between 2;8 and 3;0) in the data. By contrast, around the third birthday almost the whole of the root system is in place.

(g) *Mandarin Chinese.* Guo (1994) provides evidence that expressions of volition and ability precede other modal expressions; deontic modality follows, while epistemic modality is acquired still later on.

Although a full explanation of the root-epistemic discrepancy in the acquisition of modality requires reference to a variety of factors (e.g. input, mapping problems, syntactic aspects of modality, etc.), I want to focus on the role of ToM in the acquisition of modal concepts. First, I want to argue that there is an obvious sense in which epistemic modality hinges on metacognition. Second, I wish to point to non-epistemic modal interpretations which involve a considerable degree of mentalizing. I will use English data to illustrate throughout. [4]

Consider what is involved in standard epistemic interpretations of a modal sentence such as (1b). The speaker does not possess adequate information so as to produce a non-modal utterance, such as *You are wondering why I*

---

[4] The arguments in the next paragraphs build on Papafragou (1998a, 1998b).

disappeared. So, after accessing and processing a relevant subset of her beliefs, she draws a conclusion which is supported by the evidence she has, or at least is compatible with it. In (1b), for instance, the speaker presents a conclusion (the embedded clause) which is compatible with the relevant subset of her beliefs (and may turn out to be true). In (2b), the conclusion is entailed by the subset of the speaker's beliefs which bears on it. Therefore, in order for one to master the epistemic interpretations of the English modals, one needs to have a grasp of (a) the inferential component of the modals (broadly, the notions of compatibility and entailment which underlie those of possibility and necessity), and (b) the premises (beliefs) required for the inferencing. Consequently, the successful use and comprehension of epistemic modal operators involves actively considering one's beliefs as representations of reality, as well as assessing their adequacy and accuracy as representational means. These processes jointly presuppose a representational theory of mind.

The first uses of epistemic modals in English coincide with the emergence of mental terms such as *think,* around the second half of the third year. Initially epistemics are probably used as expressions of speaker certainty/uncertainty without a full grasp of their inferential component. This is a simpler process than the attribution of false belief; hence its earlier occurrence in development. After 4;0, expressions of epistemic modality (especially epistemic possibility) become more frequent. According to experimental evidence (Hirst and Weil 1982), children are capable of distinguishing differences in "strength" between epistemic modals by 5;0. For instance, they can recognise that *must* conveys greater speaker certainty than *should* and *should* greater certainty than *may*, whereas a non-modal utterance conveys a higher degree of certainty than epistemic *must*. Still, in order for the full content of an epistemic interpretation to be acquired, the child needs to be in a position to grasp the logical potential of the modals as well as their mentalistic aspects. For instance, the full mastery of epistemic *must* requires mastery of the notion of necessity, a step which is not completed before 11;0 to 12;0 years of age. By that time, the child's use of epistemics has reached the level of adults.[5]

The discussion so far should not be taken to imply that ToM development affects only one side of the root-epistemic distinction. This brings me

---

[5] The use of observational data to motivate the analysis is subject to the caveat that such data suffer from problems of interpretation. Still, the cross-linguistic regularity in the acquisitional pattern of modality offers more than suggestive evidence for the ToM hypothesis for epistemics. An additional piece of evidence comes from recent experimental work: Moore, Pure and Furrow (1990) showed that there is a correlation between the comprehension of the relative "strength" of modals and performance on false-belief, belief change and appearance-reality tasks.

to the second point: mentalizing is subtly implicated in some of the earliest stages of the modal system. Recall that, in language after language, the first modal notions to be expressed in children's speech are (physical) ability and volition. In English, ability in the first uses of *can* does not seem to involve an understanding of the mind but it does depend on an initial conception of the self and of the interaction with the environment. Volition and intention as expressed by *will* rely on the concept of desire (and a family of related states), which has been shown to belong to the active cognitive repertoire of the 2-year-old. Ability and volition/intention at this stage are perceived as simple causal links or forces between the child and the world. Other desire-based predicates such as *wanna* and *needta* also emerge at this period. The child's first deontic expressions appear before or around 3;0. It is worth noticing that *hafta/have (got) to*—the most common means of expressing obligation in early child speech—has predominantly non-performative uses, as evidenced by the fact that it mostly appears in the first person. That is, it is used to state a norm rather than impose an obligation. This is to be expected, since genuine performative deontics involve some consensus on the part of the interlocutors as to social relations, issues of power, authority, duty and commitment, and these are aspects of social cognition which rely heavily on complex attribution of mental states. There is evidence that accurate use of deontics starts around 7;0 years and develops till much later. Among the last members of the modal set to appear are *ought to* and *should*, which probably make heavier demands on representational resources having to do with the domain of ideals and morality.

In sum, then, it appears that modal language is driven to a considerable extent by developments in the employment of ToM. From a cognitive perspective, the root-epistemic discrepancy is linked to the fact that early root interpretations presuppose simpler (or no) conceptions of the mind than early epistemic interpretations.

3.2 Evidentiality

Evidentials broadly involve the speaker's assessment of the propositional content of the utterance in terms of its informational source (memory; observation; communication; inference) and/or the degree of speaker certainty (strong/weak). Some categories of evidentiality, therefore, seem to be particularly good candidates for an analysis in terms of ToM. An apt example comes from evidentials in Turkish. For all past tense expressions in Turkish there is an obligatory choice between two verb suffixes: -*dI* is used if the speaker was an eyewitness to the event; -*mIş* is used if the speaker has only indirectly experienced the event (through hearsay or inference):

(5)   Ahmet gel - di.

      Ahmet come - dI.

      'Ahmet came - dir/exp'

(6)   Ahmet gel - miş.

      Ahmet come - mIş.

      'Ahmet came/ must have come'

(i) inference: The speaker sees Ahmet's coat hanging in the front hall but hasn't seen Ahmet.

(ii) hearsay: The speaker has been told that Ahmet has arrived but hasn't seen Ahmet.

Aksu-Koç (1986) studied the acquisition of these suffixes by Turkish children. In one of her experiments, she showed children from 3;0 years up either illustrated stories in which a target event (e.g., the popping of a balloon) was explicitly shown or a sort of puppet show in which the event was hidden from the child but could be inferred from the perceived outcome of the story (e.g., the popped balloon). She reports that, when asked to relate the story, even children as young as 3;0-3;8 appeared to prefer -dI for directly perceived events and -mIş for inferred events. After 3;8 the reliability of the distinction in child language improved considerably so as not to differ significantly from that achieved by the oldest children in her sample (slightly over 6 years).

To test whether the use of evidentials was accompanied by genuine understanding, Aksu-Koç asked children to judge whether a doll who reported an event using either of the two suffixes had seen the event or was told about it. Performance in this task improved considerably after 4;0 years. Only 3 out of 24 children younger than 4;3 answered correctly, while all but one of the 36 older children passed the test.

It is interesting to interpret these results in light of ToM developments. As mentioned in section 2, one of the characteristics of improved ToM performance around the age of 4;0 is success in recognising the source of one's beliefs. Recall that even though 3-year-olds understand that seeing leads to knowing, they have no deep grasp of the causal relation between them. For instance, if asked to justify how they know what is in a box after having seen the contents, most 3-year-olds fail to answer correctly (their performance is low even if they are explicitly given a forced-choice question). Four-year-olds are successful in the same task. The linguistic data of this section suggest that advances in the child's commonsense theory of belief (which includes information about how beliefs are formed, updated etc.) make possible advances in the acquisition of the semantics of evidential terms.[6]

4. Alternative Hypotheses

So far, I have considered a unidirectional relationship from ToM to aspects of language. In particular, I have drawn a link between language development and the prior development of relevant cognitive resources. At this stage, it is worth asking whether the order of explanation could in some cases be reversed, or whether language development may have an effect on ToM. My purpose in what follows is to propose and examine various ways of construing and answering this question.

There is an obvious way in which language facilitates ToM development since language (linguistic communication) is an important source of information about people's mental states. For instance, verbal expressions of someone's hope, disappointment, surprise, intention and so on, can be instrumental in supporting inferences about underlying cognitive states. What is far more controversial is whether the representational and computational resources provided by language might have substantive effects on developing ToM performance, and, accordingly, what sort of implications such facilitation effects might have for the language-thought issue. Two main possibilities are worth considering.

(a) Development in language may affect the representational resources of ToM.

Different models allow different amounts of linguistic interference with the workings of ToM. On a modular account adopting a ToM mechanism (e.g., along the lines of Leslie 2000), linguistic input can only function as a trigger as far as the representational means available to ToM are concerned. On a "theory theory" account of ToM (Gopnik and Wellman 1994), linguistic input may contribute along other kinds of input to the child's construction of a model of the mind. According to the modular position, language plays a weakly causal role in the development of ToM. By contrast, the "theory theory" view allows for a strongly causal role of language in the acquisition of folk psychology. Within this framework, it is typically held that our understanding of ToM development will crucially depend on our understanding of how this development relates to the development of language (see, e.g., Bartsch and Wellman 1995: 209).

---

[6] It is known, however, that appreciation of inference as a source of knowledge may not appear consistently till after 5;0 years. It would be interesting to pursue the parallel with evidentials in tracing more specific connections between language and folk psychological knowledge.

Notice that the latter account—unlike the former—seems to leave room for the possibility that cross-linguistic differences may give rise to differences in the development of ToM. For instance, according to the "theory theory," it is in principle possible that false-belief reasoning will be enhanced (and possibly developed earlier) in speakers of languages which have specific false-belief terms. Preliminary evidence offered in Shatz, Martinez, Diesendruck, and Akar (in preparation) shows that this is incorrect. More generally, it seems that, even though the "theory theory" account is committed to the existence of a single developmental sequence in ToM development, it can tolerate age differences within that sequence due to linguistic (or other) influences. This position is hard to reconcile with the remarkable uniformity in children's performance in ToM tasks across different communities and languages (see, among others, Avis and Harris 1991). So, even though we still lack conclusive empirical evidence, it seems that the development of ToM is not substantively affected by crosslinguistic differences. This conclusion is in accordance with modular accounts but is unexpected if ToM development is truly equivalent to theory-building.

(b) Development in language may affect the computational efficiency of ToM.

This proposal seems true even though its details remain to be spelled out. In particular, it is reasonable to assume that cognitive mechanisms such as ToM may profit from the computational resources made available by a rich and highly articulated symbolic system such as natural language. For instance, it is possible that the packaging of conceptual material in lexicalised concepts such as *belief, idea, doubt,* and so on, enhances the focus and speed of processing resources and permits subtle distinctions between different mentalistic concepts. The separation of such concepts through linguistic labels arguably helps their stabilization in working memory and enables the mind to isolate and retrieve them in their own right. Beyond the lexical level, it seems plausible that the child relies on language to efficiently and speedily handle the semantic specificity and detail needed to represent embedded propositional attitudes (especially in multiple embeddings of the type "John thinks that Mary suspects that Andy hopes...").[7] Similar "performance" effects of language have been demonstrated in other areas, such as memory for complex or schematic visual

---

[7] It could be argued that the "computational enhancement" view can be taken one step further: the promotion of computational performance through the resources of the linguistic system may be so dramatic as to enable the organism to entertain (and handle) complex forms of mindreading that might have been unattainable without language. It is unclear how this position differs, if at all, from the version in (a).

stimuli (Schooler and Engstler-Schooler 1990; Gentner and Loftus 1979, respectively).

Let me turn to a set of studies which directly addresses the issue of linguistic influence on ToM. Jill de Villiers has argued on syntactic and semantic grounds that the properties of complementation in natural language provide particularly good scaffolding for understanding false belief (de Villiers 1999; de Villiers and de Villiers 2000). One argument offered for this position is that, in complementation, the truth value of the complement is independent of the truth value of the proposition in the main clause (cf. *She says/believes that the earth is flat*). Furthermore, it is argued that sentential complementation mainly occurs with communication and mental state verbs, thus providing a good entry for the child into talk about the mental life of others. In a series of studies, performance on false belief tasks was found to be predictable from knowledge of syntactic complementation; the latter was assessed by preschoolers' spontaneous speech and their ability to correctly interpret complex *wh*-questions in scenarios of the sort in (7):

(7)   The girl saw something funny at a tag sale and paid a dollar for it.
       She thought it was a toy bird but it was really a funny hat.
       What did she think she bought?

One concern raised by these studies is that the metric of mastery of complementation in (7) already involves false belief attribution, albeit of a simpler form than the usual tasks testing false belief understanding. In an extension of these studies, which partly addresses these worries, it was found that oral deaf children are profoundly impaired in false-belief understanding. This finding has been taken as strong support for the position that children are breaking through to ToM reasoning through considerable linguistic anchoring. However, there are still several ways of interpreting the results from oral deaf subjects. De Villiers herself (1999) considers the strong versions of linguistic determinism as summarised in (a), as well as some variants of the position in (b). The data at present do not point to a unique explanation but they open up interesting possibilities for further work.

5. Concluding Remarks

In this paper, I provided some conceptual motivation and a set of suggestive data to support the hypothesis that the acquisition of certain classes of linguistic items (epistemic modals and evidentials) presupposes advancements in ToM. Furthermore, I argued that, so far, there is little evidence for linguistic determinism in ToM development, although a variety of hypotheses about the relation between language development and ToM development are worth exploring further. This way of drawing the connection between language and thought is familiar from a variety of domains beyond folk psychology. For instance, an exactly parallel argument holds in the domain of space, since spatial language is generally considered to depend and draw upon previous advances in spatial cognition. Interestingly, there is no evidence for linguistic determinism in spatial reasoning, despite some recent claims to the contrary (see Li and Gleitman 1999 for some anti-Whorfian arguments).

There is still a lot to be learned about the developmental relationship between language and ToM, and empirical work has just begun in this area. As I argued above, a powerful source of new data will be crosslinguistic differences, which can prove crucial in assessing competing theoretical accounts of mentalizing. Pathological cases, such as oral deaf and autistic individuals, are another important testing ground for establishing the ontogenetic contributions of linguistic and ToM resources. Since linguistic and cognitive factors that are confounded in normal development are disentangled in these cases, data from atypical development are expected to be instrumental in the next stages of research on language and ToM.

References

Aksu-Koç, Ayhan. 1986. *The Acquisition of Aspect and Modality: The Case of Past Reference in Turkish.* Cambridge: Cambridge University Press.

Avis, Jeremy and Paul Harris. 1991. Belief-Desire Reasoning Among Baka Children: Evidence for a Universal Conception of Mind. *Child Development* 62: 460–467.

Baldwin, Dare. 1991. Infants' Contribution to the Achievement of Joint Reference. *Child Development* 62: 875–890.

Baldwin, Dare. 1993. Infants' Ability to Consult the Speaker for Clues to Word Reference. *Journal of Child Language* 20: 395–418.

Bartsch, Karen and Henry Wellman. 1995. Children Talk About the Mind. New York: Oxford University Press.

Bassano, Dominique. 1996. Functional and Formal Constraints on the Emergence of Epistemic Modality: A Longitudinal Study on French. *First Language* 16: 77–113.

Bloom, Paul. 1999. Theories of Word Learning: Rationalist Alternatives to Associationism, in W. Ritchie and T. Bhatia, eds., *Handbook of Child Language Acquisition*, 249–278. San Diego: Academic Press.

Carruthers, Peter and Jill Boucher, eds., 1998. *Language and Thought: Interdisciplinary Themes.* Cambridge: Cambridge University Press.

Choi, Soonja. 1995. The Development of Epistemic Sentence-Ending Modal Forms and Functions in Korean Children, in J. Bybee and S. Fleischman, eds, *Modality in Grammar and Discourse*, 165–204. Amsterdam: Benjamins.

de Villiers, Jill. 1999. Language and Theory of Mind: What Are the Developmental Relationships?, in S. Baron-Cohen, H. Tager-Flusberg and D. Cohen, eds., *Understanding Other Minds: Perspectives From Autism and Developmental Cognitive Neurosciences.* 2nd ed. Oxford: Oxford University Press.

de Villiers, Jill and Peter de Villiers. 2000. Linguistic Determinism and the Understanding of False Beliefs, in P. Mitchell and K. Riggs, eds., *Children's Reasoning and the Mind.* Hove, UK: Psychology Press.

de Villiers, Jill and Stanka Fitneva. 2000. Referential Transparency for Opaque Containers. Under revision.

Flavell, John. 1986. The Development of Children's Knowledge About the Appearance-Reality Distinction. *American Psychologist* 41: 418–425.

Fodor, Jerry. 1992. Discussion: A Theory of the Child's Theory of Mind. *Cognition* 44: 283–296.

Gee, Julie and Iskender Savasir. 1985. On the Use of Will and Gonna: Toward a Description of Activity-Types for Child Language. *Discourse Processes* 8: 143–175.

Gentner, Dedre and Elizabeth Loftus. 1979. Integration of Verbal and Visual Information as Evidenced by Distortions in Picture Memory. *American Journal of Psychology* 92: 363–375.

Gerhardt, Julie. 1998. The Meaning and Use of the Modals HAFTA, NEEDTA and WANNA in Children's Speech. *Journal of Pragmatics* 16: 531–590.

Gopnik, Alison and Virginia Slaughter. 1991. Young Children's Understanding of Changes in Their Mental States. *Child Development* 62: 98–110.

Gopnik, Alison and Henry Wellman. 1994. The Theory Theory, in L. Hirschfeld and S. Gelman, eds., *Mapping the Mind: Domain Specificity in Cognition and Culture*, 257–293. Cambridge: Cambridge University Press.

Guo, Jiansheng. 1994. Social Interaction, Meaning, and Grammatical Form: Children's Development and Use of Modal Auxiliaries in Mandarin Chinese. Doctoral dissertation, University of California at Berkeley.

Hirst, William and Joyce Weil. 1982. Acquisition of Epistemic and Deontic Meaning of Modals. *Journal of Child Language* 9: 659–666.

Hogrefe, Jürgen, Heinz Wimmer and Josef Perner. 1986. Ignorance Versus False Belief: A Developmental Lag in Attribution of Epistemic States. *Child Development* 57: 567–582.

Kuczaj, Stanley. 1977. Old and New Forms, Old and New Meanings: The Form-Function Hypothesis Revisited. Paper presented at the Meeting of the Society for Research on Child Development, New Orleans.

Leslie, Alan. 2000. 'Theory of Mind' as a Mechanism of Selective Attention, in M. Gazzaniga, ed., *The New Cognitive Neurosciences.* 2nd ed. Cambridge, MA: MIT Press.

Leslie, Alan. Forth. How to acquire a 'Representational Theory of Mind', in D. Sperber and S. Davis, eds., *Metarepresentation.* Vancouver Studies in Cognitive Science, Vol. 10. Oxford: Oxford University Press.

Li, Peggy and Lila Gleitman. 1999. Turning the Tables: Language and Spatial Reasoning. Submitted.

Moore, Chris, Kiran Pure and David Furrow. 1990. Children's Understanding of the Modal Expression of Speaker Certainty and Uncertainty and Its Relation to the Development of a Representational Theory of Mind. *Child Development* 61: 722–730.

O'Neill, Daniela and Janet Astington. 1990. Preschoolers' Developing Understanding of the Role Sensory Experiences Play in Knowledge Acquisition. Paper presented at the Annual Meeting of the American Educational Research Association, Boston, MA, April.

O'Neill, Daniela and Alison Gopnik. 1991. Young Children's Ability to Identify the Sources of Their Beliefs. *Developmental Psychology* 27: 390–397.

Papafragou, Anna. 1998a. Modality and the Semantics-Pragmatics Interface. Doctoral dissertation, University of London. To appear from Elsevier Science, Oxford.

Papafragou, Anna. 1998b. The Acquisition of Modality: Implications for Theories of Semantic Representation. *Mind and Language* 13: 370–399.

Papafragou, Anna. 2000. Modality and Theory of Mind: Perspectives From Language Development and Autism, to appear in F. Beukema and S. Barbiers, eds., *Modality in Generative Grammar*. Amsterdam: Benjamins.

Perkins, Mark. 1983. *Modal Expressions in English*. London: Frances Pinter.

Perner, Josef. 1991. *Understanding the Representational Mind*. Cambridge, MA: MIT Press.

Perner, Josef, Sue Leekam and Heinz Wimmer. 1987. Three-year-olds' Difficulty With False Belief: The Case For a Conceptual Deficit. *British Journal of Developmental Psychology* 5: 125–137.

Schooler, Jonathan and Tonya Engstler-Schooler. 1990. Verbal Overshadowing of Visual Memories: Some Things Are Better Left Unsaid. *Cognitive Psychology* 22: 36–71.

Shatz, Marilyn and Sharon Wilcox. 1991. Constraints on the Acquisition of English Modals, in S. Gelman and J. Byrnes, eds., *Perspectives on Language and Thought*, 319–353. Cambridge: Cambridge University Press.

Shatz, Marilyn, Henry Wellman and Sharon Silber. 1983. The Acquisition of Mental Verbs: A Systematic Investigation of the First Reference to Mental State. *Cognition* 14: 301–321.

Shatz, Marilyn, Ivelisse Martinez, Gil Diesendruck and Didar Akar. In preparation. The Influence of Language on Children's Understanding of False Belief.

Shepherd, Susan. 1982. From Deontic to Epistemic: An Analysis of Modals in the History of English, Creoles, and Language Acquisition, in A. Ahlqvist, ed., *Papers from the 5th International Conference on Historical Linguistics*, 316–723. Amsterdam: Benjamins.

Siegal, Michael. 1996. Conversation and Cognition, in R. Gelman and T. Au, eds., *Handbook of Perception and Cognition 13: Perceptual and Cognitive Development*, 243–282. New York: Academic Press.

Smoczynska, Magdalena. 1993. The Acquisition of Polish Modal Verbs, in N. Dittmar and A. Reich, eds., *Modality in Language Acquisition*, 145–169. Berlin: de Gruyter.

Stephany, Ursula. 1986. Modality, in P. Fletcher and M. Garman, eds., *Language Acquisition*, 375–400. Cambridge: Cambridge University Press. (2nd ed.) 1st ed. 1979.

Stephany, Ursula. 1993. Modality in First Language Acquisition: The State of the Art, in N. Dittmar and A. Reich, eds., *Modality in Language Acquisition*, 133–144. Berlin: de Gruyter.

Taylor, Marjorie. 1988. The Development of Children's Understanding of the Seeing-Knowing Distinction, in J. Astington, P. Harris and D. Olson, eds., *Developing Theories of Mind*, 207–225. New York: Cambridge University Press.

Tomasello, Michael and Ann Kruger. 1992. Acquiring Verbs in Ostensive and Non-Ostensive Contexts. *Journal of Child Language* 19: 311–333.

Tomasello, Michael, Randi Strosberg and Nameera Akhtar. 1996. Eighteen-Month-Old Children Learn Words in Non-Ostensive Contexts. *Journal of Child Language* 23: 157–176.

Wellman, Henry and David Estes. 1986. Early Understanding of Mental Entities: A Reexamination of Childhood Realism. *Child Development* 57: 910–923.

Wellman, Henry and Karen Bartsch. 1988. Young Children's Reasoning About Beliefs. *Cognition* 30: 239–277.

Wells, Gordon. 1979. Learning and Using the Auxiliary Verb in English., in V. Lee, ed., *Cognitive Development: Language and Thinking from Birth to Adolescence*, 250–270. London: Croom Helm.

Wells, Gordon. 1985. *Language Development in the Pre-School Years.* Cambridge: Cambridge University Press.

Wimmer, Heinz and Joseph Perner. 1983. Beliefs About Beliefs: Representation and Constraining Function of Wrong Beliefs in Young Children's Understanding of Deception. *Cognition* 13: 103–128.

Copula and Time-Stability

REGINA PUSTET

University of Munich
University of Colorado

1. Introduction

As typological research progresses, many categories of grammar writing long taken for granted lose their reliability. Among those whose universality is controversial in current functionalist analysis are the parts of speech, in particular, noun, verb, and adjective.

One of the structural features that has always served as a basis for determining the patterns of lexical class distinctions in a given language is copula usage. Cross-linguistic variation in this grammatical domain is quite pronounced, and thus offers a major challenge for typology. As will be shown in what follows, common but oversimplifying descriptions such as "the copula occurs with nouns and adjectives but not with verbs" are not an adequate tool for disclosing potential universals in the organization of the lexicon. Linguistic categorization, at least with respect to copula usage, is not necessarily in line with the traditional segmentation of the lexicon into nouns, verbs, and adjectives.

2. Method

This study operates with the following definition of "copula": A copula is a linguistic element which co-occurs with certain lexemes in certain languages when they function as predicate nucleus, and which adds neither lexical nor grammatical meaning to the predicate phrase. By virtue of the criterion of semantic emptiness copulas can be distinguished from auxiliaries and semi-copulas, elements which are similar to copulas in that they act as structural

Conceptual and Discourse Factors in Linguistic Structure.
Alan Cienki, Barbara J. Luka and Michael B. Smith (eds.).
Copyright © 2001, CSLI Publications.

components of predicate phrases, but do not form predicates on their own. Both auxiliaries, such as the English perfect marker *to have*, and semi-copulas, such as the English verb *to feel* (intransitive or "itr."), as in *to feel good*, carry semantic content, while copulas do not. Of course, the possibility that copulas convey some abstract meaning, which cannot be pinned down as easily as the meaning of auxiliaries and semi-copulas, cannot be ruled out. For instance, Langacker (1987:77) assumes that the English copula *to be* is "processual." However, there is a noticeable difference in the degree to which the addition of the copula *to be* on the one hand, and the addition of auxiliaries or semi-copulas to a given lexeme on the other, modifies the meaning of the latter. For the purpose of this study, only elements whose presence does not bring about an explicit alternation of the semantic content of a given lexeme are defined as copulas. Thus, in English, the perfect marker *to have* and the verb *to feel* (itr.) do not qualify as copulas, while the element *to be* does.

In the above definition of "copula" the notion of predicate plays a crucial role. The term "predicate" has received various interpretations in the literature. Within the present study, "predicate" is to be taken as denoting a syntactic function, which contrasts with other syntactic functions such as argument function and attribute function (cf. Croft 1991:67).

In order to assess the full range of copula usage in a given language, extensive lexical samples must be established. The statistics presented in 3.2. comprise between 1300 and 2400 lexical items per language. The major device for gathering data has been a questionnaire of about 2500 English entries. Informants were asked to translate these into their native language, if a native equivalent exists, and to indicate if the respective lexical items do or do not combine with a copula in predicate position. The first step in analyzing such complex samples is structuring them by means of a division into semantic classes. The classification used (cf. appendix 2) has been developed as a byproduct of the process of data compilation. It has been devised primarily for testing the suitability of the most popular current theory on the semantic background of lexical categorization, the time-stability hypothesis, for motivating cross-linguistic diversity in the distribution of copulas. Due to its restricted purpose, it is neither organized hierarchically, nor exhaustive; it merely covers the intransitive section of the questionnaire. No attempt at subclassifying transitive concepts has been made because the lexemic representations of the latter behave uniformly in all the languages for which statistical investigations have been conducted: They always combine with a copula. Further, the classification does not pay any respect to the traditional segmentation of the lexicon into nouns, verbs, and adjectives. As quasi-synonyms such as *fool* vs. *foolish* and *to sleep* vs. *asleep* illustrate, some concept classes are associated with more than one of the traditional parts of speech. According to their overall affiliation with the traditional parts of speech, the classes are specified as comprising nominals only ("N"), nominals and adjectivals ("NA"), adjectivals only ("A"), adjectivals and verbals ("AV"), or verbals only ("V"). Polysemous lexemes receive separate entries in the respective classes they qualify for. Further, abstract nouns, such as English *explosion, love*, and *strength* are systematically excluded from the scope of the investigation. This is mainly because not every language is furnished with abstract nouns; at least, the amount of abstract nouns found in the lexical inventories of different languages may vary considerably. One of the goals of the empirical research conducted here, however, was keeping the lexical samples as homogeneous as possible with respect to the concepts included in them. While a lexical representation of the concept 'big' can be expected to exist in any one language, this is not the case for concepts such as 'explosion', 'love', and 'strength'. Thus, abstract nouns do not make good candidates for inclusion in the list of basic semantic concepts that this study operates with.

A note on terminology: The labels nominal, verbal, and adjectival, which are employed frequently in this study, are to be understood as defined in terms of the ontological classes object/entity, event, and property.

After assigning individual lexemes to the classes listed in appendix 2, the class-internal percentages of lexemes which are compatible with a copula vs. those which are not are calculated for each language. In order to qualify for statistical analysis, a class must contain at least five lexemes. This constraint aims at keeping the language-specific lexeme classes as homogeneous as possible with respect to the amount of lexemes they comprise. In all the languages investigated, most classes contain far more than five lexemes. As a result of this constraint, some of these "minor" semantic classes have to be dropped from the language-specific statistics. In the case of the samples compiled for this particular study, choosing the specific value of five in determining minimum class size seemed most appropriate in the attempt to separate "minor" classes from other classes. On the grounds of their varying statistical inclination towards copula usage the classes can, finally, be ordered hierarchically for each language (cf. appendix 1).

3. The Data

Linguistic elements that serve as copulas may occur with a variety of predicate types. For instance, they combine with existential predicates (*there is coffee in the kitchen*), identificational predicates (*this is John*), locational predicates (*he is in the kitchen*), possessive predicates (*it is mine*), quantificational predicates in which numerals function as predicate nucleus (*there are three (houses etc.)*), and temporal predicates (*it is eight o'clock*). The above predicate types are not dealt with in this study. Only copula usage with ascriptive predicates is investigated, i.e. with predicates whose nucleus consists of a simple noun, adjective, or verb. The English lexemes listed in appendix 2 can be taken as examples of linguistic elements which can be used as the lexical base of ascriptive predicates. The resulting clause types are illustrated by examples (1) to (3).

(1)   this is a house

(2)   the house is big

(3)   the house just collapsed

Likewise, the phenomenon of copula dropping, i.e., the omission of copulas in certain grammatically defined contexts such as present tense, is not focused on explicitly. (For details on copula dropping, cf. Stassen 1994; 1997:62ff.)

It may also be worth noting that elements which are homonymous with copulas often function as full lexemes (e.g., as verbs expressing existence), or as auxiliaries that code grammatical categories such as aspect and voice.

The analyses presented in what follows, as well as the examples which represent the predicate structures found in the languages investigated, derive from consultant work with native speakers, unless otherwise indicated.

3.1. Predicate Structures

3.1.1. German

In German (Indo-European, Central Europe) copula use is obligatory with nominals (cf. example (4)) and adjectivals (cf. example (5)), but it is not admissible with verbals (cf. example (6)).

(4)   das   ist   Salz
       DEM.SG.NOM.NTR   3SG.PRS.IND.COP   salt
       'this is salt'

(5)   das   Haus   ist   klein
       DEF.SG.NOM.NTR   house   3SG.PRS.IND.COP   small
       'the house is small'

(6)   das   Schiff   sink-t
       DEF.SG.NOM.NTR   ship   sink.PRS.IND-3SG
       'the ship is sinking'

3.1.2. Mandarin

With respect to copula usage, Mandarin (Sino-Tibetan, East Asia) differs strongly from Indo-European languages. Roughly, nominals combine with the copula *shi* in predicate position (cf. example (7)), while adjectivals (cf. example (8)) and verbals (cf. example (9)) do not.

(7)   zhe   shi   niao
       DEM.P   COP   bird
       'this is a bird'

(8)   Daming hen gao
        Da-Ming very tall
        'Da-Ming is very tall'

(9)   Daming   zai   paobu
        Da-Ming   IMPF   run
        'Da-Ming is running'

In Mandarin, adjectivals cannot usually be predicated directly, i.e. without the addition of either the particle *hen* (cf. example (8)) or the nominalizer *de*. The basic meaning of *hen* is 'very'. However, in an example such as (8) an intensifying meaning is obtained only when *hen* is stressed. In combination with adjectivals which require its insertion, unstressed *hen* is semantically bleached (Li & Thompson 1981:143f.). Thus, on the basis of the definition of "copula" given in section 2., one might consider the possibility of analyzing *hen* as an element that is grammaticalizing into a copula. Adjectivals which do not require the insertion of *hen* in predicate position have to be nominalized by means of the particle *de* when they function as predicates, and they combine with the copula *shi*, as example (10) illustrates.

(10)   xiedai   shi   song de
        shoestring   COP   loose N
        'the shoestring is loose'

Since the present study aims solely at revealing a potential interdependence of copula usage and intrinsic lexical semantics, *shi - de* adjectivals are excluded from the sample. For a variety of reasons, the nominalizer *de* must be regarded as the trigger for copula use with this group of adjectivals.

It must be pointed out that the above characterization of the situation in Mandarin with respect to copula usage captures only the most basic structures encountered in the language. For instance, any adjectival is — presumably — compatible with the *shi - de* construction, but in combination with adjectivals which normally occur with desemanticized *hen* this construction conveys a pragmatic meaning, such as special emphasis. A lot more could be said about the various functions that the elements *shi*, *de*, and *hen* fulfill when they occur with adjectivals. Nevertheless, there seems to be a fundamental distinction between adjectivals which require the *shi - de* construction when semantically and pragmatically unmarked predicates are to be formed, on the one hand, and adjectivals to which *hen* must be added, on the other.

3.1.3. Lakota

The overall inclination towards copula use is comparatively weak in Lakota (Siouan, Central North America). Ascriptive predicates may require the use of the copula *hécha*. Lakota documents the phenomenon of copula dropping: *Hécha* is always optional in the third person present.

Verbals are incompatible with the copula:

(11) wa-psíce
       1SG-jump
       'I jump'

Adjectivals do not usually combine with the copula:

(12) ma-jíce
       1SG-rich
       'I am rich'

With respect to copula usage, two classes of nouns can be established: With class A copula use is obligatorily (cf. example (13)). With class B the copula is optional (cf. examples (14) and (15)).[1]

(13) Psáloka   he-má-cha
       Crow   S-1SG-COP
       'I am a Crow Indian'

(14) Lakhóta   he-má-cha
       Lakota   S-1SG-COP
       'I am a Lakota'

(15) La-má-khota
       S-1SG-Lakota
       'I am a Lakota'

3.1.4. Japanese

In Japanese (isolate, East Asia) copula use is more pervasive than in Lakota, but less common than in Indo-European languages. The sample is based on colloquial Japanese. Ascriptive predicates may require the presence of the copula *da*. Nominals always combine with the copula in predicate position (cf. example (16)), while verbals never do (cf. example (17)).

(16) Hokkaido   wa   sima   da
       Hokkaido   PB   island COP.NPST
       'Hokkaido is an island'

---

[1] Lexemes with which copula use is optional impair the statistical analysis by blurring the lexical cutoff point between lexemes which combine with copulas and those which do not. In order to avoid this, the class-internal percentages of lexemes with which copula use is optional are split between the lexemes which combine with copulas and those which do not.

(17) Taroo wa tabe-ru
      Taro   PB eat-NPST
      'Taro is eating'

Three formal classes of adjectivals can be posited on the basis of copula usage: With class A copula use is obligatorily (cf. example 18), with class B it is optional (cf. examples (19) and (20)); class C never combines with the copula. Presence vs. absence of the copula does not entail a noticeable change in meaning. Exceptions are cases of metaphorical extension as in example (21); if the adjectival predicate is to be given a metaphorical interpretation, the copula *da* is used. The basic meaning of the adjectival *kuro-* is 'black'. The reading 'guilty' is to be regarded as a derived or secondary meaning.

(18) Tyuugoku wa koodai da
      China   PB huge   COP.NPST
      'China is huge'

(19) sore   wa kuro-i
      DEM.M   PB black-NPST
      'it is black'

(20) sore   wa kuro   da
      DEM.M   PB black COP.NPST
      'it is black'

(21) kare   wa kuro   da
      3SG.MSC PB guilty COP.NPST
      'he is guilty'

3.1.5. Basque

Basque (isolate, Southern Europe) comes very close to the typological extreme of a language which employs copulas with any type of ascriptive predicate. Nominals, adjectivals, and verbals regularly occur with copulas in predicate position — with the sole exception of about three dozen verbals. Basque is furnished with two copulas. Roughly, *izan* covers the intransitive section of the lexicon, i.e. nominals (cf. example (22)), adjectivals (cf. example (23)), and intransitive verbals (cf. example (24)), whereas *ukan* is used with transitive verbals. Some scholars prefer to analyze the copulas *izan* and *ukan* as members of a single morphological paradigm, which amounts to positing a single copular element. *Izan* and *ukan* also function as full verbs. In this context, *izan* is translated as 'to be', while *ukan* is translated as 'to have'.

(22) hura   gizon-a   d-a
      3SG.ABS man-SG.ABS   3SG.ABS-PRS.COP
      'he is a man' (Saltarelli 1988:150)

(23) zakurr-a   beltz-a   d-a
      dog-SG.ABS   black-SG.ABS   3SG.ABS-PRS.COP
      'the dog is black' (Saltarelli 1988:136)

(24) bi   ordu barru   itzuli-ko   n-a-iz
      two hour inside return-FUT   1SG.ABS-PRS-COP
      'I will return in two hours' (Saltarelli 1988:191)

In addition to the above "periphrastic" inflection there exist some relics of an older "synthetic" inflection, which attaches person, number and tense/aspect/mood affixes directly to the predicate nucleus. Synthetic inflection is limited to a set of about three dozen verbals, such as *joan* 'to go' (cf. example (25)).

(25) laku-ra   n-oa
      lake-ALL   1SG.ABS-PRS.go
      'I am going to the lake' (Saltarelli 1988:22)

3.1.6. Tagalog

In contradistinction to the languages discussed so far, Tagalog (Austronesian, Oceania) never employs a copula in predicate formation.

(26) maestro ang lalaki
      teacher F   man
      'the man is a teacher' (Schachter & Otanes 1972:97)

(27) bago   ang   bahay
      new   F   house
      'the house is new' (Schachter & Otanes 1972:64)

(28) nag-hi-hi-lik   ang lolo
      AG.F-S-RED.IMPF-snore   F   grandfather
      'grandfather is snoring' (Schachter & Otanes 1972:69)

3.2. Statistics

As Lakota, Japanese, and Basque illustrate, the cutoff point between lexical items which combine with copulas on the one hand, and those which are incompatible with copulas, on the other, within language-specific lexical inventories does not necessarily coincide with the dividing lines imposed by the traditional segmentation of the lexicon into object, event, and property concepts, alias nouns, verbs, and adjectives. Rather, these cutoff points may cut across the traditional parts of speech. However, as an analytical alternative, the semantic classes listed in appendix 2 can be arranged in scales for each language on the basis of the class-internal ratio of lexemes which combine with copulas vs. those which do not; cf. Appendix 1. (The figures given in the columns marked by "#" indicate the relative rank of the respective classes. The inclination towards copula use increases as the numerical value decreases.) These language-specific hierarchies show pronounced similarities. They yield a crude implicational scale, in which "class X >> class Y" symbolizes: class X employs copulas with equal or higher frequency than class Y.

(29)   noun >> adjective >> verb

4. Conclusions

The following patterns of distribution of lexical items which combine with copulas vs. lexical items which are incompatible with copulas within language-specific lexical inventories are documented by the languages discussed above:

TAGALOG	N		A		V	
LAKOTA	N	N	A		V	
MANDARIN	N		A		V	
JAPANESE	N		A	A	V	
GERMAN	N		A		V	
BASQUE	N		A		V	V

(gray shading = +copula; blank boxes: -copula; N = nominal; A = adjectival; V = verbal)

On the basis of the grammatical descriptions about 150 additional languages, the following distributional profiles can be considered undocumented:

(a) NV: +COP / A: -COP
(b) NV: -COP / A: +COP
(c) NA: -COP / V: +COP
(d) N: -COP / AV: +COP

The fact that the latter patterns do not seem to exist corroborates the validity of the implicational hierarchy posited in (29).

The overall impression to be gained from the study outlined above is that the structural feature of presence vs. absence of copulas does not partition the lexicon randomly. The data support the initially formulated assumption that the time-stability hypothesis, which was first proposed by Givón (1979; 1984)[2] to account for parts-of-speech class differentiations in general, also provides a theoretical model that captures the regularities in cross-linguistic variation within the domain of copula usage. The implicational hierarchy N >> A >> V (cf. (29)) runs parallel to the semantic scale of time-stability. Verbals usually express fleeting events, and nominals designate permanent characteristics or class membership. Prototypical adjectivals like 'red' or 'tall' can be assigned an intermediate time-stability value.

Why do copulas, meaningless "dummy verbs", exist at all? What is the ultimate raison d'être for their systematic distribution in the lexicon? The

---

[2] Also, compare Croft (1991), Pustet (1989), and Stassen (1997), among others.

answer to these final questions is to be sought in the fact that copula usage is tied to the syntactic slot of predicate; but lexical items differ with respect to their inclination to function as predicates. Predication can be said to be most natural for verbals, less natural for adjectivals, and least natural for nominals. The predicate typically is the locus of change in a clause—a low time-stability value warrants high eligibility for predicate function. Further, unnaturalness at the semantic level is concomitant with markedness at the formal level. Thus, copula use can be regarded as a manifestation of the fundamental linguistic principle of markedness.

Acknowledgements

I am indebted to the following persons for language data and/or advice: Gunter Brettschneider, Carlos Búa, Violet Catches, Olga Chapado, Werner Drossard, Juan Gonzales, Akiko Kishimoto, Shou-Hue Kuo, Hsin-Yun Liu, Le-Ning Liu, Johanna Mattissen, Keiko Ono, Florine Red Ear Horse, Norio Shima, and Neva Standing Bear. Special thanks go to Bernard Comrie, Tom Givón, and Michael Noonan for commenting on the original 100-page version of this paper. Any errors are, of course, my responsibility.

Appendix 1: Statistics

	GERMAN			MANDARIN			LAKOTA			JAPANESE		
	#	+cop %	-cop %	#	+cop %	-cop %	#	+cop %	-cop %	#	+cop %	-cop %
action	15	0.0	100	8	0.0	100	15	0.0	100	28	0.0	100
age	1	100	0.0	4	45.5	54.5	7	39.5	60.5	6	89.2	10.8
animate entity	1	100	0.0	1	100	0.0	3	82.5	17.5	1	100	0.0
animate part	1	100	0.0	1	100	0.0	6	50.0	50.0	1	100	0.0
artefact	1	100	0.0	1	100	0.0	4	60.0	40.0	1	100	0.0
body act	13	48.9	51.1	8	0.0	100	15	0.0	100	21	45.6	54.4
body feature	1	100	0.0	5	40.5	59.5	8	26.3	73.7	9	84.4	15.6
carries substance	3	92.9	7.1	8	0.0	100	15	0.0	100	16	71.7	28.3
change of state	15	0.0	100	8	0.0	100	15	0.0	100	28	0.0	100
consistency	1	100	0.0	8	0.0	100	15	0.0	100	13	76.7	23.3
dimension	1	100	0.0	8	0.0	100	15	0.0	100	19	56.8	43.2
emotion	5	88.0	12.0	8	0.0	100	15	0.0	100	20	52.3	47.7
evaluation	1	100	0.0	8	0.0	100	15	0.0	100	11	81.6	18.4
evokes emotion	1	100	0.0	8	0.0	100	--	--	--	18	57.5	42.5
inanimate entity	1	100	0.0	1	100	0.0	5	59.5	40.5	1	100	0.0
intensity	1	100	0.0	--	--	--	--	--	--	22	42.1	57.9
location/position	10	61.1	38.9	8	0.0	100	15	0.0	100	4	90.7	9.3
material	1	100	0.0	--	--	--	--	--	--	1	100	0.0
mental process	15	0.0	100	8	0.0	100	--	--	--	28	0.0	100
mental property	1	100	0.0	8	0.0	100	15	0.0	100	12	77.7	22.3
mental value	1	100	0.0	7	2.4	97.6	--	--	--	8	87.1	12.9
motion	15	0.0	100	8	0.0	100	15	0.0	100	27	21.1	78.9
nationality/race	1	100	0.0	1	100	0.0	2	89.3	10.7	1	100	0.0
natural phenomenon	1	100	0.0	1	100	0.0	12	14.3	85.7	1	100	0.0
personality feature	1	100	0.0	2	56.0	44.0	9	18.9	81.1	2	95.6	4.4
profession	4	90.9	9.1	1	100	0.0	1	90.0	10.0	1	100	0.0
quantity	1	100	0.0	6	20.0	80.0	15	0.0	100	5	90.5	9.5
resemblance	--	--	--	--	--	--	--	--	--	7	87.2	12.8
section of entity	1	100	0.0	1	100	0.0	10	18.2	81.8	1	100	0.0

	GERMAN			MANDARIN			LAKOTA			JAPANESE		
sex	1	100	0.0	1	100	0.0	6	50.0	50.0	1	100	0.0
shape	2	95.7	4.3	3	52.0	48.0	13	7.7	92.3	10	82.5	17.5
smell/taste	8	75.0	25.0	8	0.0	100	15	0.0	100	23	41.2	58.8
social behavior	6	87.1	12.9	8	0.0	100	15	0.0	100	14	73.6	26.4
social relation	1	100	0.0	1	100	0.0	11	15.9	84.1	1	100	0.0
sound	14	12.8	87.2	8	0.0	100	15	0.0	100	26	26.9	73.1
speech	15	0.0	100	8	0.0	100	15	0.0	100	28	0.0	100
speed	11	60.0	40.0	8	0.0	100	15	·0.0	100	17	61.5	38.5
temperature	12	50.0	50.0	8	0.0	100	15	0.0	100	24	33.3	66.7
time	--	--	--	--	--	--	--	--	--	3	93.0	7.0
toponym	1	100	0.0	1	100	0.0	6	50.0	50.0	1	100	0.0
transitive	15	0.0	100	8	0.0	100	15	0.0	100	28	0.0	100
visual property/state	7	80.0	20.0	8	0.0	100	15	0.0	100	15	72.6	27.4
wealth	--	--	--	--	--	--	14	7.2	92.8	1	100	0.0
weather	9	66.7	33.3	8	0.0	100	15	0.0	100	25	28.6	71.4

Appendix 2: Semantic classification (including examples)

action (V): intransitive lexemes which are agentive, controlled, and not included in "mental process", "motion", "social behavior", "sound" and "speech". *to fight, to play, to work.*
age (NA): *new, old, young; adult, baby, boy, child, girl, man, woman.*
animate entity (N): entities which perform cell division, i.e., mainly human beings, animals and plants.
animate part (N): constitutive parts of anything that performs cell division, especially body parts; also plant parts such as *branch, leaf.*
artefact (N): *house, knife, sweater.*
body act (AV): transitory bodily states, sensations and emission processes, i.e. bodily "events" which are low in agency and more or less uncontrolled. *awake, to blush, dizzy, drunk, to faint, healthy, hungry, to itch, to perspire, pregnant, sick, to sleep, tired;* also body sounds which have a tendency to be uncontrolled, as *to breathe, to cough, to hiccup, to pant, to sneeze, to snore, to yawn.*
body feature (NA): permanent physical properties of animates. *bow-legged, color-blind, cripple(d), glutton, left-handed, midget, near-sighted.*
carries substance (A): *dirty, dusty, juicy, moldy, muddy, oily, rusty, smoky, sticky, wet;* concepts referring to the absence of a substance. *clean, clear, dry, pure.*
change of state (V): dynamic intransitive concepts. *to break (itr.), to burst, to congeal, to decay, to explode, to freeze (itr.), to grow (itr.), to harden (itr.), to melt (itr.), to rot, to rust, to shrink (itr.), to swell, to wither, to widen (itr.).*
consistency (A): *brittle, coarse, crisp, crude, elastic, firm, fluffy, fragile, hard, liquid, porous, rough, smooth, soft, solid, tender, tough, viscous.*
dimension (A): *big, broad, deep, high, huge, large, long, low, narrow, shallow, short, small, tall, thick, thin, wide.*
emotion (AV): *afraid, angry, ashamed, bold, courageous, to despair, desperate, enthusiastic, envious, to exult, furious, glad, happy, melancholic, nervous, optimistic, to panic, pessimistic, sad, serious, sullen, to worry.*
evaluation (A): *attractive, bad, beautiful, difficult, easy, excellent, good, gorgeous, noble, perfect, precious, pretty, shabby, ugly.*
evokes emotion (A): *awful, boring, despicable, disgusting, funny, horrible, impressive, miserable, pitiable, poor, ridiculous, scandalous, shocking, terrible.*
toponym (N): *canyon, cliff, hill, mountain, river, sea.*
inanimate entity (N): entity concepts such as *moon, star, stone;* substance concepts such as *clay, earth, iron, oil, rain, sand, snow, water, wood.*
intensity (A): *extreme, fierce, intensive, slight, strong, vehement, weak.*
location/position (AV): *central, distant, to hang (itr.), horizontal, to kneel, to lie, near, parallel, prone, to protrude, to sit, to squat, to stand, upright, vertical.*
material (A): *golden, wooden, woolen.*
mental property (A): *alert, attentive, careful, cautious, clever, crazy, curious, cynical, diligent, forgetful, ingenious, insane, intelligent, naive, negligent, obstinate, sagacious, skeptical, sensible, stupid, untidy, wasteful, wise.*
mental process (V): *to ponder, to think, to dream.*
mental value (A): *certain, cheap, concrete, dangerous, detrimental, direct, dubious, evident, exact, exceptional, expensive, extreme, false, general, guilty, important, innocent, legal, likely, logical, mysterious, necessary, normal, paradox, possible, real, right, safe, secret, simple, special, strange, sufficient, sure, trivial, true, useless, wrong.*
motion (V): *to dance, to dangle, to drive (itr.), to fall, to float, to fly (itr.), to go, to move (itr.), to rise, to run (itr.), to sink, to swim, to walk (itr.).*
nationality/race (NA): *American, French, Frenchman, Italian.*
natural phenomenon (N): non-material entity concepts such as *fire, ghost, lightning, shadow;* also time concepts like *day, evening, morning, night, noon, summer.*
personality feature (NA): *coward, crank, dreamer, genius, gossip, loser, macho, maverick, timid.*

profession (N): *actor, artist, politician, scientist, teacher, thief.*

quantity (A): *all, few, many, much, numerous, several.*

resemblance (AV): *alike, to differ, different, (to) equal, heterogeneous, homogeneous, similar.*

section of entity (N): sections of or formations on entities belonging mainly to the classes "artefact" and "toponym". *bump, center, edge, end, hole, point.*

sex (NA): *boy, female, girl, hermaphrodite, male, man, woman.*

shape (NA): *angular, arch, bent, blunt, circle, circular, cone, concave, conical, cross, cube, cubic, flat, hollow, oval, pointed, round, sharp, straight, triangle, triangular.*

smell/taste (AV): *acidic, bitter, fetid, fragrant, pungent, rancid, salty, to smell (itr.), sour, stale, to stink, sweet, tangy.*

social behavior (AV): *aggressive, arrogant, to brag, brusque, cordial, cruel, faithful, frank, friendly, generous, harsh, honest, humble, jealous, kind, to lie, nasty, obedient, obstinate, opportunistic, polemic, polite, to pout, rebellious, selfish, shy, sincere.*

social relation (N): focal examples: terms of relationship; also: *ally, boss, enemy, foreigner, friend, orphan, widow.*

sound (AV): *to call, to croak, to crunch, to cry, to growl, to hiss, to holler, to howl, to hum, to laugh, loud, to moan, to purr, to rattle, to ring, to rustle, to scream, to shout, silent, to sing, to tinkle, to whisper, to whistle.*

speech (V): *to babble, to speak, to stammer, to talk.*

speed (AV): *fast, to hurry (itr.), slow.*

temperature (AV): *to boil (itr.), to burn (itr.), cold, cool, hot, tepid, warm.*

time (A): *early, late, permanent, recent, simultaneous.*

transitive (V): lexemes which obligatorily require more than one argument. This is, of course, not a conceptual definition of transitivity, but rather, a structural one. Nevertheless, transitivity can be defined at a purely conceptual or semantic level as well (Hopper & Thompson 1980). Structural and semantic transitivity can be expected to correlate (Langacker 1988:99f.), so that structural transitivity can be taken as an indicator of conceptual or semantic transitivity. This treatment of transitivity can be justified by the fact that a structure-based definition of transitivity is very successful in separating lexemes which combine with copulas from those that do not in all the languages investigated in the present study with the sole exception of Basque. As a rule, (structurally) transitive lexemes do not admit copulas. Exceptions are relational nominals such as body parts and terms of relationship. As a consequence, for such lexemes, which require the presence of two arguments when used in predicate position and are therefore transitive, the separate semantic classes "animate part", "section of entity", and "social relation" are established. Thus, "transitive" merely constitutes a default class which is resorted to because it is convenient and very effective in handling part of the bulky data corpus compiled for this study. Typical examples of concepts which tend to be realized as transitive lexemes in the languages investigated -- and, possibly, in any one language -- include *to cut, to hit, to make, to take.*

visual property/state (AV): color terms; also visual impressions like *to blink, to glimmer, to glitter, to glow, iridescent, to radiate, to shine, to sparkle, speckled, striped, transparent.*

wealth (NA): *millionaire, poor, rich.*

weather (AV): *cloudy, foggy, to hail, to rain, rainy, to snow, sultry, sunny, stormy.*

Abbreviations

ABS = absolutive; AG = agent; COP = copula; DEM = demonstrative; ERG = ergative; F = focus; FUT = future; IMPF = imperfective; IND = indicative; M = medial; MSC = masculine; N = nominalizer; NOM = nominative; NPST = non-past; NTR = neuter; P = proximate; PART = particle; PB = predication base; PRS = present; RED = reduplication; S = part of stem; SG = singular

References

Bhat, D.N.S. 1994. *The Adjectival Category*. Amsterdam, Philadelphia: Benjamins.

Bhat, D.N.S. and Regina Pustet. Forthcoming. Adjective., in G. Booij, Ch. Lehmann and J. Mugdan, eds., *Morphology. A Handbook on Inflection and Word Formation*. Berlin, New York: Mouton de Gruyter.

Croft, William. 1991. *Syntactic Categories and Grammatical Relations*. Chicago, London: University of Chicago Press.

Croft, William. 1999. Some Contributions of Typology to Cognitive Linguistics, in T. Janssen and G. Redeker, eds., *Cognitive Linguistics: Foundations, Scope, and Methodology*. Berlin, New York: Mouton de Gruyter.

Dixon, R. M. W. 1977. Where Have All the Adjectives Gone? *Studies in Language* 1:19-80.

Givón, Talmy. 1979. *On Understanding Grammar*. New York etc.: Academic Press.

Givón, Talmy. 1984. *Syntax. A Functional-typological Introduction*. Vol. I. Amsterdam, Philadelphia: Benjamins.

Hashimoto, Anne Yue. 1969. The Verb 'to be' in Modern Mandarin, in J. W. M. Verhaar, ed., *The Verb 'be' and its Synonyms*, vol. IX. Dordrecht: Reidel.

Hengeveld, Kees. 1992. *Non-verbal Predication*. Berlin, New York: Mouton de Gruyter.

Hopper, Paul J. and Sandra A. Thompson. 1984. The Discourse Basis for Lexical Categories in Universal Grammar. *Language* 60:703-752.

Hopper, Paul J. and Sandra A. Thompson. 1980. Transitivity in Grammar and Discourse. *Language* 56:251-299

Hopper, Paul J. and Sandra A. Thompson. 1985. The Iconicity of the Universal Categories 'noun' and 'verb', in J. Haiman, ed., *Iconicity in Syntax*. Amsterdam, Philadelphia: Benjamins.

Langacker, Ronald. 1987. Nouns and Verbs. *Language* 63:53-94.

Langacker, Ronald. 1988. The Nature of Grammatical Valence, in B. Rudzka-Ostyn, ed., *Topics in Cognitive Linguistics*. Amsterdam, Philadelphia: Benjamins.

Li, Charles N. and Sandra A. Thompson. 1977. A Mechanism for the Development of Copula Morphemes, in C. N. Li, ed., *Mechanisms of Syntactic Change*. Austin, London: University of Texas Press.

Li, Charles N. and Sandra A. Thompson. 1981. *Mandarin Chinese. A Functional Reference Grammar*. Berkeley etc.: University of California Press.

Payne, Thomas. 1997. *Describing Morphosyntax: A Guide for Field Linguists*. Cambridge: Cambridge University Press.

Pustet, Regina. 1989. *Die Morphosyntax des "Adjektivs" im Sprachvergleich.* Frankfurt a. M.: Lang.

Saltarelli, Mario. 1988. *Basque.* London: Croom Helm.

Schachter, Paul. 1985. Parts-of-speech Systems, in T. Shopen, ed., *Language Typology and Syntactic Description*, vol. I. Cambridge: Cambridge University Press.

Schachter, Paul and Fe Otanes. 1972. *Tagalog Reference Grammar.* Berkeley: University of California Press.

Stassen, Leon. 1994. Typology versus Mythology: The Case of the Zero Copula. *Nordic Journal of Linguistics* 17:105-126.

Stassen, Leon. 1997. *Intransitive Predication.* Oxford: Clarendon.

Thompson, Sandra A. 1988. A Discourse Approach to the Cross-linguistic Category 'adjective', in J. A. Hawkins, ed., *Explaining Language Universals.* Oxford, NewYork: Blackwell.

Vogel, Petra M. and Bernard Comrie, eds. 2000. *Approaches to the Typology of Word Classes.* Berlin, New York: Mouton de Gruyter.

Wierzbicka, Anna. 1986. What's in a Noun? (Or: How Do Nouns Differ in Meaning from Adjectives?). *Studies in Language* 10:353-389.

Prosodic Integration in Spanish Complement Constructions*

IVO SÁNCHEZ

University of California, Santa Barbara

1. Introduction

Semantic constituency, or the semantic relationship between a syntactic head and its dependent arguments has become a central issue for recent syntactic theories. In the received model of constituency, the semantic relationship between heads and dependent arguments is seen as a set of static, invariable configurations. Accordingly, syntactic frameworks that adopt this model of constituency adopt one invariable constituency configuration for a given type of constituency relation. In this vein, the early generative framework proposed the invariable constituency schema [V [S][O]] for the constituency relations holding between the clausal constituents subject, verb and object, whereas Tesnière (1939) proposed the alternative schema [S [V O]] (see Lazard 1998: 97).

In contrast with this view of constituency, some recent functional approaches such as Givón (1990), Langacker (1987; 1993; 1995), Tao (1997) and Helasvuo (forthcoming) have proposed a dynamic view of constituency that allows for alternative constituency configurations of the same combination of constituents. Furthermore, these frameworks also allow for different possible 'degrees of integration' between constituents grouped under a single higher level constituent. These models posit that the formal expression of

*I am indebted to Sandra Thompson, Steven Fincke, Patricia Clancy, Mira Ariel and two anonymous reviewers for very helpful comments on this paper. All remaining errors are solely my own.

semantic integration is iconically encoded by the conflation of different prosodic and morphosyntactic trappings from different coding means such as the
linear juxtaposition of constituents, different morphosyntactic options, and,
in Langacker (1987), by the integration of constituents under the same prosodic unit.

Langacker bases his discussion on the role of prosody as a coding
means of integration on isolated examples. However, the recent work of Tao
(1997) on Mandarin and Helasvuo (forthcoming) on Finnish has proved that
different types of constituency relations between the same types of constituents are indeed partially encoded by their integration in the same prosodic
unit in naturally occurring discourse. For instance, Helasvuo has found that
in Finnish conversation, core arguments that are supposedly semantically
closer to their predicates occur more frequently integrated with their verbs in
a same intonation unit[1]. Conversely, oblique arguments occur most of the
time prosodically non-integrated with their verb, in a different intonation
unit. Thus, she has shown that prosody iconically encodes different degrees
of semantic cohesion between heads and dependent elements in natural discourse along with other morphosyntactic coding means.

Within this same line of research, this paper aims to contribute to the
burgeoning study of the dynamic nature of constituency in spoken discourse
and the role of prosody as one of its main coding means. It also addresses
the relationship of prosody with other concurrent morphosyntactic coding
strategies of constituency as well as other alternative functions of intonation
units, such as the allocation of informational content, that play an important role in the prosodic implementation of constituency relations. The focus of the study is the degree of prosodic integration between complementation constructions within the same or several intonation units in casual
Spanish conversation. It also addresses the degree of co-occurrence of this
type of prosodic integration with other morphosyntactic means of constituency such as the presence vs. the absence of subordinators.

Thus, in Spanish conversation, one finds some tokens of complement
constructions that occur integrated with their matrix in the same intonation
unit, such as the complement construction *pues yo creo que fui* 'I think I
went' in line 5 in (1): (Each line in examples represents an intonation unit.
See Appendix A for further transcription conventions).

(1)   (MINA: 8:58)

1   JOSE: ..Te estuvimos `buscando en La ^Gloria el otro día\.
             'We were looking for you in La Gloria the other day

2   OSCAR: .. Qué día fue/?
             What day was that?

3   JOSE: El ^sábado\.

---

[1] See definition of intonation unit in section 2.

Saturday

4   OSCAR: … El sábado pa^sado/ ?

last saturday

5 →   … Pues yo creo que ^fui\.

I think I went.'

One also finds instances of prosodically non-integrated complementation constructions such as *yo creo que le ha creado un trauma* 'I think that he's been traumatized by it.' in lines 1 and 2 in (2) that span over two different intonation units.

(2)   (DIVINA 3:36)

1 --> OSCAR: … Yo ^creo/,

'I think

2 -->   que le ha `creado un ^trauma\,

that he's been traumatized by it.

3   .. Y tiene que gastarse siete mil pelas en un psi^cólogo\.

and has to spend 7,000 pesetas in a therapist.'

A first hypothesis for the differences in the prosodic implementation of the two constructions is based on their different degrees of semantic integration. Semantic integration is defined as correspondences or relations of semantic identity between subcomponents of the two constructions (i.e. Lehmann's 1988 'interlacing'). Thus, in the first construction, there is a semantic correspondence of co-referentially between the subject *yo* 'I' of the matrix *yo creo* 'I think' and the subject of its complement *que fui* 'that I went' expressed in the agreement suffix *-i* on the verb. Conversely, the second example shows a lack of correspondences between the arguments of the matrix, i.e. the subject *yo* 'I' and the arguments of the complement *le* 'to him' and *un trauma* 'a trauma'. Thus, the prosodic integration of the first example correlates with its high semantic integration, whereas the lack of prosodic integration of the second example correlates with its lower degree of semantic integration.

As suggested by Ono and Thompson (1995) for English conversation, the prosodic integration of complement constructions might not be limited to a reflection of their degree of semantic integration. Additional pragmatic and cognitive factors such as limits on the amount of information allowed in each intonation unit such as Chafe's (1987; 1994) "one-new-idea-per-intonation-unit constraint" might be playing an important role in the prosodic implementation of these constructions. Thus, for example, the integrated complement in (1) contains a single highly recoverable argument *yo* 'I', whereas the non-prosodically integrated complement in (2) contains the three arguments *yo, le,* and *un trauma* 'a trauma' of which the latter is newly activated and thus non-recoverable. These examples thus suggest that the implementation of a single construction in one or several intonation units might also respond to cognitive limits on the maximum amount of new information typically allowed per intonation unit.

As Lehmann (1988) and Givón (1990) have shown, semantic integration is encoded by a varied array of morphosyntactic trappings crosslinguistically, such as finite vs. non-finite morphology on the complement verb, equi-deletion of the complement subject in cases of coreferentiality with the subject of main clause, occurrence or absence of subordinators, etc.

Thus, recent functional literature suggests two alternative hypotheses to account for the prosodic implementation of complement constructions: one based on degrees of semantic integration or interlacing between the two clauses, and a second hypothesis based on the degree of informational content of the construction as a whole. In addition, it remains unclear what the degree of co-occurrence of prosody and other morphosyntactic coding means of integration is. The present study seeks to determine the degree of relevance of both semantic and informational factors for the prosodic integration of complements, and the relationship of prosody to other ways in which integration in complementation is coded morphosyntactically.

The study is organized as follows: Section 2 provides a brief description of the corpus employed and the method of selection of the constructions collected for the database. Section 3 provides a quantitative study of the degree of correspondence between the prosodic integration of complements with their degree of semantic integration. Section 4 is concerned with the degree of correspondence between prosodic integration and informational constraints. Section 5 deals with prosodic integration vis-à-vis other devices by which integration is coded morphosyntactically, and Section 6 provides a general discussion on the findings in the preceding sections.

2. Data and Method of Selection

2.1 Data

The data employed in this study consist of a sample of the first 560 complement constructions that occurred in a corpus of about four hours of casual Spanish conversation. The corpus was collected in Madrid (Spain) during the Christmas period of 1996. All the conversations took place between native speakers of both sexes that had a good personal knowledge of each other.

2.2 Selection

The 560 tokens of complement constructions were selected from the four hours of data according to the semantic crosslinguistic definition of complement construction provided by Noonan (1985):

'By complementation we mean the syntactic situation that arises when a notional sentence or predication is an argument of a predicate. For our purposes, a predication can be viewed as an argument of a predicate if it functions as the subject or the object of that predicate.' (1985: 42)

Thus, we selected as instances of complementation constructions in Spanish those clauses in the data that were the notional subject or object of a main, finite predicate.

2.3 Intonation Units

Intonation Units are defined in Chafe (1987:22) as "a sequence of words combined under a single, coherent intonation contour, usually preceded by a pause." For the discrimination of intonation units, I followed Du Bois et al. (1991; 1993) who provide five main cues to identify the boundaries between intonation units:

a) Intervening pauses between units.
b) A coherent intonational contour throughout the unit.
c) A shift upward in the overall pitch at the beginning of each unit.
d) Anacrusis in the first syllables of the unit.
e) Lengthening of the final syllable of the unit.

At least for the purposes of this study, I consider intonation units to be largely equivalent to 'tone groups' (Crystal 1969), 'intonation groups' (Cruttenden 1983) and 'intonation phrases' (Couper-Kuhlen 1986).

In the following sections, I will discuss the rest of the relevant constructs employed in the study with examples of representative tokens from the corpus. I will begin in the next section by addressing the notion of semantic integration in complement clauses.

3. Prosodic vs. Semantic Integration

In this section I will define and illustrate prosodic and semantic integration in Spanish complementation constructions and I will provide a measurement of the degree of convergence of these two types of integration for the tokens in the corpus employed.

Complementation constructions are considered prosodically integrated if both the matrix and the complement clauses occur in the same intonation unit. The notion of semantic integration is found in Givón (1990), Langacker (1987) and Lehmann (1988), who state that two component structures are notionally integrated if they have correspondences (identity relations) holding between some of their constituents. For complementation constructions, semantic integration might be operationalized in terms of two factors:

a) One or more of the arguments of both the matrix and the complement verb have the same discourse referent.
b) Both verbs refer to the same token of a state or event.

Example (3) illustrates a complement construction both prosodically and semantically integrated according to the above definition:

(3)   (MINA: 2:53)

1   TINO: Porque no me haces un espiritismo de esos ?,
             'Why don't you do one of those sorceries on me?

2   Y me dices como va a se=r

3   lo de= ^Miguel
             And tell me how is going to be the thing with Miguel.

4 → OSCAR: (9.) Porque os tengo que ver ^juntos
             Because I have to see you guys together.'

The complement construction in (3) is integrated semantically since the subject of its matrix predicate *tener* and the subject of its complement verb *ver* refer to the same discourse entity, the speaker Oscar. Furthermore, the semantic content of the matrix *tener* is clearly integrated with the meaning of the complement *ver* in the construction: '*tener* + *que* + Verb', since *tener* provides a deontic modality to the event denoted by its complement. Thus, instead of constituting a different event, this matrix elaborates a facet of the event denoted by the complement.

Contrarily, example (4) illustrates a complementation construction that is neither prosodically nor semantically integrated.

(4) (AMOR 4:10)

1   JM: (0) la carta es una preciosidad.
           'The letter is just beautiful

2   ... La carta,
           the letter

3   .. a mí se me saltaron las lágrimas
           tears came to me

4 →   ... (H) de ver como ^alguien,
           from seeing how somebody

5 →   ... puede ser tan ^listo, /
           could be so perceptive'.

The subject of the matrix predicate *ver* 'see' and the subject of the complement *ser* 'be' refer to two different discourse entities: the speaker and the writer of the letter respectively. Furthermore, the verb *ver* and the verb *ser* refer to distinct events and states respectively.

In order to obtain an approximate idea of the degree of correlation between semantic integration with prosodic integration, the 560 complement constructions in the database were tagged for the referential identity of their subject arguments and the events expressed in their predicates. Figure 1 summarizes the results obtained from this measurement.

**Figure 1: Prosodic Integration vs. Semantic Integration
(same vs. different subject and event).**

Semantic Integration	Same I.U.		Different I.U.		Total by Row
Same Subject and Event	**172**	**(95%)**	25	(5%)	197
Same Subject but Other Event	**161**	**(78%)**	43	(22%)	204
Different Subject and Event		(45%)	86	(55%)	159
Total by Column		= 406		= 154	= 560

Figure 1 shows that there is a tendency for complement constructions to be encoded prosodically integrated in general. Completely and partially semantically integrated constructions (one subject but two events) also occur prosodically integrated most the time (95% and 78% respectively). Conversely, constructions which are not semantically integrated occur non-prosodically integrated to a larger degree. These results, therefore, strongly suggest that semantic integration is a relevant factor for the prosodic implementation in terms of integration of complement clauses with their matrixes.

However, the figure also shows that 25 semantically integrated constructions occur prosodically non-integrated and 73 semantically non-integrated constructions occur prosodically integrated, amounting to 17% of the cases out of the total that deviate from the prediction. These cases suggest the possibility that a complementary factor might bear on the prosodic integration of complements. As we have noted before, Chafe (1987; 1994), Clark (1996), and Kotschi (1996) have pointed to the important role of intonation units as the prosodic format for the allocation of combinations of given and new information in unrehearsed discourse. In the next section, I will consider this role of prosody as a possible independent factor that might account for the prosodic implementation of deviant cases from the results obtained in figure 1.

4. Prosodic Integration vs. Information Packaging

Chafe (1987; 1994), Clark (1996), and Kotschi (1996) have discussed the role of intonation units as units of processing and verbalization of information in discourse. In this role, intonation units constitute domains that typically contain combinations of given and new information implemented in an average of five or six words per unit. Chafe has also noted that there are severe limits in the amount of new information that intonation units contain, suggesting that typically, intonation units only contain one new information chunk or idea.

As suggested by Ono and Thompson (1995) for English conversational data, Chafe's findings might have direct implications for the prosodic implementation of complement constructions in a single vs. several intonation units. In order to obtain an approximate idea of the degree to which the information packaging function of intonation units correlates with the prosodic integration of complement constructions, the 560 tokens in the database were tagged for the amount of information that they carried.

Although Chafe's original formulation of new information was presented in terms of 'information chunks' or 'ideas', for our current purposes, I have operationalized the amount of new information in intonation units in terms of two pragmatic properties of the nominal arguments of the construction. These two properties are their 'activation state' (Chafe 1987; 1994) and their degree of 'identifiability' (Du Bois 1980).

Chafe (1994:72) defines the activation state of a referent in terms of its relative location in the interlocutors' consciousness. In this respect, the referents of noun phrases can be given or new. Given referents are those that are presented by the speaker as if they had already been activated in the interlocutors' consciousness at the moment of the utterance of their noun phrase. New referents are those that are presented as if they had to be activated at the moment of the utterance of their noun phrase. Observe the following excerpt:

(5)   (MINA: 8:58)

1   ... Pues yo creo que ^fuí\.
                  'I think I went.

2   JOSE: Oye /,
                  'hey,

3   Cuéntame que pasó con Jose
                  tell me what happened with Jose

4   y una amiga tuya/?
                  and a friend of yours

5   OSCAR: Elvira/ ?
                  Elvira?

6   JOSE: Creo que sí\
                  I think so.'

The referent of the pronoun *yo* 'I' the 3SG.PST verbal agreement suffix '*-í*' of the verb *fuí* in line 1, and the third person singular dative clitic pronoun *-me* in line 3, are examples of given noun phrases since their referent, the current speaker, is active in the conversation at the moment of utterance. Contrarily, the noun phrases *Jose* and *una amiga tuya* 'a friend of yours', in lines 3 and 4 respectively, are examples of new referents since they are introduced for the first time into discourse by means of the utterance of these noun phrases. Note that the construction *Pues yo creo que fuí* 'I think I went' is prosodically integrated, whereas the construction *Cuentame que pasó con José y una amiga tuya* 'Tell me what happened with Jose and a friend of yours' is implemented in two intonation units.

The degree of identifiability of referents was discerned according to the definition of the term in Du Bois (1980):

> Identifiability is a property of the relation between reference and referent and cannot apply to either a reference or a referent alone. If a noun phrase is said to be identifiable, this means simply that the hearer can establish a link between the noun phrase and the concept it refers to. (1980:218)

Thus, an identifiable referent is one that the speaker assumes the listener can identify. Given referents are always identifiable, since the interlocutor can always identify them by means of their previous occurrence, whereas new referents might be identifiable usually by means of prior context or a semantic frame, or non-identifiable. In (5), *Jose* is identifiable and thus encoded as a proper noun, however, the referent of *una amiga tuya* is still non-identifiable and coded as an indefinite noun phrase. Observe that in the following intonation units in lines 5 and 6 there is an attempt to establish this referent as identifiable for the speaker Oscar.

In order to obtain an idea of the relationship between the prosodic integration of complement constructions and the amount of information carried, the nominal arguments of the 560 tokens of the construction in the sample were coded for their activation state and their identifiability. Figure 2 summarizes the results of this measurement.

Figure 2: Prosodic Integration vs. Information Flow of all Arguments in the Construction.

Information Flow	Same I.U.		Different I.U.	Total by row
All Given Arguments	362	(79%)	99 (21%)	460
At least One New, Identifiable	44	(59%)	30 (41%)	74
At least One New, Non-Identifiable	0	(0%)	25 (100%)	25
Total by Column	= 406		= 154	= 560

Figure 2 shows that the occurrence of new information in the construction correlates with lack of prosodic integration for the 25 tokens of constructions with at least one new and non-identifiable referent. The correlation of constructions with all recoverable information (both given and identifiable) is quite high (79%). However, 21% of clauses from the set in which all arguments are given and identifiable are not prosodically integrated. The 74 constructions intermediate in terms of information load, that include new but identifiable referents, occur prosodically integrated to a slightly greater degree.

Thus, these results compared to those of Figure 1 suggest two important conclusions:

1. The introduction of new information unequivocally influences the verbalization of a complementation construction in several intonation units.

However, this perfect correlation of introduction of new information and lack of prosodic integration could not be taken as the sole factor relevant to prosodic integration since it only operates on a small number of clauses (5% of constructions).

2. Semantic integration and informational content jointly account for the prosodic integration of complements as two intertwined functional dimensions of intonation units in spontaneous discourse for the grammatical domain of complementation.

Now that we have established the two main factors that account for the prosodic integration of complement constructions in Spanish conversation, we might turn to consider prosodic integration with the means of morphosyntactic coding employed for signaling integration.

5. Prosodic Integration vs. the Morphosyntactic Encoding of Integration

Lehmann (1988) and Givón (1990) provide an array of morphosyntactic coding devices that signal the degree of semantic integration between matrixes and their complements in different types of complementation constructions crosslinguistically. As these two authors note, these morphosyntactic cues iconically represent the degree of semantic proximity between the two clauses. Thus, predicates of complementation constructions that have a high degree of semantic integration occur more proximate to each other formally than those that have a lower degree of integration.

In Spanish, three main morphological cues signal a high degree of semantic integration. Complements with the same referential subject of their matrixes do not occur with an overt complement subject (equi-deletion), the subordinate verb is in a non-finite form, and tends to occur without intervening complementizers, such as *que* 'that' (see Givón 1990 for a more detailed discussion). Thus, the semantically integrated example in (3) *Os tengo que ver juntos* 'I have to see you guys together' has an equi-deleted subject, the subordinate verb *ver* 'see' is in infinitival form and there is not a complementizer intervening between the two clauses. Conversely, the non-semantically integrated example in (4) contains two different subjects, a finite modal form *puede* 'can' and the complementizer *como* 'how'.

In order to estimate whether these morphosyntactic cues to semantic integration correlate with the degree of prosodic integration of the constructions in the database, we tagged the 560 tokens for the three features: a) finiteness of the subordinate verb, b) equi-deletion, and c) presence vs. absence of complementizer. Figure 3 shows the results obtained from this measurement.

Figure 3: Prosodic Integration vs. Morphosyntactic Encoding of Integration.

	Morphosyntactic Features	Same I.U.	Diff. I.U.	Row
More Integrated Morphosyntax	Non-Finite, Equi-D., No Complementizer	205 (92%)	20 (8%)	225
Less Integrated Morphosyntax				
	Non-Finite, Equi-D., Complementizer	52 (96%)	2 (4%)	54
	Non-Finite, No Equi-D., No Complementizer	6 (85%)	1 (15%)	7
	Finite, No Equi-D., No Complementizer	7 (13%)	50 (87%)	57
	Finite, No Equi-D., Complementizer	136 (62%)	81 (38%)	217
		= 406	= 154	= 560

Figure 3 shows that the complement constructions with a more integrated morphosyntax (i.e. non-finite subordinate verb, equi deletion, and lack of complementizer) occur prosodically integrated most of the time (92% and 96%). Lower degrees of syntactic integration, as seen in the group with finite complement verb, nominative subject marking and the absence of a complementizer, correlate with the lack of prosodic integration. However, the correlation of these constructions is weaker for the group of least syntactically integrated constructions (38% of the time).

The examination of the 136 morphologically non-integrated constructions that occurred prosodically integrated, however, showed that 98% of them included all given participants amongst their arguments. Example (1) above illustrates this specific pragmatic and morphosyntactic type of construction.

Thus, we might conclude that although in general terms there is a high degree of correlation between morphosyntactic and prosodic integration, this correlation is always mediated by the informational load of the construction. That is, prosody in terms of intonation units serves the double function of signaling the integration of complex constructions and the implementation of canonical combinations of given and new information.

6. Final Remarks

In the previous sections I have aimed to present empirical proof for the role of prosody, more specifically, intonation units, as a coding means of the semantic integration between the two clausal constituents of complementation constructions in naturally occurring spoken Spanish. This role of intonation units as a coding means of integration in complement constructions has been further evidenced by their co-occurrence with other morphosyntactic devices such as equi-deletion, finiteness of the subordinate verb, and the presence of complementizers.

I have also aimed to show that a second functional role of prosody, the packaging of information in spoken discourse, is largely accomplished in conjunction with its role as a coding means of semantic integration, showing in many cases its primacy over semantic integration for the prosodic integration of a given token of the construction.

Finally, this study comes as a further investigation in the line of Tao (1997) and Helasvuo (1998) on the flexible and gradient nature of dependency relations between constituents in spontaneous discourse. I hope it has shown, by means of quantitative analyses, the need for a view of the relationship between means of coding and functional domains which embraces a likely polyfunctionality of the former.

References

Chafe, Wallace. 1987. Cognitive Constraints on Information Flow, in Russel Tomlin, ed., *Coherence and Grounding in Discourse*. Amsterdam: John Benjamins.

Chafe, Wallace. 1994. *Discourse, Consciousness, and Time*. Chicago: The University of Chicago Press.

Clark, Herbert. 1996. *Using Language*. Cambridge: Cambridge University Press.

Couper-Kuhlen, Elizabeth. 1985. *An Introduction to English Prosody*. Tubingen: Niemeyer.

Cruttenden, Alan. 1983. *Intonation*. Cambridge: Cambridge University Press.

Crystal, David. 1969. *Prosodic Systems and Intonation in English*. Cambridge: Cambridge University Press.

Du Bois, John. 1980. Beyond Definiteness. The Trace of Identity in Discourse, in Wallace Chafe, ed., *The Pear Stories. Cognitive, Cultural, and Linguistic Aspects of Narrative Production*. Norwood, N.J.: Ablex.

Du Bois, John, Susanna Cumming, Stephan Schuetze-Coburn, Danae Paolino, eds. 1991. *Discourse Transcription*. Santa Barbara Papers in Linguistics. Vol. 4. Santa Barbara, CA: Department of Linguistics of the University of California, Santa Barbara.

Du Bois, John, Stephan Schuetze-Coburn, Susanna Cumming, and Danae Paolino. 1993. Outline of Discourse Transcription, in J. A. Edwards and M. D. Lampert, eds., *Talking Data: Transcription and Coding in Discourse Research*. Hillsdale, NJ: Lawrence Erlbaum.

Givón, Talmy. 1990. *Syntax. A Functional-Typological Introduction. Vol. II.* Amsterdam: John Benjamins.

Helasvuo, Marja-Liisa. Forthcoming. *When Discourse Becomes Syntax: Noun Phrases and Clauses as Emergent Syntactic Units in Finnish Conversational Discourse*. Amsterdam: John Benjamins.

Kotschi, Thomas. 1996. Procedimientos de producción y estructura informacional en el lenguaje hablado, in Thomas Kotschi, Wulf Oesterreicher, and Klaus Zimmerman, eds., *El Español Hablado y la Cultura Oral en España e Hispanoamérica*. Frankfurt am Main: Vervuert; Madrid: Iberoamericana.

Langacker, Ronald. 1987. *Foundations of Cognitive Grammar. Vol. I. Theoretical Prerequisites*. Palo Alto, CA: Stanford University Press.

Langacker, Ronald. 1995. Conceptual Grouping and Constituency in Cognitive Grammar, in Linguistic Society of Korea, ed., *Linguistics in the Morning Calm 3*, 149-172. Seoul: Hanshin.

Langacker, Ronald. 1997: Constituency, Dependency, and Conceptual Grouping. *Cognitive Linguistics* 8: 1-32.

Lazard, Gilbert. 1998. *Actancy*. Berlin: Mouton de Gruyter.

Lehmann, Christian. 1988. Towards a Typology of Clause Linkage, in John Haiman, and Sandra Thompson, eds., *Clause Combining in Grammar and Discourse*. Amsterdam: John Benjamins.

Noonan, Michael. 1985. Complementation, in Timothy Shopen, ed., *Language Typology and Syntactic Description*. Cambridge: Cambridge University Press.

Ono, Tsuyoshi, and Sandra Thompson. 1995. What Conversation Can Tell Us about Syntax, in Phillips W. Davis, ed., *Alternative Linguistics*. Amsterdam: John Benjamins.

Tao, Hongyin. 1997. *Units in Mandarin Conversation*. Amsterdam: John Benjamins.

APPENDIX A: Transcription Notations
(Based on Du Bois et al. 1991).

1. Transitional continuity

,	Continuing intonation (slightly falling)
.	Terminal intonation (falling)
?	Appeal (slightly rising)
--	Truncated intonation unit.

2. Accent and lengthening

^	Primary accent
`	Secondary accent
=	Lengthening of the preceding sound

3. Tone

/	Rising
\	Falling
_	Level
/\	High-low
\/	Low-high

4. Other

@	laughter
<X X>	Uncertain hearing
..()	Pause (length indicated in parentheses)

Some Aspects of Path-Like Iconicity in German Separable Verb Constructions

MICHAEL B. SMITH
Oakland University

1. The General Issue and Some Relevant Data

A classic problem in German syntax has been the difficulty in accounting for the separability of verb prefixes from their bases in some constructions and the lack of separability of the same prefixes in other constructions, as illustrated by the examples in (1). The prefix *ab* separates from the verb base and occurs in sentence final position in the present (1a) and simple past (1c) tenses; the fact that separation is obligatory in these tenses is shown in (1b) and (1d).

(1) a.   Inge   fährt   um   vier   Uhr   ab
          Inge   drives   at   four   o'clock   away
          'Inge leaves (by vehicle) at four o'clock.'

     b.   *Inge abfährt   um   vier   Uhr

     c.   Inge   fuhr   um   vier   Uhr   ab
          Inge   drove   at   four   o'clock   away
          'Inge left (by vehicle) at four o'clock.'

     d.   *Inge abfuhr   um   vier   Uhr

Conceptual and Discourse Factors in Linguistic Structure.
Alan Cienki, Barbara J. Luka and Michael B. Smith (eds.).
Copyright © 2001, CSLI Publications.

But the prefix remains attached to the verb in other constructions, such as the future (2a) and with modal verbs (2c). The impossibility of separation in these constructions is shown in (2b) and (2d).

(2)   a.

Hans	wird	morgen	mit	dem	Zug	abfahren
Hans	will	tomorrow	with	the	train	away-drive

'Hans will leave tomorrow by train.'

    b.

*Hans	wird	morgen	mit	dem	Zug	fahren	ab

    c.

Hans	will	morgen	mit	dem	Zug	abfahren
Hans	wants	tomorrow	with	the	train	away-drive

'Hans wants to leave tomorrow by train.'

    d.

*Hans	will	morgen	mit	dem	Zug	fahren	ab

Separable prefixes may derive from a variety of different lexical classes, including: adverbs (*ab, vorbei, zurück, vorwärts*), verbs (*spazieren, stehen*, etc.), or nouns (*auto, rad, ski*, etc.). Traditional German grammars typically identify the position of the separated prefix (sometimes referred to as one of a number of kinds of predicate complements) as the posterior limit of the sentence field (cf. Lederer 1969:477ff.), with the conjugated part of the verb occupying the anterior limit of this field. More recent generative accounts have proposed variations on an analysis in which the prefix plus verb combination is generated in clause final position, with the conjugated form of the verb moved to second position under certain circumstances (thereby stranding the prefix at the end of the clause when the verb is moved) (Olsen 1985 provides a historical overview of representative accounts of this type).

But what, if anything, might these word order facts signify? Is there a semantic motivation for prefix separation in German, or is the separability vs. nonseparability of the prefixes simply an arbitrary feature of a particular construction, as is tacitly assumed in traditional accounts of German syntax? This paper draws on some basic German data to propose a semantically-based account for the word-order facts from the perspective of cognitive grammar (CG) (Langacker 1987; 1991a,b). It addresses the question "...to what extent can 'grammar' be considered a system of formal structures that is autonomous from its function?" (Croft 1995:492), and argues that such autonomy is untenable. If there is a nonarbitrary relationship between prelinguistic conceptual (semantic) categories and syntactic or morphological ones in human languages (such as the separability vs. nonseparability of the German separable verb prefixes), then it should be possible to identify a semantic correlation between a prefix's separability in a given construction and its semantic contribution (together with that of the verb base) within that construction.

I will argue that reinterpreting the basic facts within CG provides a better understanding of how the morpho-syntactic distribution and patterning of the prefixes in various construction types correlates with their meaning contribution to the clause, i.e. that there is an *iconic* relationship between the meaning and form (i.e. syntactic patterning) of separable prefixes which has hitherto gone unnoticed. I will show that the separability vs. non-separability of the prefix in different constructions is not completely arbitrary, but almost always semantically motivated (if not strongly predictable), and that the linguistic content conveyed by the prefixes helps structure (at least to some extent) the linguistic forms in which they occur.

2. Some Theoretical Notions

2.1 Cognitive Grammar (CG)

I will assume the general outlines of the CG framework described in Langacker (1987; 1991a; 1991b), and also the approach to cognitive linguistics found in Lakoff (1987) and Lakoff and Johnson (1980). These approaches to language all agree that much of "grammar" is inherently meaningful, not autonomous or accidental—i.e. that "grammatical structure reduces to patterns for the structuring and symbolization of conceptual content, and that all valid grammatical constructs have some kind of conceptual import" (Langacker 1991b:338).

They view the meaning of a linguistic predication as involving not only its objective content (as is generally espoused by most logic-based approaches to semantics), but also how that content is construed by the speaker-conceptualizer (a crucially important tenet in linguistic semantics known as *imagery*). Grammatical constructions therefore involve the grammaticization (or encoding) of conventional imagery; i.e. grammar involves the structuring and symbolization of conceptual content, and a grammar is defined as "a structured inventory of conventional linguistic units" (Langacker 1987:57). Each individual construction type in a speaker's grammar is thus assumed to have its own unique meaning.

It should be noted, however, that in spite of the close connection assumed to hold in language between meaning and form, the framework does not claim that meanings predict grammatical behavior. Rather, CG assumes that absolute predictability is unrealistic and unnecessary in showing that semantico-conceptual structure often shapes and *motivates* (though does not strongly predict) morpho-syntactic structure, i.e. "[c]ognitive grammar does not claim that grammar is *predictable* from meaning, but rather that it is meaningful because it embodies and symbolizes a particular way of construing conceptual content" (Langacker 1991:517).

2.2 Image Schemas

Lakoff and Johnson (1980), Lakoff (1987), and Johnson (1987) suggest that much of what we call "grammar" is organized around certain cognitively fundamental pre-linguistic conceptions called *image schemas* (e.g. container-content, source-path-goal, link, balance, cycle, center-periphery, part-whole, etc.), which are grounded in everyday physical or bodily experience. Image schemas are mental "structures for organizing our experience and comprehension" which lend "pattern and order to our actions, perceptions, and conceptions...a recurrent pattern, shape and regularity in, or of, these ongoing ordering activities" (Johnson 1987:29).

Image-schematic patterns can also be viewed as experiential gestalts that emerge throughout sensorimotor activity as we manipulate objects, orient ourselves spatially and temporally, and direct our perceptual focus for various purposes (Johnson 1991).[1] CG assumes that speakers have the ability to relate and then metaphorically extend prelinguistic image-schematic conceptions, which are grounded in a concrete physical domain, to more abstract domains, including those relevant to the structuring of conceptual content for purposes of grammatical coding (i.e. the internal structure of an image schema can be projected into more abstract domains via metaphor). Image schemas "play an important role in structuring cognitive domains...that support the characterization of basic grammatical constructs" (Langacker 1991b:399).

Lakoff and Johnson (LJ) note, for example, that spatial metaphors can "apply directly to the form of a sentence.... [t]his can provide automatic direct links between form and content, based on general metaphors in our conceptual system" (LJ 1980:126). Thus, part of a sentence's meaning can stem from the precise form the sentence takes due to this nonarbitrary linking between form and meaning, and "[l]inguistic forms are themselves endowed with content by virtue of spatialization metaphors" (LJ 1980:126).

Among the metaphors discussed by LJ in this context are MORE OF FORM IS MORE OF CONTENT, illustrated in (3), and CLOSENESS IS STRENGTH OF EFFECT, illustrated in (4-5).

(3)   a. He ran and ran and ran and ran

       b. He is very very very tall

---

[1]Gibbs and Colston (1995) note that there appears to be independent evidence for the psychological reality of image schemas and their transformations: "A large body of research can be interpreted as supporting the claim that image schemas are indeed psychologically real and function in many aspects of how people process linguistic and nonlinguistic information" (1995: 347).

Note how in (3a) the repetition of the verb *ran* implies more running than if the verb had only been mentioned once, and in (3b) the repetition of *very* implies a greater degree of tallness than if it were only used once.

(4) a. Harry is not happy

  b. Harry is unhappy

(5) a. I taught Greek to Harry

  b. I taught Harry Greek

LJ note that (4a) could be neutral with respect to happiness or sadness, but that (4b) implies a stronger negative: in (4b) Harry is definitely sad. The close morphological attachment of the negative morpheme to the adjective in (4b) is thus viewed as having a stronger effect than the looser syntactic association between the negative morpheme and the adjective in (4a). The closer proximity of *Harry* and *Greek* in (5b) likewise signifies a much stronger effect--i.e. Harry actually learned Greek—than indicated in (5a), in which Harry may not have learned what I tried to teach him.

3. Motivating a German Spatialization Metaphor

My claim is that the syntactic behavior of separable prefix verbs reflects a spatialization metaphor in German involving the source-path-goal image schema in which DISCONTINUITY OF FORM IS ICONIC FOR A PATH. This is motivated, since such verbs prototypically profile concrete path-like notions. I assume here the CG notion that all verbs profile processual relations of various kinds, in that they involve "a series of relational configurations that necessarily extend through conceived time and are scanned sequentially" (Langacker 1991a:81). These relations may encompass both highly concrete and also quite abstract senses. Many verbs with concrete senses (including separable verbs) actually profile path-like notions conceived as unfolding in the physical world (cf. example (1) above with *abfahren* 'depart'), in which case it is easy to see how the path notion is involved in the verbs' meaning.

Other verbs have meanings which are usually characterized against more abstract domains which primarily evoke mental relationships of various kinds (cf. a separable verb like *beitragen* 'contribute'). In such cases, the path-like notion is usually still relevant in the literal interpretation of the morphemes comprising the verb, but the verb has taken on a more abstract sense as a result of a semantic extension of the original path-like meaning via metaphor into a more abstract realm of conceptualization (cf. *beitragen*'s literal morpheme-by-morpheme translation as 'carry by'). Nevertheless, a residual path-like notion is still present even in abstract verbs, if only in the sense that they profile relations construed to unfold directionally through time (often with a clear goal in mind).

The syntactic separability of the prefix from the verb (i.e. the discontinuity of form shown in (1a, c)) can be construed generally as iconically evoking, in the grammar, the notion of a directional path, due to the fact that paths are prototypically conceived as lengths which involve a physical separation of the source and goal. The linear separation of the verb prefix from its verb base within a syntactic string can thus be construed as a linguistic rendering of the physical separation of one part of a linear path from another, e.g. the linear separation of a starting point of a path from its goal. The fact that the prefixes often specify spatial aspects of either the source or the goal of the paths profiled by the verbs in their concrete or literal senses is also significant (cf. also Drosdowski 1984:419ff.).[2]

The evidence also suggests—to some extent—a semantically relevant difference between the syntactic constructions in which the prefix separates as opposed to those in which it does not separate from the verb (though the correlation here is less than absolute and there are apparent exceptions). Separation of the prefix from the verb base in some constructions evokes the idea that the conceptual salience of the path is especially strong and highlighted in those constructions. The non-separation of the prefix tends to occur in constructions reflecting situations in which the conceptual salience of the profiled path is downplayed for some reason (more details will follow). This difference may constitute an additional layering of semantic information within the morpho-syntax over and above the fact that the verbs in question profile (i.e. designate) some kind of path notion (either concrete, abstract, or metaphorical).[3]

3.1 Constructions with Separable Prefixes Profile *Actual Paths*

Note that in constructions in which the prefix separates from the verb the path profiled by the verb is either in the process of being actualized (or realized) (as in the present tense) or has already been actualized (as in the past and perfect tenses): i.e. the path is *actual*. By this I mean that the path notion evoked by the verb is construed as more immediately relevant, highlighted, or accentuated in these constructions than in others. Note also that in all of the constructions involving actual separation of the prefix from the verb base, the separable verbs are grounded (finite verbs), i.e. they make

---

[2]Later examples will show that some separable prefixes can specify more specific information about the path itself which may not be overtly characterized in the verb base alone.

[3]A caveat is in order: This analysis does not attempt to explain why some prefixes are separable and others (such as *be-*, *ent-*, *ver-*, etc.) are not separable, but simply addresses the iconic motivation of prefix separability in some constructions and suggests what the separability vs. the inseparability of the separable prefixes in different construction types might signify. Inseparable prefixes will not be discussed in this paper.

reference to the immediate speech event and its participants via tense and agreement (cf. Langacker 1991a:321). The following subsections illustrate these cases in some detail.

3.1.1 Prefix Separation in Matrix Present and Simple Past Tense Clauses

Examples of this type were illustrated above in (1a) and (1c). The sentences in (6) below additionally exemplify prefixes specifying the *source* of the path profiled by the verb. They are in the present tense and the paths are construed as actual:

(6)   a.   Hans   holt   mich   jetzt   ab

                Hans   gets   me   now   from

                'Hans is picking me up now'

        b.   Inge   geht   nicht   oft   mit   ihren   Freundinnen   aus

                Inge   goes   not   often   with   her   girlfriends   out

                'Inge doesn't go out much with her girlfriends.'

The verbs in (6c) and (6d) are in the simple past tense, and again the paths are construed as actual:

(6)   c.   Hans   holte   mich   gestern   ab

                Hans   got   me   yesterday   from

                'Hans pick   ed me up yesterday'

        d.   Inge   ging   nicht   oft   mit   ihren   Freundinnen   aus

                Inge   went   not   often   with   her   girlfriends   out

                'Inge didn't go out much with her girlfriends.'

Other separable verbs with prefixes specifying the starting point (source) of the path (with a concrete spatial sense) include the following: *abfliegen* 'fly away', *abmalen* 'portray, copy by painting' (imitation of a standard) (lit. 'paint from'), *abreisen* 'travel from or away', *abschreiben* 'copy, transcribe' (lit. 'write from'), *abspringen* 'jump from or off', *ausschrauben* 'screw out', and *aussteigen* 'climb out/off'. Not surprisingly, most involve the prefixes *ab* 'from' and *aus* 'out of, from', which well reflect the notion of a starting point.

One also finds examples of separable verbs with prefixes specifying the source of the path which further evoke a more abstract inchoative sense: *abblühen* 'cease blooming, fade.' (lit. 'bloom from or away'), *aufblühen* 'blossom, open up' (vs. *blühen* 'bloom'), *aufleuchten* 'flash, light up' (vs. *leuchten* 'shine'), *anbrennen* 'begin to burn, catch fire; set fire to', *anbrechen* 'start, open', *ausruhen* 'rest', *einschlafen* 'fall asleep' (note that *aus-*

ruhen and *einschlafen* even gain a perfective sense with the emphasis placed by the prefix on the path's starting point).

The sentences in (7) exemplify prefixes specifying the *goal* or *endpoint* of the path profiled by the verb in the present tense, where the path is construed as actual:

(7) a. Inge   kommt   heute   mit   dem   Zug   an
         Inge   comes   today   with   the   train   on
         'Inge arrives today by train'.

     b. Wir   nehmen die   Bücher jetzt weg
         we   take   the   books now   away
         'We're taking the books away now.'

The path is again actual in the simple past tense in (7c) and (7d):

     c. Inge   kam   gestern   mit   dem   Zug   an
         Inge   comes   yesterday with   the   train   on
         'Inge arrived yesterday by train'.

     d. Wir   nahmen die   Bücher weg
         we   take   the   books away
         'We took the books away.'

There are many additional separable verbs with prefixes specifying the endpoint (goal) of the path in a concrete spatial sense, and some, such as *anblicken* 'look at' and *anschauen* 'look at, watch', in which the path is construed more abstractly as a kind of mental attention directed toward a goal. Many often also have a clear *perfective* or *completive* sense which reflects the fact that reaching the endpoint or goal of a path evokes completion, a notion which may then be invoked in more abstract contexts. Here are some additional examples (many more are easy to find): *abstellen* 'put down/away', *anfliegen* 'fly to', *angreifen* 'lay hands on, seize hold of', *ankommen* 'arrive' (lit. 'come to'), *anrufen* 'call up', *anschalten* 'turn on (a machine)', *aufblasen* 'blow up, inflate', *(etwas) aufessen* 'eat up (something)', *aufschreiben* 'write down', *aufschwellen* 'inflate, swell up', *aufstehen'* get up, stand up', *aufwachen* 'wake up', *ausfüllen* 'fill out', *durcharbeiten* 'work through, complete', *durchschlafen* 'sleep through (without interruption)', *durchbringen* 'carry through (complete)', *einfressen* 'eat up', *einfrieren* 'freeze up', *einreisen* 'travel into', *einsteigen* 'climb/get in/on', *eintreten* 'enter, step in', *freimachen* 'set free', *heimgehen* 'go home', *totschießen* 'shoot dead', *totschlagen* 'kill (dead)', *vorstellen* 'place in front of, introduce', *vorziehen* 'draw in front of, prefer', *weggehen* 'go away', *zueilen* 'run to', *zufahren* 'drive to', *zuhören* 'listen to', *zurück-gehen* 'go back', *zurückkommen* 'come back'.[4]

The present tense sentences in (8) exemplify prefixes which seem to specify some more specific aspect of the nature of the path itself, involving either the means or the manner in which the action is effected. In (8a) the prefix *rad-* (which derives from the noun meaning 'wheel') specifies more exactly the means of the driving activity profiled by the verb *fahren*; in (8b) the prefix *durch-* makes more specific the manner notion that the reading activity (profiled by *lesen*) is construed to directionally traverse the newspaper from start to finish. In each example the paths are construed as actual:

(8) a. Ich fahre   heute   mit   meinen   Freunden   rad
         I   drive   today   with   my   friends   wheel
         'I'm cycling (bike-riding) today with my friends.'

     b. Mein Vater   liest   jetzt   die   Zeitung   durch
         my   father reads   now   the   newspaper   through
         'My father is now reading through (perusing) the newspaper.'

The verbs in (8c) and (8d) below are in the simple past tense, and the paths are also construed as actual. In (8c) the prefix *mit-* accentuates the idea (already implicit in the verb base) that the book accompanies the teacher at each step along the way, i.e. it reinforces the idea of the book's being in the teacher's possession for the duration of the path. In (8d) the path profiled by the verb base *bleiben* 'remain' represents a limiting case in which the path's linear extension is zero. Nevertheless, the prefix *stehen* 'stand' (from the verb with the same meaning) further specifies the kind of activity profiled by the verb base.

     c. Der   Lehrer   brachte   sein   Buch   mit
         the   teacher   brought   his   book   with
         'The teacher brought his book along.'

     d. Die   Uhr   blieb   plötzlich   stehen
         the   clock   remained   suddenly   stand
         'The clock suddenly stopped (i.e. remained standing).'

Here are some additional separable verbs with prefixes which seem to evoke a more specific aspect of the nature of the path itself, involving either the means or the manner in which it is effected: *durchgehen* 'go through',

---

[4]Note that the verbs with the prefix *durch-* also seem to evoke an aspect of the manner in which the action profiled by the verbs is effected (as will be discussed more fully in the following paragraphs).

durchfahren 'drive through', *durchreisen* 'travel through', *mitkommen* 'come along', *mitnehmen* 'take with/along', *schilaufen* 'ski, go skiing', *spazierengehen* 'go walking', *umdrehen* 'turn around', (the prefix specifies the exact nature of the turning action), *vorbeilaufen* 'walk past/by', *vorbeigehen* 'go past/by', *weiterfahren* 'drive on'.

3.1.2 Prefix Separation in Past Participles in Perfect Tenses

The prefixes are also separated from the verb by the past-participial prefix *ge-* in all perfect tenses (the present perfect is shown in (9a) and the past perfect in (9b)):

(9)   a.   Hans ist   gestern   mit   dem   Zug   abgefahren

               Hans is   yesterday   with the   train   away-driven

               'Hans left yesterday by train.' (prefix specifies source of path)

      b.   Inge hatte ihrem   Vater   zugehört

               Inge had   her   father   to-listened

               'Inge had listened to her father.' (prefix specifies goal of path)

Note that in these examples the entire verb complex consisting of the auxiliary in second position and the past participle in sentence-final position is grounded (by the auxiliary verb) and the path is construed as actual (i.e. as having been completed).

3.1.3 The Separability of the Prefix in Some Other Typical Constructions

The present tense is often used to refer to future time, as shown in (10) below. The separability of the prefix in these cases does not present a problem to the analysis I am proposing, but simply requires a minor adjustment in which the verb's path is construed as imminent to the moment of speaking (even though it is not yet objectively actualized):

(10) a.   Hans   fährt   morgen   mit   dem   Zug   ab

             Hans   drives   tomorrow with   the   train from

             'Hans will leave tomorrow by train'.

      b.   Wir   fahren   nächste   Woche   ab

             we   drive   next   week   from

             'We're leaving next week.'

The notion of a path's actualization being imminent also seems relevant for yes/no questions (11a-b) and content questions (11c-d) in the present tense:

(11) a.   Fängt   die   Klassenstunde   pünktlich   um 10 Uhr   an?

| | begin the | class | | promptly | at | 10 clock | on |

'Does the class begin promptly at 10 o'clock?

b. Kommt der Zug immer pünktlich an?
   comes the train always punctually on
   'Does the train always arrive on time?'

c. Was bringen die Leute mit?
   what bring the people with
   'What are the people bringing along?'

d. Wann fährt der nächste Zug ab?
   when drives the next train away
   'When does the next train depart?'

Separable verb prefixes also separate in imperatives (12). Because imperatives are usually construed as being actualized either at the moment of speaking or very soon thereafter, they are similar to presents used as futures with respect to evocation of the idea that the path's actualization is imminent; this then motivates the separation of the prefix.

(12) a. Steigen Sie bitte schnell in den Zug ein
     climb you please quickly in the train in
     'Please get into the train quickly!'

   b. Gehen Sie sofort ab
      go you immediately from
      'Go away from here immediately!'

   c. Bereiten wir jetzt unsere Hausarbeit vor
      prepare we now our homework before
      'Let's prepare our homework now!'

Content questions in all past tenses (simple past and perfect tenses) illustrated in (13) also exemplify paths construed as actualized:

(13) a. Wie spär fuhr der letzte Zug ab?
     how late drove the last train from
     'How late did the last train leave?'

   b. Wer hat mein Heft weggenommen?
      who hast my notebook away-taken
      'Who took away my notebook?'

c. Wo   hatte Inge das   Formular   ausgefüllt?
   where   had   Inge the   form   out-filled
   'Where had Inge filled out the form?'

Both the simple past and perfect tense forms of yes/no questions in (14) generally specify the path-like notion as actualized, though there are interpretations in which this may not necessarily be true:

(14) a. Kam   der   Zug   pünktlich   an?
        came   the   train punctually   on
        'Did the train arrive on time?'

     b. Hat   Hans das   Heft   mitgebracht?
        has Hans the   notebook   with-brought
        'Has Hans brought the notebook along?'

Note that in (14a) there is a clear implication that the train did arrive at some time in the past, though its punctuality is being questioned. But a different choice of adverb (such as *eigentlich* 'actually') or omission of the adverb altogether could imply doubt as to whether the train's path was actualized at all. And in (14b) there are at least three interpretations which depend upon which constituent is being questioned: the path is construed as actualized if it is the identity of the bringer or what was brought that is in question; the path is not necessarily so construed if what is being questioned is whether the bringing activity took place at all. But, more often than not, the path is or can be construed as actualized in these constructions, which plausibly motivates prefix separation for the construction as a whole. Exceptions of this type must be viewed as limiting cases in which, occasionally, the syntactic patterning (i.e. prefix separation) has become conventionalized (grammaticalized) and need not always strongly reflect semantic criteria. Such a situation poses no problem for a usage-based theory such as CG.

3.2 Constructions without Prefix Separation Profile *Virtual Paths*

In other syntactic environments the prefix does not separate from the verb. Semantically, this is motivated because the path profiled by the verb in these environments is construed as *virtual*; i.e. it has not yet been construed as actualized (or even imminent) relative to the moment of speaking (ground), but is rather subordinated conceptually to another concept profiled by some other predication. Significantly, in the future tense and with modal auxiliaries, the separable verb appears unseparated and in its infinitival (ungrounded) form.

3.2.1 Prefix Nonseparability in the Future Tense

In the future tense the grounding predication is a grammaticalized usage of the verb *werden* 'become', which appears in second position with the appropriate person and number agreement morphology; the separable verb appears in clause final position in its infinitival form without prefix separation:

(15) a. Hans wird morgen mit dem Zug abfahren

Hans will tomorrow with the train away-drive

'Hans will leave by train tomorrow',

b. Ich werde meine Bücher mitbringen

I will my books with-bring

'I'll bring my books along.'

In these sentences the actions of leaving and bringing (something) along are not yet construed as having taken place: they are thus virtual. Their possible realization (actualization) is construed to be at some time subsequent to the moment of speaking (if at all). The lack of physical separation of the prefixes from their bases iconically evokes the notion that the path-like actions have not yet occurred (and indeed may not occur).

3.2.2 Prefix Nonseparability with Verbs Used with Modal Auxiliaries

With modal auxiliaries the grounded modal verb that agrees with the subject appears in clause second position, and the separable verb appears in its infinitival form in clause final position in the present (16a) and simple past (16b) tenses without prefix separation:

(16) a. Inge muß mit dem Zug abfahren

Inge must with the train away-drive

'Inge must depart by train';

b. Wir wollten die Zeitung durchlesen

we wanted the newspaper through-read

'We wanted to read through the newspaper.'

The lack of prefix separation in modal constructions is motivated semantically in much the same way as for the future tense. The actions profiled by the dependent infinitives, which are syntactically subordinated under the modal verbs, are also semantically subordinated under the modals: they are construed as virtual (not yet actualized) and as dependent upon circumstances of necessity (16a), desire (16b), etc. Thus, in (16a) Inge's departure by train, though construed as necessary, has not yet occurred at the moment of speaking, nor is its realization guaranteed. In (16b), though our desire to read through the newspaper is construed to have been relevant at some point in the past, there is no guarantee that the event ever took place.

3.2.3 Prefix Nonseparability on Grounded Verbs in Subordinate Clauses

At first glance data like the following might seem to pose a problem for the analysis. The grounded separable verb forms in the present (17a-d) and simple past (18a-d) tenses in subordinate clauses do not separate from their verb bases, even though it seems as though the processes profiled by the separable verbs in each case are actual (as was claimed for earlier data involving the present and past tenses in matrix clauses). What might account for the lack of separation here?

(17) a. | Ich | glaube, | daß | Hans | jetzt | ankommt |
          |-----|---------|-----|------|-------|---------|
          | I | believe | that | Hans | now | arrives |

        'I believe that Hans is now arriving'.

    b. *Ich glaube, da8 Hans jetzt kommt an

    c. | Du | weißt, | daß | wir | die | Bücher | wegnehmen |
          |-----|--------|-----|-----|-----|--------|-----------|
          | you | know | that | we | the | books | away-take |

        'You know that we are taking away the books.'

    d. *Du weißt, daß wir die Bücher nehmen weg

(18) a. | Er weiß, | daß | ich | mit | dem | Zug | abfuhr |
          |----------|-----|-----|-----|-----|-----|--------|
          | he knows | that | I | with | the | train | away-drove |

        'Hans knows, that I departed by train.'

    b. *Er weiß, daß ich mit dem Zug fuhr ab

    c. | Die | Kinder | wissen, | daß | ich | ankam |
          |-----|--------|---------|-----|-----|-------|
          | the | children | know | that | I | arrived |

        'The children know that I arrived.'

    d. *Die Kinder wissen, daß ich kam an

The motivation for the lack of prefix separation with subordinate-clause separable verbs in the present and past tenses is similar to that given for its nonseparability in the future tense and with modal auxiliaries. Because the actions profiled by the separable verbs in the subordinate clauses are conceptually (and thus grammatically) subordinated under matrix verbs of believing or knowing, which themselves profile mental states about these actions, the relevance of the subordinated actions vis-à-vis the ground is consequently reduced in conceptual salience (i.e. backgrounded), and may thus be viewed as virtual relative to the grounded matrix verbs. Notice that, under this analysis, though both the matrix and subordinate verbs are assumed to profile states and/or actions (because they designate such processes), what apparently counts for prefix separation (or its absence) is the degree of conceptual salience of one clause profile relative to the other.

Data of this type seem to require an adjustment in how the notions *actual* vs. *virtual* path are to be understood. A path known to have been actualized may still be conceptually virtual relative to some other conceptualization. Prefix separation is therefore only likely in case the path-like notion is highly salient conceptually and has not been mediated through some other conceptualization, regardless of whether it is construed to have been objectively actualized or not. This means that the notion of *actuality* must take into account not only whether the path has actually been objectively realized, but also the degree of relevance of this actualization to the ground. This crucial additional characterization is a matter of imagery and demonstrates the importance of construal in the structuring of grammar.

3.2.4 Prefix Nonseparability in Present Participles

I think the analysis also accounts for the nonseparability of the prefix in the present participial forms of separable verbs. Though by themselves the participles profile events which are in the process of actualization, they are invariably subordinated conceptually under a grounded verb and as such are construed as virtual with respect to this verb.

(19) a. Der   ankommende Zug   ist sehr   spät

        the   arriving   train   is   very   late

        'The arriving train is very late'

    b. Die   aussteigenden Passagiere   sind   sehr   müde

        the out-climbing   passengers   are   very   tired

        'The disembarking passengers are very tired.'

Thus, in the examples in (19) above the paths traced by the train (19a) and the passengers (19b) are indeed actual in one sense, but they are nevertheless conceptually subordinated to the states profiled by the grounded verbs of being and their associated adjectives (*spät* and *müde*).

3.2.5 More on Motivating Prefix Nonseparability in Some Constructions

In the data given in 3.2.1–3.2.4 above, the modal, future auxiliary *werden*, or matrix verb (*glauben* 'believe' and *wissen* 'know' in this case) can be viewed as establishing a conceptual mental space (cf. Fauconnier 1985) involving some kind of "judgment" (necessity, belief, futurity, etc.) within which the path profiled by the separable verb might potentially occur.

The subordination of the path notion (or its abstract analog) within such mental spaces in effect distances the actualization of the path from the ground, thereby rendering it less salient and thus virtual relative to the conceptualization set up by the grounded "judgment" verbs. This is true even when a path-like verb itself is grounded within its own subordinate clause, since this clause is subordinate to, and thus less salient than, the overall conceptualization set up by the grounded matrix verb.

These observations allow us to make the generalization that prefix separation almost always implies that the path-like notion is highly salient and that the path has been objectively actualized (or its actualization is strongly imminent).[5] Lack of prefix separation may or may not imply objective actualization of the path, but it does imply a lower degree of relevance (conceptual distancing) of that actualization with respect to the ground.

3.3 Semantic Extensions of Path-Like Separable Verbs via *Metaphors*

As already noted, the path-like notion evoked by a verb may be realized at varying degrees of abstractness. The mostly concrete path-like separable prefix verbs discussed above were chosen to represent prototypical members of the separable verb category, and as such they likely motivate the separability of the prefix for all verbs in the category.

This is due to the CG assumption of a prototype model of categorization (not a criterial attribute model), in which some members of a category may be less prototypical than others, because they lack some characteristics found in prototypical members. Many (if not most) non-prototypical separable verbs (i.e. those not having clear path-like meanings) can be motivated as fitting into the separable verb category because their standard meanings often reflect semantic extensions of path-like notions via metaphors into more abstract realms of conceptualization (indeed the non-metaphorical meanings of many of these verbs directly reflect their path-like origins). Even those separable verbs whose path-like senses are hard to discern almost invariably evoke some kind of residual path-like notion, if only in the sense that they profile relations construed to unfold directionally through time (often with a clear goal in mind).

Here is a representative sampling of separable verbs whose senses in the modern language apparently derive from more concrete path-like senses via metaphors of various kinds (in most cases the relationship between the presumed original concrete meanings given in parentheses and the metaphorically-extended ones are obvious): *anfangen* 'begin' (lit. 'seize on'),

---

[5]Certain readings of some past tense yes/no questions may be exceptions (cf. (14) in section 3.1.3 above).

anziehen 'put on (clothes)' (lit. 'pull on'), *aufmachen* 'open' (lit. 'make on'), *ausziehen* 'take off (clothes)' (lit. 'pull off'), *beitragen* 'contribute' (lit. 'carry by'), *durcharbeiten* 'work through, finish' (also has a perfective sense), *einladen* 'invite' (lit. 'load in'), *einpacken* 'wrap, pack, put away' (lit. 'pack in'), *einschlafen* 'fall asleep' (lit. 'sleep in(to)'), *fernsehen* 'watch TV' (lit. 'see far'), *kennenlernen* 'become acquainted with' (lit. 'learn by knowing'), *nachahmen* 'imitate' (lit. 'imitate after/to'), *umkommen* 'die' (lit. 'come around'), *vorbereiten* 'prepare' (lit. 'ready (something) before'), *vorkommen* 'happen' (lit. 'come in front of'), *weiterschlafen* 'continue sleeping'. Note, for example, the metaphor evoked by the verb *einschlafen* which involves the notion of moving into the state of sleep (and which is echoed by the English expression 'to fall asleep'), and the metaphor evoked by *einpacken* in which literal movement of an entity into something has come to represent the notion of packing or wrapping in general.

Note also that with the prefixes exemplified in (20-22) below, which can be either separable or inseparable, the meanings of the former are almost always more concrete (i.e. evoke more concrete path-like notions) than those of the latter. When used inseparably the prefixes are unstressed and the meanings are almost always more abstract and metaphorical. The following data are from Lederer (1969:72): (a) versions are separable, (b) versions are inseparable:

(20) a. Die Mutter schneidet den Apfel durch
the mother cuts the apple through
'Mother cuts through the apple'

b. Das Schiff durchschneidet die Wellen
the ship traverses/crosses the waves
'The ship traverses the waves.'

(21) a. Er setzte die Leute mit seinem Boot über
he set the people with his boat over
'He's transported the people with his boat'

b. Ich habe den Brief ins Deutsche übersetzt
I have the letter into-the German translated
'I've translated the letter into German.'

(22) a. Er hält die Hand unter (etwas)
he holds the hand under (something)
'He holds his hand under (something).'

b. Er   unterhält   seine Familie

    he   under-holds   his   family

    'He supports (or entertains) his family.'

While space limitations preclude any more detailed examination of the metaphorical senses of these verbs and others like them, they are certainly worth further study.

4. Problematic Cases and/or Apparent Exceptions to the Analysis

I would like to briefly note some apparent exceptions to the analysis developed to this point. In (23–26) below the prefix separates from the verb base, even though the path-like verb seems to be conceptually subordinated to some other concept expressed by a grounded matrix verb. Based on the analysis given so far, we would expect the prefix not to separate in such contexts, because the paths profiled by the separable verbs, though sometimes objectively actualized (as in (23b) and in (24)), are virtual relative to the grounded matrix verbs.

The sentences in (23) illustrate prefix separation from the verb base in the perfect tenses in dependent clauses (present perfect in (23a) and past perfect in (23b)):

(23) a. Ich   glaube, daß   Hans   angekommen   ist

        I   believe that   Hans   arrived   is

        'I believe that Hans (has) arrived.'

    b. Du   weißt, daß   er das   Buch   weggenommen   hatte

        you   know that   he the   book   away-taken   had

        'You know that he had taken away the book.'

The sentences in (24) show prefix separation in past participles used adjectivally (the adjectival participles in these examples profile the endpoints of actions which are construed as already having been objectively actualized):

(24) a. Sie kam zu mir   mit   ausgestreckten   Armen

        she came to me   with   out-stretched   arms

        'She came to me with outstretched arms.'

    b. Der   abgefahrene Zug   war   spät

        the   departed   train was   late

        'The departed train was late.'

In infinitival constructions the prefix is separated from the verb base by *zu* 'to' (and the verb is in its infinitival form), as shown in (25) and (26)

(25) a. Hans beeilte sich, um   uns   pünktlich abzuholen
          Hans hurried   REFL around us   on-time   pick-up
          'Hans hurried in order to pick us up on time.'

      b. Inge sagte es, ohne   mich   anzusehen
          Inge said it without   me   on-to-see
          'Inge said it without looking at me.'

(26) a. Hans   versuchte abzufahren
          Hans   tried   from-to-drive
          'Hans tried to leave (by vehicle)'.

      b. Er   bat   mich, das   Buch mitzubringen
          he   asked me   the   book with-to-bring
          'He asked me to bring the book along.'

Despite their apparent exceptionality, I think that such data may be principled exceptions. Note that in each case the verb prefix is separated from the verb base by another prefix: either the past participial prefix *ge-* or the infinitival prefix *zu-*. *Ge-* highlights the endpoint (the final state) of the path profiled by the verb, and *zu-* is also endpoint focused and directional, highlighting that portion of the path which nears the endpoint (cf. Smith 1987; 1993a; 1993b; 1995 for more information about the meaning of *zu* and its role with respect to endpoint focus and dative case assignment in German).

Since the verbs in these constructions already have prefixal morphemes which refer in some way to the endpoint of the path or process profiled by the verb, the iconic contribution of the separation of the separable prefix from the verb base may simply be overridden in these cases. That is, the separability vs. nonseparability of the prefix is rendered moot and the analysis I have developed may simply not apply—i.e. is not relevant—in these kinds of constructions. Perhaps further research will be able to clarify the problem.

It is important to note that, from the CG perspective, the existence of apparent exceptions to an analysis does not necessarily entail the incorrectness of that analysis in cases where it otherwise seems valid. It may simply be a fact that a schema (or generalization) may not extend to all instances of a category. The CG conception of grammar as usage-based allows for the grammatical relevance of partial generalizations where applicable, and the lack of such generalizations where they are not applicable. Recalcitrant cases may be, at worst, either exceptions to the rule, or they may simply elude analysis at present. In any event, we must allow for the possibility that some grammatical patterns may not be strongly motivated semantically, but are simply arbitrary.

It is also important to point out in this regard that the existence of verbs with inseparable prefixes which also seem to evoke path-like notions (such as *entfliehen* 'flee, escape'), and also verbs without prefixes at all which evoke path-like notions (such as *gehen* 'go', *kommen* 'come', *rennen* 'run', etc.) should not be taken as evidence against a path-like analysis for separable verbs. While there may be a correlation between prefix separability and a strong evocation of a path-like notion, and while the path notion can serve as an explanation or semantic motivation for the separability of a prefix where it occurs, this is not the same thing as saying that all path-like meanings must be evoked by verbs with separable prefixes, which is patently untrue.

5. Conclusions

I have argued that German grammar has a spatialization metaphor involving a grammaticalized use of the source-path-goal image schema in which DISCONTINUITY OF FORM IS ICONIC FOR A PATH. The syntactic separability of the prefix from the verb can be construed, therefore, as iconically evoking, in the grammar, the notion of a directional path, whose conceptual salience is highlighted in those constructions where the prefix actually separates (actual paths), but is downplayed in those where it does not separate (virtual paths). Obviously, this idea presupposes the notion that all separable verbs evoke a "path" of some kind, which may vary in its degree of abstractness. The separability vs. nonseparability of the prefix is not arbitrary, but almost always semantically motivated (if not strongly predictable).

The analysis also suggests that whether a path is construed as actual or virtual seems to partially depend upon how it is construed relative to the ground, which functions somewhat like a conceptual reference point (cf. Langacker 1993): separable verbs profiling virtual paths (whose prefixes do not separate) are usually subordinated conceptually to other grounded verbs (even when the path verbs themselves are grounded within their own clause), whereas verbs profiling actual paths in which the prefixes actually do separate are not construed as subordinated to other grounded verbs.

In addition, there appears to be good evidence that the separable verb category in German has a prototype structure. Prototypical examples with clear path-like meanings are the prime motivation for separation of the prefix with such verbs. Less prototypical (or more abstract) separable verbs are more peripheral members of the separable verb category, and it is likely that in certain peripheral cases the separability of the prefix is completely grammaticalized and no longer has any appreciable semantic content (as is probably the case with yes/no questions in the past tenses).

Analyses of this kind argue strongly for the idea that grammatical structure cannot be insightfully analyzed independently of meaning. There is often a (sometimes very subtle) relationship between grammatical structure and conceptual structure in languages which many current autonomist theories overlook.

References

Croft, William. 1995. Autonomy and Functionalist Linguistics. *Language* 71:490–532.

Drosdowski, Günther. 1984. *Grammatik der deutschen Sprache*. Mannheim: Bibliographisches Institut.

Fauconnier, Gilles. 1985. *Mental Spaces. Aspects of Meaning Construction in Natural Language*. Cambridge, MA/London: The MIT Press.

Gibbs, Raymond W., Jr. and Herbert L. Colston. 1995. The Cognitive Psychological Reality of Image Schemas and their Transformations. *Cognitive Linguistics* 6:347–378.

Johnson, Mark. 1987. *The Body in the Mind*. Chicago: The University of Chicago Press.

Johnson, Mark. 1991. Knowing through the Body. *Philosophical Psychology* 4:3–18.

Lakoff, George and Mark Johnson. 1980. *Metaphors We Live By*. Chicago and London: The University of Chicago Press.

Lakoff, George. 1987. *Women, Fire, and Dangerous Things: What Categories Reveal About the Mind*. Chicago: The University of Chicago Press.

Langacker, Ronald W. 1987. *Foundations of Cognitive Grammar, Vol. I: Theoretical Prerequisites*. Stanford: Stanford University Press.

Langacker, Ronald W. 1991a. *Concept, Image, Symbol:The Cognitive Basis of Grammar*. Berlin/New York: Mouton de Gruyter.

Langacker, Ronald W. 1991b. *Foundations of Cognitive Grammar, Vol. II: Descriptive Application*. Stanford: Stanford University Press.

Langacker, Ronald W. 1993. Reference-point Constructions. *Cognitive Linguistics* 4:1–38.

Lederer, Herbert. 1969. *Reference Grammar of the German Language*. New York: Charles Scribner's Sons.

Olsen, Susan. 1985. On Deriving V-1 and V-2 Structures in German, in Jindřich Toman, ed., *Studies in German Grammar*, Dordrecht-Holland: Foris Publications, 133–163.

Smith, Michael B. 1987. The Semantics of Dative and Accusative in German: An Investigation in Cognitive Grammar. Doctoral dissertation, University of California, San Diego.

Smith, Michael B. 1993a. Aspects of German Clause Structure from a Cognitive Grammar Perspective. *Studi Italiani di Linguistica: Teorica e Applicata 22*: 601–638.

Smith, Michael B. 1993b. Cases as Conceptual Categories: Evidence from German, in Richard A. Geiger and Brygida Rudzka-Ostyn, eds., *Conceptualizations and Mental Processing in Language* (Cognitive Linguistics Research 2), Berlin/New York: Mouton de Gruyter, 531–565.

Smith, Michael B. 1995. Semantic Motivation vs. Arbitrariness in Grammar: Toward a More General Account of the DAT/ACC Contrast with German Two-Way Prepositions, in Irmengard Rauch and Gerald F. Carr, eds., *Insights in Germanic Linguistics I: Methodology in Transition* (Trends in Linguistics, Studies and Monographs 83), Berlin/New York: Mouton de Gruyter, 293–323.

Access Path Expressions in Thai

KIYOKO TAKAHASHI

Chulalongkorn University

1. Introduction

This paper investigates the so-called 'access paths' in Thai.[1] Access paths are a category that Talmy (1996) terms fictive motion (i.e. less palpable motion) or what Langacker (1986; 1987; 1998) calls abstract or subjective or virtual motion (i.e. motion on the part of the conceptualizer). These terms refer to motion that does not physically occur but is evoked in the conceptualizer's mind. Talmy (1996: 251) comments that fictive motion is neither seen at the fully concrete level of palpability nor felt at the fully abstract level of palpability. It is rather sensed at the semiabstract level of palpability. That is, the motion itself is intangible but experienced as present in association with other entities seen at the fully concrete level. Fauconnier (1997) and Langacker (1998) describe fictive motion in terms of conceptual "blending" (cf. Fauconnier & Turner 1996). The blended structure of fictive motion comprises two simultaneous mental spaces: an actual space for the described stationary scene and a virtual space with an imaginary mover.

The category of access paths is one among several main categories of fictive motion (cf. Talmy 1996). The physical concrete entities associated with the access paths are entities located with respect to another entity. An access path emerges as we fictively connect the located entity(s) with the reference entity. In Talmy's (1996: 242) view, "access

[1] An earlier version of this paper was presented to the fourth Conference on Conceptual Structure, Discourse, and Language, held at Emory University in October 1998. I am very grateful to Yo Matsumoto and Krisadawan Hongladarom for their helpful comments, and I gratefully acknowledge the comments of two anonymous reviewers of this paper. Thanks are also due to Dale R. Kvalheim and John C. Maher for stylistic suggestions.

Conceptual and Discourse Factors in Linguistic Structure.
Alan Cienki, Barbara J. Luka and Michael B. Smith (eds.).

paths are a depiction of a stationary object's location in terms of a path that some other entity might follow to the point of encounter with the entity." But the same can not be said of the Thai counterparts. For one thing, the described entity or entities may not be located at the endpoint of the path, but may stretch over the path (see Section 4). What is more, Thai speakers do not imagine a concrete entity moving along an access path, but what moves along the path is only their focus of attention (see Section 5).

In the following examples, (1) and (2) exemplify access path expressions in English and Thai, respectively:[2]

(1) a. [The bike] is *across the street from the church.* (Talmy 1983: 251)

     b. Twenty minutes *down the road* is [the hotel].

     c. There was [a fire] last night *across the river, through the canyon, and over the mountain.* (Langacker 1986: 468)

     d. [The city] lies many miles *across the desert.* (Matsumoto 1996: 366)

(2) a.
thàt	tɛ̀ɛ	klùm	nùm		maa
move a little	from	group	young man		come
khâaŋ lăŋ	pen	[klùm	mɛ̂ɛ bâan]		
side back	COP	group	housewife		

'Back from the group of young men (toward some reference point) is the group of housewives'

     b.
lǝǝy	càak	khǎw	mǎacuu	pay	cà?	mii
pass	from	hill	Maju	go	MOD	exist
[thaaŋ jêɛk		pay	sùu	thâm	lɔ̂ɔt	
side road		go	towards	cave	go through	
jày]						
large						

'Beyond the Maju hill (away from some reference point),

---

[2] The data used for this study were derived mainly from published literary works and a computerized corpus of the Thai language including literary works, magazines and newspapers, and partly from interviews with Thai native speakers studying at the linguistics department of Chulalongkorn University, Bangkok. The corpus belongs to the National Electronics and Computer Technology Center (NECTEC), National Science and Technology Development Agency (NSTDA), Ministry of Science, Technology and Environment, Thailand. I would like to thank the organization for permission to use the corpus for this study.

In all the examples, noun phrases representing located entities are inside brackets; verb or prepositional phrases representing access paths are italicized; and copulative, existential and locational verbs are underlined.

Abbreviations in the glosses are: CLA(ssifier); CON(junction); COP(ula); MOD(al); NEG(ative); PRON(oun, including relative pronoun); REC(iprocal); TOP(ic).

there is a side road to the large tunnel'

c. [sǔan phǎasǒmdèt]   nán   cà?   <u>jùu</u>   *hàaŋ*

park   Pasomdet   TOP   MOD   lie   remote

ʔɔ̀ɔk   *pay*   raaw   sɔ̌ɔŋ   kilooméet

exit   go   approximately   two   kilometer

'Pasomdet Park is about two kilometers away (from some reference point)'

In this paper I will examine the forms and functions of access path expressions in Thai and further consider semantic constraints on those expressions. Specifically, I will discuss: (a) how Thai—a serial verb language—encodes the access paths; (b) for what purposes Thai speakers use access path expressions; and (c) how Thai speakers' construals, with respect to the access paths, affect the structure of Thai access path expressions.

2. Distinct Construction Types

This section elaborates syntactic structures encoding access paths in Thai. Thai access path expressions in (3), (4) and (5), respectively, include <u>khɯɯɯ</u> / <u>pen</u> 'to be, namely' (copulative verb), <u>mii</u> 'to have, to exist' (existential verb), and <u>jùu</u> 'to lie, to stay' (locational verb). One of these three verbs inevitably occurs in the expressions. For convenience, we will name these three subtypes of expression Copulative type, Existential type, and Locational type.

(3) a. *klay* *ʔɔ̀ɔk* *pay* <u>pen</u> [kɔ̀? lǎay kɔ̀?]

        far   exit   go   COP   island   many   CLA

        'Far off are many islands'

  b. *troŋ*   *khâam* *tiaŋ nɔɔn* *sǔay*

        straight   cross   bed   beautiful

        khɔ̌ɔŋ thəə <u>khɯɯɯ</u> [hɔ̂ɔŋ nám rǔurǎa]

        of   PRON   COP   bathroom   gorgeous

        'Opposite to her beautiful bed is a gorgeous bathroom'

(4) *lúk*   *loŋ*   *pay*   *tây*   *phǔɯn nám*   *ʔan*

    deep   descend go   under   surface water   PRON

    jîŋ jày dùt kan <u>mii</u> [phuukhǎw] <u>mii</u>

    great   likewise exist   mountain   exist

    [hùp hěew]

    valley

    'Deep under the surface of the great sea, likewise, are mountain(s) and valley(s)'

(5) lɔɔn   lɛɛ   duu   [thalee ʔan   dam   pen
     PRON   look   see   sea   PRON   dark   COP

     ŋaw]   sûŋ   <u>jùu</u>   *klay*   *pay*   *càak*   *naytaa*
     shadow   PRON   lie   far   go   from   eye

'She looked at the dark sea which was far away from her eyes'

There are two distinct syntactic structures for the access paths in Thai, namely Copulative / Existential type vs. Locational type. The table below shows the orders among their three main constituents (a), (b) and (c). No other order for the constituents is possible.

	1	2	3
Copulative type:	(c) *Path VP/PP*	(a) <u>Copulative</u> <u>V</u>	(b) [Theme NP]
Existential type:	(c) *Path VP/PP*	(a) <u>Existential</u> <u>V</u>	(b) [Theme NP]
Locational type:	(b) [Theme NP]	(a) <u>Locational</u> <u>V</u>	(c) *Path VP/PP*

(a) <u>Copulative V</u>   copulative verb <u>khɯɯ</u> / <u>pen</u>

     <u>Existential V</u>   existential verb <u>mii</u>

     <u>Locational V</u>   locational verb <u>jùu</u>

(b) [Theme NP]   noun phrase naming located entity(s)

(c) *Path VP/PP*   verb or prepositional phrase encoding fictive path

Compare the syntactic structures of English access path expressions, as in (1), with those of Thai access path expressions, as in (2). The similarities between them are as follows. First, Existential verbs precede Theme noun phrases, as in (1c) and (2b). Second, Locational verbs occur after Theme noun phrases and before Path verb or prepositional phrases, as in (1d) and (2c). There are also differences between them. First, English Copulative verbs may occur after Theme noun phrases and before Path prepositional phrases, as in (1a). However, Thai Copulative verbs always occur after Path verb or prepositional phrases and before Theme noun phrases, as in (2a). Second, while English Path prepositional phrases normally follow Existential verb phrases, as in (1c), Thai Path verb or prepositional phrases always precede Existential verb phrases, as in (2b). Third, noun phrases indicating distance are placed at the beginning of English Path prepositional phrases, as in (1d), while they are placed at the end of Thai Path verb or prepositional phrases, as in (2c). These syntactic contrasts between the two languages, however, are not specifically observed in access path expressions; rather, the contrasts are natural consequences of the different principles of grammatical structures in the two languages.

(6) lists all the types of components of verb or prepositional phrases expressing the fictive path (Path VP/PP). Examples in (7) illustrate how these components are combined in a Path VP/PP.

(6)   a.   Locative noun (i.e. noun indicating the spatial position of its determining noun) which can be interpreted into English preposition or adverb (e.g. nǔa(...) 'above(...) (north),' tây(...) 'below(...) (south)') or locative preposition (e.g. tèɛ... 'from...,' tân tèɛ... 'from (to set up + from)...,' troŋ khâam... 'opposite (straight + to cross)...,' troŋ kan khâam... 'opposite (straight + REC + to cross)...'), and its attendant noun phrase naming the reference entity.

        b.   Space-descriptive verb which is semantically equivalent to the English adjective (e.g. klay 'far,' hàaŋ 'remote,' sǔuŋ 'high,' tàm 'low,' nǔa 'northern,' tây 'southern,' lúk 'deep')

        c.   Locative co-verb (i.e. locative preposition derived from motion verb) (e.g. càak... 'from (to leave)...,' ləəy... 'beyond (to overstep)...,' thàt 'next (to move a little)'), normally accompanied with object noun phrase indicating the reference entity, with the exception of thàt which requires no object noun phrase

        d.   Directional verb 1 representing direction that results from interaction between the path and the outside world (i.e. khâw 'into some enclosed space (to enter),' ʔɔ̀ɔk 'out of some enclosed space (to exit),' khûn 'upward (to ascend),' and loŋ 'downward (to descend)'), which precedes Directional verb 2

        e.   Directional verb 2 representing direction with respect to some reference point (i.e. maa 'toward some reference point (to come)' and pay 'away from some reference point (to go)'), which follows Directional verb 1

        f.   Noun phrase indicating distance (e.g. sɔ̌ɔŋ kiloomêet 'two kilometers') or direction (e.g. bûaŋ bon 'above (toward + upper part)') and/or adverbial indicating degree (e.g. lék nɔ́ɔy 'a little'), which is capable of being placed at the end of Path VP

(7)   a.   *nŭa*   *khûn*   *pay*   bûaŋ   bon   khɯɯ

          above   ascend   go   toward   upper part   COP

          [kǐŋ   kâan   khɔ̌ɔŋ   takhòp   jày]

          twig   stem   of   Takop tree   big

          'Up above are branches of a big Takop tree'

     b.   *klay*   *ʔɔ̌ɔk*   *pay*   lék nɔ́ɔy   khɯɯ   [rɯan

          far   exit   go   a little   COP   house

          máy]

          tree

          'Far off a little is a wooden house'

     c.   *thàt*   *pay*   mây   klay   càak   kan

          move a little   go   NEG   far   from   REC

          nák   kɔ̂   cà?   pen   [laan   sùríjan]

          very   then   MOD   COP   yard   Suriyan

          'Next, not very far (from some reciprocal reference point), is the Suriyan yard'

The Path PP in (7a) is composed of the locative noun nŭa 'above (north)' (6a) and the directional verbs 1 and 2 khûn pay 'upward (to ascend) + away from some reference point (to go)' (6d, e) which are followed by the adverbial bûaŋ bon 'above (toward + upper part)' (6f). The Path VP in (7b) is composed of the space-descriptive verb klay 'far' (6b) and the directional verbs 1 and 2 ʔɔ̌ɔk pay 'out of some enclosed space (to exit) + away from some reference point (to go)' (6d, e) which are followed by the adverbial lék nɔ́ɔy 'a little' (6f). And the Path VP/PP in (7c) is composed of the locative co-verb thàt 'next (to move a little)' (6c) and the directional verb 2 pay 'away from some reference point (to go)' (6e) which are followed by the modifying phrase mây klay càak kan nák 'not very far from some reciprocal reference point' (6f).

       Pattern 1:   6a   (+ 6d)   + 6e
       Pattern 2:   6b   (+ 6d)   + 6e   (+ 6a/6c)
       Pattern 3:   6c   (+ 6d)   + 6e   (+ 6c)
       Pattern 4:   6c   + 6c   (+ 6e)

The predicates with locative nouns/prepositions (6a) as well as the predicates with space-descriptive verbs (6b), i.e. Patterns 1 and 2, are used only for expressing abstract motion. For example: nŭa khûn pay 'above (north) + upward (to ascend) + away from some reference point (to go)' in (7a) expresses abstract upward motion of someone's gaze or focus of attention ('above') but not physical upward motion of someone. On the other hand, the predicates with only directional verb phrases (6d, e) and/or co-verb phrases (6c), i.e. Patterns 3 and 4, may be used for expressing either abstract or physical motion. An interpretation of them is dependent on the particular context. For example: thàt pay 'next (to move a little) + away from some reference point (to go)' in (7c) is capable of expressing either abstract motion of someone's gaze or focus of attention ('next') or physical motion of someone ('to move a little'). As far as Thai access path expressions are concerned, however, an abstract motion reading is appropriate (see Section 5).

3. Two Subtypes of Copula

Thai has two copulas, i.e. pen and khuɯɯ. Komolwanig and Sawada (1993: 96) point out that the distinction between the two copulas is a matter of cognitive pragmatics. The following are grammatical and pragmatic factors distinguishing the two copulas (Komolwanig & Sawada 1993: 104-5).

	Grammatical level	Pragmatic level
pen	[+ modal]	[+ speaker's commitment]
khuɯɯ	[- modal]	[- speaker's commitment]

The first copula pen occurs in expressions involving the speaker's hypothesis (or supposition) and reasoning (or inference). pen thus primarily functions at the pragmatic level: it marks the speaker's subjective, modal attitude at the speaking time. In other words, this modal copula marks a high degree of speaker commitment in giving the relevant information. Concurrently, pen identifies entities at the logical level, that is, it either describes their qualities or typifies them. The second copula khuɯɯ, in contrast, does not pertain to the speaker's subjective evaluation or recognition. This nonmodal copula objectively identifies (or denotatively categorizes) things without any connotation of the things implied, and does not co-occur with adverbials of epistemic modality (e.g. khon 'probably,' ʔàat 'may').

Endorsing Komolwanig and Sawada's categorization of Thai copulas, I will divide Thai copulative sentences for access paths into two subtypes: (a) the modal copulative type using pen, which implies the speaker's commitment in conveying information about the identified thing(s) (the referent of Theme NP); and, (b) the nonmodal copulative type using khuɯɯ, which does not. Consider (8a) below. The first serial verbs express the fictive path that terminates at the pond and the second and third copulative verb phrases express the pond's properties. The former nonmodal copulative verb phrase khuɯɯ sàʔ pathom '(it) is the

Patom pond' represents the objective identification (or categorization) of the pond as one having the name of Patom, while the latter modal copulative verb phrase pen sà? nám kwâan '(it) is the wide pond' represents the subjective identification (or categorization) of the pond as one being wide in size. Other combinations are also possible, as in (8b, c). Thus, the described thing's intrinsic or objective properties have nothing to do with the selection of the copulas. The selection depends entirely on the speaker's subjective recognition.

(8) a. *tàm*   *loŋ*   *maa*   khuɯɯ   [sà?   pathom]

         low   descend   come   COP   pond   Patom

         pen   [sà?   nám   kwâaŋ]

         COP   pond   water   wide

         'Down below is the Patom pond, a wide pond'

    b. *tàm*   *loŋ*   *maa*   pen   [sà?   pathom]

         low   descend   come   COP   pond   Patom

         'Down below is the Patom pond'

    c. *tàm*   *loŋ*   *maa*   khuɯɯ   [sà?   nám   kwâaŋ]

         low   descend   come   COP   pond   water wide

         'Down below is the wide pond'

4. Functions of Thai Access or "Trace" Path Expressions

Analysis of Thai corpus data together with interviews with Thai native speakers concerning access path expressions show that Thai speakers prefer to use the expressions to describe a spatial relationship between two stationary objects, viz. one is located with respect to the other, in terms of a linear path connecting with each other. The reference object may be named by a noun phrase after a locative noun (e.g. tây... 'below... (south)'), as in (4), or after a locative preposition (e.g. tɛ̀ɛ... 'from...,' troŋ khâam... 'opposite (straight + to cross)...'), as in (2a) and (3b), or after a locative co-verb (e.g. càak... 'from (to leave)...'), as in (2b) and (5); or it may be alluded to by such a lexical item as kan implying reciprocal relationship, as in (7c); or it may be unmentioned if it is obvious from the context, as in (2c), (3a), (5), (7a, b), and (8).

Additionally, the access paths in Thai can describe another kind of spatial relationship: a number of objects or a single object indefinitely extending in a space specified by the reference object in a certain way. (9) below, for example, describes a number of resort hotels that stand in line along the road beyond Thungsalaengluang National Park. That is, the described locus is not necessarily at the endpoint of the fictive path, but it may extend over the fictive path. The term "access paths" is not quite felicitous for such fictive paths. We can call them "trace paths" instead.

(9) táŋ tèɛ   ʔùtthajaan hèŋ châat   thûŋ salěɛŋlǔaŋ

     from   national park   Tungsalaengluang

     pen   *tôn*   *maa*   cà?   *mii*

     COP   beginning   come   MOD   exist

     [riisɔ̀ɔt   plùuk sâaŋ   jùu]   dooy talɔ̀ɔt

     resort hotel   build   lie   throughout

     'Beyond Thungsalaengluang National Park are resort hotels built along the way'

Furthermore, it has been found that the different subtypes of Thai access or trace path expressions convey different kinds of information. The following are random samples. The Copulative type of sentence in (3a) introduces islands that have a distant relationship with the covert reference entity. The Existential type of sentence in (4) introduces mountain(s) and valley(s) that spread out in the deep sea. The Locational type of sentence in (5) introduces the precise location of Pasomdet Park. The Existential type, on the one hand, describes something that has a specific spatial relationship with the reference entity. The entity(s) to be located by the Existential type (e.g. 'mountain(s) and valley(s)' in (4)) is assumed to be nondefinite but specific. That is, it is what the speaker wants to convey to the addressee.[3] The Locational type, on the other hand, describes an exact location of something with respect to the reference entity. The entity(s) to be located by the Locational type (e.g. 'Pasomdet Park' in (5)) is assumed to be generic or definite. That is, it is part of the general knowledge of both the speaker and the addressee. The Locational type presupposes that not only knowledge of the reference entity but also knowledge of the located entity(s) is shared by the speaker and the addressee.

(10) a. Informational Structure for Existential Type:

          given   □

          new   □ ----------------------> 0

---

[3] In terms of informational status, Ekniyom (1982: 120) claims that a noun phrase following the existential verb mii is characterized by the feature [-given] which corresponds to the feature [-definite] with the subfeature [-generic].

b.   Informational Structure for Locational Type:

given   □   0

new   □ ----------------------> 0

The schematic informational structures of the Existential type and the Locational type are shown in (10a) and (10b), respectively. Notations for the pictorial primitives are as follows: The square □ on the left side represents the reference entity; the sign **0** on the right side represents the located entity; and the line between the square □ and the sign **0** represents the fictive path. The upper figures represent given information relevant to new information and the lower figures represent new information introduced by an access or trace path expression.

As for the Copulative type, both of the above two informational structures are applicable. The Copulative type, however, highlights the speaker's identification. The entity(s) to be located by the Copulative type (e.g. 'islands' in (3a)) must have some specific nature recognized or identified by the speaker. With the modal copula pen, the nature is attributed to the speaker's subjective evaluation; with the nonmodal copula khɯ̄ɯ, it is not.

There is another important point we have to clarify with regard to the use of access or trace expressions in Thai. Namely, Thai speakers use access or trace path expressions for describing something's locus, but not directing someone to somewhere or reporting someone's travel to somewhere.[4] When Thai speakers show a way or state a travel course, they utter sentences like those in (11), which include an agentive verb (khàp 'to drive') and/or a verb referring to the result of an actual or hypothetical process denoted by the agentive verb (thɯ̌ɯŋ 'to reach' expressing the agent's arrival at the destination, phóp / cəə 'to encounter' expressing the agent's coming across something on her way, hěn 'to see' expressing the agent's visual perception of the scene emerging as she travels); and, possibly including the temporal conjunction mɯ̂a 'once, when.'

(11)	a.	khàp	rót	pay	pramaan	sɔ̌ɔŋ
		drive	car	go	approximately	two
		chûamoоŋ	kɔ̂	cà?	thɯ̌ɯŋ	sǔan
		hour	then	MOD	reach	park

---

[4] Langacker (1987: 170-1) states that English access path expressions like 'The Linguistic Hall of Fame is across the plaza, through the alley, and over the bridge' would be used for giving directions to the addressee.

phăasŏmdèt

Pasomdet

'You drive about two hours and then you will reach Pasom-det Park'

b. | mɯ̂a | khâam | mɛ̂ɛ nám | | paasík | pay | kɔ̂ |
    |------|-------|---------|--|--------|-----|-----|
    | CON | cross | river | | Pasik | go | then |

cà?	{phóp / cəə / hĕn / pen}		sanăam	jâa
MOD	{encounter/ encounter/ see/ COP}		field	grass

kwâaŋ	jày
wide	large

'Once you cross the Pasik river, you will {encounter/ see/ find that it is} a wide grass plot'

The verbs khàp 'to drive' and thɯ̆ŋ 'to reach' in (11a) express the un-named agent's drive to Pasomdet Park for about two hours. Here how the agent goes to the park is the focus, while the park functions as the background of the drive, that is, the destination. The temporal conjunction mɯ̂a 'once, when' in (11b) overtly marks a dynamic process, namely the unnamed mover's travel to somewhere. In short, the sentences in (11) foreground someone's movement through time. These dynamic expressions are distinguished from access or trace path expressions which describe an entity's or entities' locus per se. Someone's "potential" motions expressed in (11) are rather similar to motions along coverage paths in Thai (cf. Takahashi 1998) and motions along access paths in English (see Section 5; cf. Matsumoto 1996).

5. Thai Speakers' Construal of Access or Trace Paths

Access or trace path expressions describe stationary entities' spatial rela-tionships in terms of a path linking the located entity(s) with the refer-ence entity, along which some other entity fictively moves. What, then, is imagined to fictively move along the path? Opinions vary as to the nature of the imagined moving entity. According to Talmy (1996: 242), the entity fictively moving along the access paths can be imagined as being (a) a person or (b) the focus of a person's attention. Likewise, Langacker (1987: 171) divides the abstract motion regarding the access paths into two categories according to the degree of specificity in the properties of the imagined moving entity: (a) potential motion, i.e. either projected motion of a specific mover or hypothetical motion of an arbitrary mover; (b) subjective motion, i.e. the conceptualizer's sequen-tial scanning of the linear path. The projected motion is more specific (less abstract), the hypothetical motion is less specific (more abstract), and the subjective motion is by no means specific (the most abstract).

Matsumoto (1996: 368-9), on the other hand, claims that the imagined entities traveling over the access paths should be human beings or at least concrete entities such as cars. The unacceptable or less acceptable sentences in (12) support this view.

(12)   a. * [The village] is *over the valley from us.* (Brugman 1981 cited in Matsumoto 1996: 368)

   b. */OK   [His office] is *{across/ through} this wall.* (Matsumoto 1996: 368)

   c. ? [The cloud] is 1,000 feet *up from the ground.* (Talmy 1996: 242)

(12a) is not acceptable because we cannot go over a valley to get to the village on the other side of it. For most English speakers, (12b) is not acceptable, either, because we, except those who have power to easily go through a wall, cannot cross a wall separating offices. An English native speaker told me that (12c) also sounds odd, although it is taken up as a good instance by Talmy. The reason is, he commented, that we can hardly imagine some kind of motion that would allow us to reach the clouds.

I argue that the access or trace paths proper in Thai do not entail a concrete mover, but what shifts along the path is the speaker's focus of attention alone. Thai speakers use access or trace path expressions to describe entities' spatial relationships in terms of a linear path between the entities traced by their gaze. There are some pieces of evidence in favor of this opinion. First, access or trace path expressions in Thai resist temporal modification. For example, the temporally modified sentences in (13a) and (13b) that respectively contain the time phrases raaw sɔ̌ɔŋ chûamooŋ 'about two hours' and jîisìp naathii 'twenty minutes' are abnormal. This pertains to the highly abstract nature of subjective motion involved in the expressions. It is so abstract as to be of no duration.

(13)   a. ?? [sǔan phǎasǒmdèt]   nán   cà?   jùu   hàaŋ

   park   Pasomdet   TOP   MOD   lie   remote

   ʔɔ̀ɔk   pay   raaw   sɔ̌ɔŋ   chûamooŋ

   exit   go   approximately   two   hour

   (intended meaning) 'Pasomdet Park is about two hours away'[5]

---

[5] To some Thai native speakers, however, (13a) is acceptable although they admit that it is somewhat awkward and does not appear in written Thai. The difference in the degree of acceptability between (13a) and (13b) appears to come from the different semantic properties of the two space-descriptive verbs hàaŋ 'remote' and tàm 'low.' While tàm 'low' denotes purely static spatial notion, hàaŋ 'remote' may express a remote relationship arising from some previous actual motion (e.g. resultant remoteness between the departure point and the destination of someone's long travel). Since hàaŋ

b. *tàm   loŋ   maa   jìisĭp   naathii   khuɯɯ

    low   descend come   twenty   minute   COP

[sà?   pathom]

pond   Patom

(intended meaning) 'Twenty minutes down (the road) is the Patom pond'

Secondly, verbs denoting a specific manner of motion and a specific moving entity (e.g. bùŋ 'to rush,' dəən 'to walk,' lɯ́ay 'to crawl (snake-like animal)') as well as verbs denoting a specific configuration of the path of motion (e.g. wók 'to meander,' wian 'to circle') do not appear in Thai access or trace path expressions. It may be ascribed to the fact that the shift of the conceptualizer's focus of attention (or mental tracing) involved in the expressions is never substantial and therefore its contour must not be complicated (but ideally straight).

(14) a. [The vacuum cleaner] is *down around* behind the clothes hamper. (Talmy 1996: 242)

    b. [khrɯ̂aŋ   dùut   fùn]   jùu   lăŋ   takrâa

        machine   suck   dust   lie   back   hamper

    'The vacuum cleaner is behind the hamper'

The English access path expression in (14a), which includes the preposition 'around' indicating the curved path of motion, does not have a Thai counterpart. English speakers imagine that someone's arm stretches down around behind the clothes hamper and eventually reaches the vacuum cleaner. Thai speakers do not imagine such a concrete motion of someone to locate the vacuum cleaner in this setting, but they would employ a purely static spatial expression like (14b) for describing the vacuum cleaner's location.

Thirdly, either maa 'toward some reference point (to come)' or pay 'away from some reference point (to go)' appears in Thai access or trace path expressions, with some exceptions (see below). It follows that most of the expressions involve the speaker or conceptualizer's vantage point independent of the located and reference entities. The entities' spatial relationship tends to be described from a particular point of view. In other words, the spatial relationship is largely designated in the relative frame of reference (Levinson 1996: 142-5).

However, the locative preposition troŋ (kan) khâam... 'opposite (straight (+ REC) + to cross)...' does not, and the locative co-verbs thàt càak... 'next to (to move a little + to leave)...' and ləəy càak... 'be-

---

'remote' possibly induces us to imagine some temporally developing process, (13a) might seem compatible with temporal modification.

yond (to overstep + to leave)...' may not, co-occur with maa / pay. These lexical items, like English prepositions (e.g. across), express entities' spatial relationships irrespective of a vantage point (troŋ (kan) khâam... 'opposite...' denoting an oppositional relationship, thàt càak... 'next to...' denoting a proximal relationship, and ləəy càak... 'beyond...' denoting a front-rear relationship). These spatial relationships are binary: they are sufficiently designated by the two parts, i.e. the located entity and the reference entity, and need not involve a viewpoint distinct from the two parts. In this regard, these lexical items are similar to locative nouns (e.g. lăŋ... 'in back of... (back),' nâa... 'in front of... (face),' bon... 'above..., on... (upper part)') which denote a contiguous relationship between the located entity and the reference entity by referring to the reference entity's intrinsic configuration.

Whether or not a verb or prepositional phrase in an access or trace expression in Thai includes maa / pay, however, the phrase does indeed indicate the starting point and direction of some abstract motion.[6] Therefore, we may safely state that the access or trace paths in Thai are mentally traced in a certain direction by the speaker or conceptualizer.

6. Conclusion

The semantic conditions on Thai access or trace path expressions discussed in this paper can be summarized below.

First, neither noun phrases indicating duration (e.g. sɔ̌ɔŋ chûamooŋ 'two hours') nor adverbials indicating velocity (e.g. rew 'quickly,' cháa 'slowly') can be encompassed in the expressions. This restriction is presumably due to Thai speakers' construals of the access or trace paths. Thai speakers bring in an access or trace path only when they need to locate entity(s) with respect to another entity in such a way that they mentally trace the linear path between them. No physical mover along this fictive path is imagined. The expressions lack temporal notion, for they do not involve any physical, concrete motion.

Second, motion verbs that appear in the expressions are limited to six versatile directional verbs and some locative co-verbs. The sense of motion incorporated in these verbs has been more or less bleached out. Thai verbs of motion proper, on the other hand, generally represent substantial motion with specific manner and/or path as far as their meanings are confined to the spatial domain. Since motion verbs in Thai tend to require such a high degree of concreteness or substance of motion, they cannot be used for encoding the access or trace paths along which a nonconcrete, intangible entity—the speaker's focus of attention—moves.

Third, the expressions must include a verb or prepositional phrase

---

[6] No intermediate point on the path is specified, though. To relate entities to each other, it is not necessary to refer to a specific intermediate point between the entities.

whose components together overtly or covertly indicate the starting point and direction of the shift of the speaker's focus of attention (or mental tracing) along the access or trace path.

Thai speakers' construals of access or trace paths are strictly spatial (or atemporal), that is, they do not imagine a concrete mover along the paths. Since the involved moving entity is their own gaze (or their focus of attention), the access or trace paths in Thai are highly abstract and subjective phenomena. We have seen that such strictly spatial and highly abstract construals do condition Thai access or trace path expressions.

All languages might have access path expressions which are used for spatially linking entities in a setting that is arbitrarily structured. But it is possible that the degree of abstractness and subjectivity of the expressions varies among languages.

References

Brugman, Claudia. 1981. The Story of Over. Master's thesis, University of California, Berkeley.

Ekniyom, Peansiri. 1982. A Study of Informational Structuring in Thai Sentences. Doctoral dissertation, University of Hawaii.

Fauconnier, Gilles. 1997. *Mappings in Thought and Language*. New York: Cambridge University Press.

Fauconnier, Gilles and Mark Turner. 1996. Blending as a Central Process of Grammar, in A.E. Goldberg, ed.,*Conceptual Structure, Discourse, and Language*. Stanford: CSLI.

Komolwanig, Komol-orn and Naoko Sawada. 1993. A Contrastive Study of Copulative Sentences in Japanese and Thai—from the Viewpoint of Cognitive Pragmatics. *Gengo Kenkyuu* 103: 92-116.

Langacker, Ronald. 1986. Abstract Motion. *Proceedings of the Twelfth Annual Meeting of the Berkeley Linguistics Society*, 455-471.

Langacker, Ronald. 1987. *Foundations of Cognitive Grammar Vol.1*. Stanford: Stanford University Press.

Langacker, Ronald. 1998. Virtual Reality. Paper presented at the Conference of Linguistic Association of Canada and the United States. Claremont Graduate University, California, July 29, 1998.

Levinson, Stephen C. 1996. Frames of References and Molyneux's Question: Crosslinguistic Evidence, in P. Bloom, M.A. Peterson, L. Nadel and M.F. Garrett, eds., *Language and Space*. Cambridge: MIT Press.

Matsumoto, Yo. 1996. How Abstract is Subjective Motion? A Comparison of Coverage Path Expressions and Access Path Expressions, in A.E. Goldberg, ed., *Conceptual Structure, Discourse, and Language*. Stanford: CSLI.

Takahashi, Kiyoko. 1998. Functions of Resultative Fictive Motion (Advent Path) Expressions and Potential Fictive Motion (Coverage Path) Expressions in Thai and Semantic Constraints on the Expressions. *Proceedings of the 116th General Meeting of the Linguistic Society of Japan*, 136-

141.

Talmy, Leonard. 1983. How Language Structures Space, in H. Pick and L. Acredolo, eds., *Spatial Orientation: Theory, Research, and Application*. New York: Plenum Press.

Talmy, Leonard. 1996. Fictive Motion in Language and "Ception," in P. Bloom, M.A. Peterson, L. Nadel and M.F. Garrett, eds., *Language and Space*. Cambridge: MIT Press.

Switch Reference and Zero Anaphora: Emergent Reference in Discourse Processing

LIANG TAO

Ohio University

1. Introduction

This study proposes a unified account of language and cognition by means of a cross-linguistic study of the switch-reference pattern. The study proposes that the grammatical coding, or lack of such coding in this pattern, may reflect how much inference speakers use in reference tracking, i.e., the more grammatical coding a language uses in its reference presentation, the less inference its speakers may rely on in processing discourse information, and vice versa. As an illustration to support the argument, the study proposes the following two hypotheses:

A.   Gricean Principle in reference presentation (the Gricean Continuum)

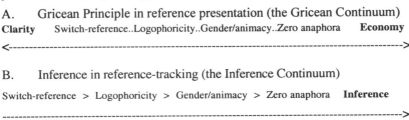

Clarity   Switch-reference..Logophoricity..Gender/animacy..Zero anaphora   **Economy**

<--->

B.   Inference in reference-tracking (the Inference Continuum)

Switch-reference > Logophoricity > Gender/animacy > Zero anaphora   **Inference**

--->

The two continuums together answer the two inter-related questions of:
• why languages present referents with different grammatical structures,

Conceptual and Discourse Factors in Linguistic Structure.
Alan Cienki, Barbara J. Luka and Michael B. Smith (eds.).
Copyright © 2001, CSLI Publications.

- whether people use an equal amount of inference to conduct reference tracking in discourse processing.

The Gricean Continuum answers the first question. It illustrates a formal realization of a pragmatic competing motivation regarding grammatical coding of switch reference cross-linguistically. The arrows indicate the motivations to reach both clarity and economy.

The Inference Continuum answers the second question. It proposes an increased amount of inference being used for reference tracking with the decrease of formal grammatical coding of switch reference. The two continuums are explained in detail in Sections 2 and 3.

The pattern of switch reference is illustrated in example 1, which indicates that the grammatical subject of a clause may be the same or different from the subject of an adjacent clause.

(1)   NP Subject1......, NP Subject1(same) / 2(different).....

This study tries to examine different grammatical structures that code this pattern cross-linguistically, focusing on the canonical switch reference languages in comparison with Mandarin Chinese, a language with abundant use of zero anaphora, to support the two continuums.

2. Gricean Principle in Reference Presentation

2.1 The Gricean Continuum

Previous studies discuss the switch reference pattern by focusing on the canonical switch-reference languages (e.g., Haiman and Munro 1983; Stirling 1993). The only exception is Givon (1983b) who gives the pattern a typological account by suggesting that reference presentation in the switch reference pattern follows the theory of topic continuity (Givon 1983a). However, as explained later in section 2.2.3, this theory does not adequately describe anaphoric choices in discourse. The current study proposes to look at the pattern from a different perspective by proposing the Gricean Continuum.

The Gricean Continuum illustrates a pragmatic competing motivation (Du Bois 1985; 1987) striving for both clarity and economy in reference presentation cross-linguistically. Languages all use anaphoric devices such as full noun phrases, pronouns, and/or zero anaphora to code referents. In addition, languages may also use other grammaticalized coding such as morphological markers on the predicate verb to indicate the referentiality of a noun phrase. This study proposes that cross-linguistically, the grammaticalized devices for reference presentation follow the pragmatic competing motivation to achieve both maximum clarity and economy in communication. This competing motivation can be explained by Grice's theory of conversational cooperative principles (Grice 1975). Formally, this motivation engenders diverse grammatical patterns along a continuum centering on reference presentation in the switch reference pattern. The Gricean continuum is repeated below.

(2)   Gricean Principle in reference presentation (the Gricean Continuum)

Clarity   Switch-reference..Logophoricity..Gender/animacy..Zero anaphora   **Economy**

<--->

The dots in the continuum indicate grammatical forms that are not cited, and the arrows illustrate the competing motivations. On the left side of the continuum are languages with the most grammaticalized coding, on the right side are those with the least coding of the same discourse phenomenon. The arrows indicate the competing motivations striving to achieve both explicitness and clarity (with more grammaticalized coding) and economy (with less or no grammaticalized coding) in reference presentation. For instance, to achieve clarity in reference presentation, the canonical switch-reference languages use morphological markings to indicate whether the subjects of two adjacent clauses share the same or different referents. On the other hand, to achieve maximum economy, languages like Mandarin Chinese may use abundant zero anaphora to code the same type of nominal information. As a support to the continuum, let us first look at the switch-reference patterns in different languages.

2.2 Examples Supporting the Gricean Continuum

2.2.1 Switch-Reference

To the left end of the Gricean Continuum are languages with the canonical switch-reference system. These languages have the most markings for referential status in discourse. The canonical switch-reference languages are mostly verb-final languages with a set of morphological markings on the predicate verb to indicate that the grammatical subject of the clause is the same or different from the subject of an adjacent clause (e.g., Ulcha [a Manchu-Tungus language, Nichols 1979], Lenakel [an Austronesian language, Lynch 1983], Kiowa [an American Indian language, Watkins 1993], and so forth). The 'marking' clauses are often subordinate clauses, so the switch-reference markers are sometimes taken as indications of sentence boundaries (Comrie, personal communication). In some languages there are clause-chains that are considered co-subordination because these clauses are in a dependency relationship, yet none of them is embedded in the other (Foley & Van Valin 1984:242; Stirling 1993:15).

What are special among these languages are the grammaticalized morphological markings. Even if two full noun phrases are present as grammatical subjects, the switch-reference markers are still present, as illustrated in example 3. Here SS and DS are markings for 'same subject' and 'different subject' respectively in two adjacent clauses.

(3) Central Pomo (Mithun 1993:121)[1]

  a. Subject (clause 1)=Subject (clause 2) (SS)

     ?a- ...c=àw=yó-**ba** down   ?-c=há´-c=-**ba**

     I.AGT in=go-SAME down   by.gravity-sit-INCH-SAME

     ma?á qa´-yú?c='i-w

     food biting-begin-P

     I came into the house, (I) sat down, and (I) started to eat.

  b. Subject (clause 1)=/=Subject (clause 2) (DS)

     ?a- ...c=àw=yó-w=**li** háyu=?el ?úda-w t≤o- sé-c=-mad=a

     I.AGT in=go-p=**DIFF** dog=the really 1.PAT glad.to.see-AFF=IMM

     I came into the house, and **my dog** was really glad to see me.

    Central Pomo is a Native American language spoken in Northern California. The language manifests the switch reference pattern with three pairs of aspectual markers. The pair of markers in Example 3 (-**ba** (SS) and -**li** (DS)) is used in realis constructions. These examples show that the referential status of the subjects is clearly marked by the morphological suffixes to the verbs. Notice that in (3b), even though the identity of the second referent is shown clearly by a full NP (my dog), the DS marker is still used, a fact indicating the grammaticalized pattern of switch reference.

    Such grammaticalized morphological markings prevail among the canonical switch-reference languages. One of these languages, Amele (a Papuan language), is especially interesting because its discourse pattern reflects the speaker's pragmatic effort striving for both clarity and economy. With provision for marking subject and object on the verb, the language allows overt pronouns to be dropped. In some circumstances the verbal agreement markings can also be omitted, leaving the verb stem in a highly elliptical expression. Yet at the other extreme, the language has extensive switch-reference markings. The two extremes reflect the effort to achieve both clarity and economy in reference presentation within this language. It should be noted, however, that the grammaticalized switch reference markers still prevail in Amele discourse.

    Amele has extensive clause chaining, with mostly subordination and some coordination of the clauses. But the switch-reference markers do not consistently correspond to the referentiality of referents. The DS marker also marks event-shift between clauses.

---

[1]The abbreviations that appear in the glosses of this example are the following: AFF: emotional affect; AGT: agent; DIFF: different subject; IMM: immediate; INCH: inchoative; P: perfect aspect; PAT: patient.

(4) Amele (Roberts 1987:250, cited in Stirling 1993:217)

    Deel ijed **he-do-co-b**   uqa cesel-I   h-on.

    Day three finish:3Sg:DS:3Sg 3Sg return-Pred come:3Sg:RemP

    After three days he came back.

In this example, the DS marker does not indicate coreferentiality, and there is no reference switching. According to Stirling, the DS marker here indicates a shift in time. In addition, the specific verb phrase 'he-do-co-b'—he finished it-DS—is considered a recapitulation clause which marks the completion of a series of events plus the beginning of a new episode. Thus, according to Stirling, the switch-reference markers serve to indicate the degree of agreement or dis-agreement between some **structured eventuality indices**. An SS marker indicates no change in eventuality, a DS marker indicates a shift in the parameters of the next eventuality, the default of which is a change in the Protagonist, but changes in Actuality or Location are also possible (p.234). Stirling's claim is supported in Mithun's study of Central Pomo, which also proposes that the primary function of the switch-reference markers is to show the aspectual relationship between two clauses, and switch reference is their secondary function. (For a detailed discussion, see Mithun 1993).

    Stirling proposes that from the native speaker's point of view, the switch-reference markers in Amele may have the following effect on the speaker (5a) and the hearer (5b):

(5) Reference markers in Amele (Stirling 1993:152)

      a. if time, place, event sequence, mood changes, use DS; otherwise, if reference changes, use DS; otherwise, use SS.

      b. if SS is used, assume same reference, and general continuity of event (unless otherwise indicated); if DS is used, assume disjoint reference; if this doesn't work, assume some other change.

    Stirling's proposal predicts both the speaker's intention in choosing the reference markers (5a) and the hearer's cognitive strategies to track nominal referents in discourse processing (5b).

    Although Stirling claims that in Amele, the primary function of these switch-reference markers is to indicate the status of eventuality, the fact these markers are taken as **the starting point** in discourse formation (5a) and reference interpretation (5b) indicates the importance of these grammaticalized markers in forming Amele discourse on the one hand, and language users' dependency on these markers in their processes of discourse information on the other. Taking the switch reference markers as the starting point for reference tracking is in line with studies of other canonical switch reference languages (e.g., Haiman & Munro 1983). Therefore, what these switch reference languages have in common is their grammaticalized morphological markings on the verbs to indicate referentiality. Functionally, the switch-reference markers act as indices for referential status and discourse events associated with the referents. Cognitively, a grammaticalized pattern marking referential identities and the possible range of nominal referents can facilitate reference tracking.

2.2.2 Logophoricity and Others

Languages in the middle of the Gricean Continuum have some, but not extended, marking systems just for switch reference. Some of them (e.g., some West African languages) have a set of logophoric pronouns whose function is to indicate coreferential status of third persons. The logophoric pronouns are used in subordinate clauses with a set of special verbs (e.g., logocentric verbs of saying); therefore these languages mark referential status of third persons in a given set of discourse patterns, unlike the switch-reference markings which occur in all occasions in the canonical switch reference languages. The next example from Igbo illustrates such use of a logophoric pronoun. The number associated with each pronoun indicates the same or different referents.

(6) (Comrie 1983:21)

    a. ó sìrì nà ò byàrà

        he said that he came

        He1 said that he2 came.

    b. ó sìrì nà yá byàrà

        he said that LOG came

        He1 said that he1 came.

From example (6), we can see that the English translations of the two expressions are ambiguous without the numbers indicating referentiality; thus the logophoric pronouns evidently may facilitate reference tracking.

Some languages do not have grammatical markings just to signal reference switching. Instead they use different verbal morphology or gender marking to help track a particular referent across clauses (Foley & Van Valin 1984; Van Valin & LaPolla 1997). In languages like English, Tzutujil and Tepehua, a change in voice may indicate that the referent being tracked is the undergoer instead of the actor.

(7). Change of voice (Foley & Van Valin, 1984:354)

    John went to work and ___ talked to his boss and ___ was given a promotion.

Gender is also used to code referential status. Here are two examples from English.

(8). Gender marking

    a. (Givon 1983b:59) He gave presents to the king and the queen. *Hé* thanked him, but *shé* just grunted.

    b. (E-mail from one of the author's friends) Now is when you should be in Athens. The weather has been beautiful without the humidity. I hope *it* has left us for good.

English has a M/F gender distinction in its pronominal system; thus, the use of stressed pronouns in (8a) is sufficient to code the switch of subject referents between the king (he) and the queen (she). Spanish also seems to employ stressed pronouns to indicate switch reference.

    Note that in theory, the pronoun *it* in example (8b) may have two referents (the weather and the humidity). Yet given the actual discourse context, there is only one referent of the pronoun that can be interpreted.

    In addition to the languages mentioned above, there are other languages that have extensive grammaticalized agreement markings (e.g., subject-verb agreement, person, number, and gender agreement, etc.). These languages include Italian, French, German and Turkish.

    All the languages discussed above have one thing in common: they all have certain grammaticalized devices (morphological markings, voice changes, agreement, or specific forms of pronouns) to code referents. We now examine the right side of the Gricean continuum: languages with minimal referential markings. Data from Mandarin Chinese are used to illustrate that zero anaphora may also occur in a switch reference pattern.

2.2.3 Zero Anaphora

On the right side of the Gricean Continuum are languages with the least grammatical coding for referential status. Unlike any of the languages discussed before, these languages allow extensive use of zero anaphora in the switch reference pattern, achieving maximum economy in the discourse grammar. Mandarin Chinese is discussed as an example of such a language.

    Zero anaphora is a figurative term for an empty grammatical slot standing for some previously mentioned nominal referent. The expressions containing zero anaphora are elliptical and, without filling in the omitted referents, these expressions cannot be interpreted fully. The referent of the zero is always recoverable from the discourse context. In this study, the verb 'to code' is used figuratively for the function of zero anaphora. Example (9), from an oral narrative, illustrates such use of zero anaphora.

(9) (Changsha: 1)

    ta\1 jiù tiào dao   dìshang lái,   **02** dàodi¨ gei¨ **ta\1** zhua\ahu le.

    It   then jump:arrive ground:on:come, to-end by it catch-stop-Asp

    It1 then jumped down, (02) finally was caught by **it1**.

In the center of the narrative, there are a cat and a moth. The pronoun 'it' refers to the cat. The subject of the second clause, which should be the moth, is not mentioned. Such elliptical expression is considered a zero anaphor. The zero anaphor has a definitive referent, the moth, but without the prior discourse context, the expression can only be interpreted as 'someone/something was finally caught by it.' In other words, without the prior context, such elliptical expression is unacceptable in any language because it cannot make sense.

Notice that the two clauses in example (9) form a switch reference pattern: the subject of the second clause is different from that of the first clause. There is no morphological coding indicating such a switch, yet the subject of the second clause is presented with a zero; thus the expression reaches maximum economy in reference presentation.

The next example also comes from a natural conversation. It again illustrates the use of zero anaphora in the switch reference pattern, but the interpretation of the zero requires special inference.

(10) (Beijing: 82-83)

(A and E were talking about an incident in E's university where some guns were stolen)...

1. E: Bù yíding sh' xuésheng ná da.   Rénjie shi//:::
        Neg definite be student   take-Nom they   be

2. A: (To G, a 20 month-old baby) //Chi\ dia¨r, a
                                        Eat bit Inter

3. G: eeh. (noise)

4. E: Xi\gua   bú   cuò.
         Water melon   Neg bad

5. A: Ní   sho¨ushang búshì   yo¨u ma.
         2sg. Hand:on   Neg:be have Q

-->6.   Yo¨u yíg'1 xíng le.   Zuìhuò   02 zha¨ozháo   méi?
         have one:Cl enough:Asp Most:end   look:find Neg/Q

7. E: Méi ne. Xiànzài 02 yìzhí   zha¨obúdào.   …
         Neg yet now   one:straight   look:Neg:find

1. E: It may not be the students who took (them).   They
         were//...

2. A: //Have a little (watermelon).

3. G: (noise)

4. E: The watermelon tastes pretty good.

5. A: Don't you already have one piece in your hand?

-->6.   One piece1 is enough.   Were (the **guns2**) recovered/
         found eventually?

7. E: Not yet. Till now (they2) still haven't been found.

Line 6 of example (10) is the focus of this discussion. There are three important issues here: (a) Although the adjacent clauses are not related syntactically, semantically or pragmatically, from the linear arrangement of the expressions there is a switch of grammatical subjects in the adjacent expressions ('One piece of watermelon' and 'the guns'). (b) Both subjects of the two clauses are coded by zero anaphora. (C) The referent of the second subject zero is not in the immediately preceding clause, but in the prior discourse context of Line 1[2]. The occurrence pattern of zero anaphora, as illustrated in this example, entails that in a conversation, Chinese speakers are actively involved in the interactive communication in a particular cognitive mode: The speaker has to make sure that the referent of zero anaphora can be tracked down in the discourse context, and the hearer has to be able to know what exact referents have been omitted.

Abundant use of zero anaphora, as illustrated in the elliptical expressions in examples (9) and (10), achieve maximum economy in communication. Such uses of zero are common in Chinese discourse; therefore, the Chinese discourse pattern for reference presentation falls onto the right side of the Gricean Continuum.

According to the theory of topic continuity (Givon 1983a; 1983b), the switch of a referent may break the continuity of a discourse topic, in which case a pronoun or even a full NP should be used in the next clause to code the referent that is different from the one in the previous clause. Such prediction presumes a linear mental representation of reference presentation. However, as examples (9) and (10) illustrate, reference presentation may be linear, yet its cognitive representation has to be multi-dimensional because the speaker and hearer are able to interact beyond the immediately preceding expression to track the reference of some zero to a prior discourse context (Fox 1984; Tao 1993; 1996).

2.3. Interim Summary

The examples discussed in this section illustrate the cross-linguistic competing motivations striving for maximum clarity and economy in reference presentation. This study believes that the motivations exist in all languages. However, because the competition may not (and probably cannot) be balanced within a language, different coding systems are grammaticalized, as illustrated in the Gricean Continuum.

3. The Role of Inference

This study proposes the Inference Continuum as an answer to the question whether an equal amount of inference is used in the processes of reference tracking. Given the different coding systems for reference presentation among languages, it is hardly surprising that language users may rely on different means to process discourse information. However, this view has not been taken seriously in the studies of reference processing. Current theo-

---

[2]The zero in the second clause of Line 6 is called a 'return pop'. For a detailed discussion of a return pop, see Fox 1988; Tao 1993; 1996.

ries of discourse comprehension take inference as a general human practice in discourse processing (e.g., Kintsch 1988; Givon 1998). The Inference Continuum proposes that inference is *not* used equally among people with different language experience. The view is supported from the following two aspects: emergent reference in Chinese discourse processing and experimental comparisons of speakers of different languages.

3.1 Emergent Reference

This study proposes that because of abundant use of zero anaphora in Chinese, Chinese speakers are specifically attuned to local discourse cues associated with different referents. Consequently, the speaker is able to resort to zero anaphora for maximum economy in reference presentation; and the hearer is able to track the referents of zero from the cues associated with each referent. Such practice is termed 'emergent reference'.

Emergent reference refers to a set of cognitive strategies used by hearers/readers of a zero anaphora language to perform reference tracking in discourse processes. To successfully comprehend any discourse with abundant zero anaphora, the hearer/reader is attuned to locally distributed discourse cues associated with each referent. These cues help activate inferential processes from which the identification of the referent emerges out of the zero. The stages of the inferential processes are defined and summarized below (Tao 1993; 1996; Tao & Healy 1996a; 1999).

(11) Emergent Reference

   a. *Cue identification*: When processing discourse information with missing referents, language users are attuned to specific cues provided by the local discourse context; cues that are unique to the referents;

   b. *Reference reinterpretation*: While processing discourse, individual NP referents become part of knowledge patterns that are reinterpreted with information from these distributed local cues;

   c. *Information integration*: By integrating the cues to the recurring zero anaphors, which now serve as the referents in question, the referents that are 'missing' due to the use of zero anaphora emerge with new information built upon the local cues.

The model of 'emergent reference' is based on the theory that referent information is *indexical* in that it is constructed from the local discourse context (Heritage 1984; Fox 1994). From this premise, it follows that language comprehension is highly context-sensitive: The identity of a particular referent coded by a zero anaphor actually comes out with the help of a set of local discourse cues; referents thus 'emerge' out of the local discourse context into language users' discourse comprehension. The cues mainly come from (but are not limited to) the verbs.

Let us re-examine examples (8) and (9) to see how these cues work. In (8), the specific cues allow the two referents to be reinterpreted as the predator (the cat) and the victim (the moth). With the expression 'finally caught by it,' the referent of the zero has to be the victim, hence the moth. In example (9), the two zeros at line 6 are the watermelon and the guns. The latter carries the cues from the prior context to be the 'missing object'. With the expression 'recover/find', the referent of the 'missing object' is activated. In both examples, the cues and their associated reinterpretations are indexical: they are associated with the referents *only* in the local discourse context (i.e., the cat may not always be the predator).

In her discussion of English conversational discourse, Ervin-Tripp (1993:242) points out that native English speakers 'look for cues' to conduct reference tracking as well, indicating that discourse cues play an important role in language comprehension cross-linguistically. People may question why this study proposes the model of 'emergent reference' as a unique cognitive practice for speakers of zero anaphora languages. The reasons are the following.

First, language users all possess similar cognitive capacity in language processing; so the discourse cues are available to all language users. Second, even though inference always plays an important role in discourse processing (e.g., Givón 1990; Gordon & Chan 1995; Gordon & Hendrick 1998; Kintsch & van Dijk 1978; van Dijk & Kintsch 1983), the amount of attention paid to different linguistic or nonlinguistic cues varies among speakers of different languages. In other words, the degree to which speakers activate different discourse cues in discourse processing is language specific. The first assumption is shared by many previous studies of discourse processing, yet the second one poses a specific theoretical hypothesis that has not to date been fully addressed.

3.2 The Inference Continuum

3.2.1 The Continuum

In theory, all languages allow certain degrees of ambiguity in discourse, and all language users are able to apply inference in their interactive communication. Yet different discourse patterns may foster different cognitive strategies in speakers' language production and comprehension (Tao & Healy 1996a; 1996b; 1998). This proposition is illustrated in the Inference Continuum, repeated below.

(12)   The Inference Continuum

Switch-reference > Logophoricity > Gender/animacy > Zero anaphora   **Inference**

-->

According to this continuum, the less grammatical coding a language offers, the more inference its speakers may have to rely on in their processes of reference tracking. In other words, with regard to reference management and reference tracking, the type and amount of inference speakers utilize should be drastically different based on specific grammatical features of their native languages.

3.2.2 Support for the Continuum

Studies of prosody in spoken language comprehension find that speakers with different language experience rely on different acoustic cues for spoken word processing (Cutler, Dahan and van Donselaar 1997). The Inference Continuum suggests that the same practice also exists in reference tracking during discourse processing.

Bates and MacWhinney (1989) propose with their competition model that people with different language experience rely on different cues (e.g., word order or animacy) in sentence processing. But their studies focus on processes of isolated sentences with little or no zero anaphora present. Other experimental studies show that inference has been an important part of discourse processing, especially in the task of reference tracking. For example, Gordon and Chan (1995), Gordon and Hendrick (1998), Kinstch (1988), Kinstch and van Dijk (1978), and Sanford (1985) have all obtained the results that native English speakers use discourse context to track the referentiality of pronouns. However, these studies tested native speakers of the same language to presume uniform human language processes.

Aaronson and Ferres (1986) find that Chinese-English bilinguals perceived English words as semantically richer than did monolingual English speakers. They attribute the results to the fact that Chinese grammar affected subjects' processes of English because Chinese discourse contains a greater deal of elliptical expressions and Chinese speakers pay more attention to word meaning in their language processing. This study reinterprets their findings by proposing that word attributes were rated higher by Chinese speakers because they are more attuned to the cues from words and their context to extract discourse information in their language processes, a practice that they have developed due to highly elliptical expressions (including zero anaphora) in Chinese discourse.

As a more direct evidence to support the Inference Continuum, Tao and Healy specifically compared native speakers of different languages as to their cognitive strategies in tracking reference (e.g., Tao 1993; Tao & Healy 1996a; 1996b; 1998). The studies compared native speakers whose languages contain abundant use of zero anaphora (Chinese and Japanese) with those whose languages do not use much zero (Dutch and English). All are fluent in English. English texts were used in different formats, including (but not limited to): a. Normal English discourse, and b. English texts with multiple omissions of nominal referents corresponding to the use of zero anaphora in Chinese.

When participants were asked to fill in the missing referents, native speakers of Chinese, English, and Japanese could all track the referents in the elliptical expressions. However, when asked to rate English passages with multiple instances of zero anaphora whose occurrence follows the information flow (e.g., Chafe 1994; 1998; Tao 1993), native Chinese and Japanese speakers both indicated the texts were much more comprehensible than did the native English and Dutch speakers. More importantly, when participants were asked to answer multiple-choice comprehension questions related to the passages with multiple instances of zero anaphora, the native Chinese speakers scored significantly higher than did the native English speakers (Tao and Healy 1996b).

The results of these experiments support the hypotheses that, first, the discourse pattern of a language helps form language processing strategies in its native speakers. Secondly, speakers transfer their cognitive strategies in processing their first language onto processing their second language; and thirdly, such transfer helps the second language learners to comprehend passages in the second language when the passages resembled the discourse patterns of their first language. Aaronson and Ferres' study (1986) also confirms the first two hypotheses.

The results of these experiments support the claim that although inference is used in discourse processing by all language users, the degree and magnitude to which native speakers of different languages are attuned to local discourse cues may vary. As a result, in discourse processing, inference does not play an equal role to speakers of all languages. Du Bois (1985:363) maintains that 'Grammars code best what speakers do most.' This claim can be explained in the following fashion: If grammar codes referentiality (e.g., the canonical switch reference languages) specifically, it entails that its speakers use this coding most to track referents and their associated events. Yet if grammar allows abundant use of zero anaphora, it entails speakers of this language use a high degree of inference in their processes of reference information. The Inference Continuum is proposed to capture the essence of this belief.

4. Conclusion

This study hopes to put inference into a cross-linguistic perspective by examining the impact of language patterns on its speakers. To better understand how and why grammar is formed so differently from both the speaker's and the hearer's points of view, it is imperative to conduct comparative studies of speakers with different language experience.

References

Aaronson, Doris and Steven Ferres. 1986. Sentence Processing in Chinese-English Bilinguals. *Journal of Memory and Language* 25:136–162.

Bates, Elizabeth and Brian MacWhinney. 1989. Functionalism and the Competition Model. In B. MacWhinney and E. Bates, eds. *The Cross-Linguistic Study of Sentence Processing*, 3–37. New York: Cambridge University Press.

Chafe, Wallace. 1994. *Discourse, Consciousness, and Time: The Flow and Displacement of Conscious Experience in Speaking and Writing*. Chicago: The University of Chicago Press.

Chafe, Wallace. 1998. Language and the Flow of Thought, in M. Tomasello, ed., *The New Psychology of Language*. Mahwah, NJ: Lawrence Erlbaum Press.

Comrie, Bernard. 1983. Switch-reference in Huichol: A Typological Study, in J. Haiman and P. Munro, eds., *Switch-reference and Universal Grammar*, 17–37. Philadelphia: John Benjamins.

Cutler, Anne, Delphine Dahan, and van Donselaar, Wilma (1997). Prosody in the comprehension of spoken language: A literature review. *Language and Speech*, 40, 141–201.

Du Bois, John. 1985 Competing Motivations, in J. Haiman, ed.. *Iconicity in Syntax*. 343-365. Philadelphia: John Benjamins

Du Bois, John. 1987. The Discourse Basis of Ergativity. Language 63: 805–855.

Ervin-Tripp, Susan. 1993. Conversational Discourse. In Gleason, J. B. and N. Ratner, eds., *Psycholinguistics*, 237–270. New York: Harcourt Brace Publishers.

Foley, William A., & Robert Van Valin. 1984. *Functional Syntax and Universal Grammar*. Cambridge: Cambridge University Press.

Fox, Barbara. 1994. Contextualization, Indexicality, and the Distributed Nature of Grammar. *Language Science*, 16: 1–37.

Givon, Talmy. ed., 1983a. *Topic Continuity in Discourse: A Quantitative Cross-Linguistic Study*. Philadelphia: John Benjamins.

Givon, Talmy. 1983b. Topic Continuity in Discourse: The Functional Domain of Switch Reference, .in J. Haiman & P. Munro, eds., *Switch Reference and Universal Grammar*. Philadelphia: John Benjamins.

Givon, Talmy. 1990. *Syntax*. Amsterdam: John Benjamins.

Givon, Talmy. 1998. The Functional Approach to Grammar, in M. Tomasello, ed., *The New Psychology of Language*. Mahwah, NJ: Lawrence Erlbaum Press.

Gordon, Peter. C. & Davina Chan, 1995. Pronouns, Passives, and Discourse Coherence. *Journal of Memory and Language* 34: 216–231.

Gordon, Peter C. & Randall Hendrick. 1998. The Representation and Processing of Coreference in Discourse. *Cognitive Science* 22:4.389–424.

Grice, Paul H. 1975. Logic and Conversation, in P. Cole & J. L. Morgan eds., *Syntax and Semantics 3: Speech Acts*. 41–58. New York: Academic Press.

Heritage, John. 1984. *Garfinkel and Ethnomethodology*. Cambridge: Polity Press.

Haiman, John & Pamela Munro, eds. 1983. *Switch Reference and Universal Grammar*. Philadelphia: John Benjamins.

Kintsch, Walter. 1988. The Role of Knowledge in Discourse Comprehension: A Construction and Integration Model. *Psychological Review* 95:153–182.

Kintsch, Walter & Teun. A. van Dijk. 1978. Toward a Model of Text Comprehension and Production. *Psychological Review* 85:363–394.

Lynch, John. 1983. Switch-Reference in Lenakel, in J. Haiman & P. Munro, eds., *Switch-reference and Universal Grammar*, 209–221. Philadelphia: John Benjamins.

Mithun, Marianne. 1993. "Switch-reference": Clause Combining in Central Pomo. *International Journal of American Linguistics* 59:119–136.

Nichols, Johanna. 1979. Syntax and Pragmatics in Manchu-Tungus Languages, in P. Clyne, et al., eds., *The Elements: A Parasession on Linguistic Units and Levels*, 420–428. Chicago: CLS.

Roberts, John. 1987. *Amele*. Descriptive Grammar Series. London: Croom Helm.

Sanford, Anthony. J. 1985. Aspects of Pronoun Interpretation: Evaluation of Research Formulations of Inference, in G. Rickheit & H. Strohner, eds., *Inferences in Text Processing*, 183–204. Amsterdam: North-Holland.

Stirling, Lesley. 1993. *Switch Reference and Discourse Representation*. Cambridge: Cambridge University Press.

Tao, Liang. 1993. Zero Anaphora in Chinese: Cognitive Strategies in Discourse Processing. Doctoral dissertation, University of Colorado, Boulder.

Tao, Liang. 1996. Topic Discontinuity and Zero Anaphora in Chinese Discourse: Cognitive Strategies in Discourse Processing, in B. Fox ed., *Studies in Anaphora*, 485–511. Philadelphia: John Benjamins.

Tao, Liang & Alice F. Healy. 1996a. Cognitive Strategies in Discourse Processing: A Comparison of Native Chinese and Native English Speakers. *Journal of Psycholinguistic Research* 25:597–616.

Tao, Liang & Alice F. Healy. 1996b. Information Flow and Zero Anaphora. Paper presented at the Annual Convention of the Psychonomics Society. Chicago, Nov. 1996.

Tao, Liang and Alice F. Healy. 1998. Anaphora in Language Processing: Transfer of Cognitive Strategies by Native Chinese, Dutch, English and Japanese Speakers, in A. F. Healy & L. Bourne Jr., eds., *Foreign Language Learning: Psycholinguistic Studies on Training and Retention*, 193–211. Mahwah, NJ: Lawrence Erlbaum.

van Dijk, Teun A. and Walter Kintsch. 1983. *Strategies of Discourse Comprehension*. New York: Academic Press.

Van Valin, Robert & Randy LaPolla. 1997. *Syntax: Structure, Meaning and Function*. Cambridge: Cambridge University Press.

Watkins, Laura. 1993. The Discourse Functions of Kiowa Switch-Reference. *International Journal of American Linguistics* 59:137–164.

Index